Dan—

Words cannot contain the immensity of my gratitude for the work and growth in my life through your presence in it. You have fathered me in ways you will never know, and likely in ways you didn't even intend. Thank you for holding hope for me and so many others. And thank you for contributing to this work! Here's to hunting...

Chris

Praise for *Man Maker Project*

"From incarceration to abuse to just plain missed opportunities, so many boys in our country become 'chronological men' who never arrive at manhood. What is needed, urgently so, is a field guide for fathers, mentors, and teachers of boys. Chris Bruno has given us the kind of book to carry into the terrain where boys become men. I would trust Chris with the five boys most precious to me—my grandsons. This book is for fathers, mentors, grandfathers, teachers, and anyone who cares about even just one boy."

—*Dr. Keith Anderson*
President of The Seattle School of Theology and Psychology

"A boy's world is a dangerous and treacherous place, filled with traps and sharks. I often hear men describe the bewildered and lost experience of entering adulthood, feeling that they should know how to be a man, but with no guide, map, or support. How deep is the longing to have another man just a few steps ahead of them, showing them how to do it, what is important, what to look out for—with a particular longing for someone to see their heart and tell them that they can do it. Chris Bruno has given men a great gift in Man Maker Project. This is a stunning work, borne of Chris's own story and his passion for his son. It is a feast of narratives that prove the struggle into manhood is not only worth it, but can display the kindness of God. This is a meaty feast, worthy of all men and fledgling men."

—*Jan Meyers Proett*
Author of *The Allure of Hope, Listening to Love,*
and *Beauty and the Bitch: Grace for the Worst in Me*

Praise for *Man Maker Project*

"For centuries, men in most cultures knew they had a sacred responsibility to guide the boys of their community into healthy manhood. This practice is largely unknown in our own culture. Most men intuitively know they want to pass on some significant teaching about masculinity to their boys, but they have no idea what. In *Man Maker Project*, Chris Bruno invests his own passion, insight, and experience into this crucial topic. He provides tangible, long-term, meaningful experiences that dads will immediately connect with and use. This book is truly a gift to those boys, their dads, and our culture."

—*Craig Glass*
President of Peregrine Ministries,
Colorado Springs, CO

"*Man Maker Project* is an answer to many fathers's prayers. 'How do I lead my son into becoming a man?' is a question I've heard from men for many years. I now have a book I will enthusiastically recommend to all the fathers I know. Chris not only outlines a practical path for fathers to follow, but he also reveals how fathers can step into the fullness of who they are as men. You will be enlightened, inspired, and connected to God's powerful plan for you as a father. I'm excited for the many sons who will become men of God through the influence of this important book."

—*Bob Hudson*
Founder and director of Men at the Cross Ministries
Golden, CO

"Every man should read *Man Maker Project* because it speaks into the struggles and doubts of all men. As a pastor and father of two pre-teen boys, I found myself challenged and provoked. It is here that most books on manhood end, but Chris goes further to give practical steps for creating a learning and experiential environment for sons. This book has given me the tools to be a better man and a better father."

—*Brent Rood*
Pastor at Seed Church in Lynnwood, WA, and
Founding member of 3Strand Church Network

Praise for *Man Maker Project*

"I knew from experience that Chris Bruno is a fine therapist. He gently and profoundly guided me through my own heart and my work as a jail chaplain and gang pastor. I now know he is also a fine writer. I'm buying a box of *Man Maker Project* and giving copies to all my colleagues. I'm also putting this book to practice with the young men I pastor out of crime, and mailing copies to guys I love still sitting in their prison cells."

—Chris Hoke
Tierra Nueva Gang Initiative, and Author of
Wanted: A Spiritual Pursuit Through Jail,
Among Outlaws and Across Borders

"This is a book that strikes home for me. As a father of three boys, I see the challenges we dads face in parenting our sons. We need perspectives like Chris's to bring clarity to this difficult task. This is an incredibly helpful book for all fathers and sons. *Man Maker Project* will help us, as sons, confront and reflect on our own masculine development; it will help us, as fathers, raise the next generation of men."

—Samuel Rainey
Therapist and author,
Nashville, TN

"I know for a fact that Chris is not scared off by anyone's life, and that's a gift to all who need somebody they can entrust both their scars and their substance to. Chris has earned the authority by which he attracts that trust. He's spent much of his adult life reaching out to people in the most extreme circumstances and environments, offering genuine solace and peace they might never have hoped for. This same clear authority is evident in his writing to men, writing that is tenderly inviting and immovably challenging in equal measure. That combination makes Chris, to me, a living reminder of God's merciful strength, and that's something all men could use."

—Scott Sawyer
Author of *Earthly Fathers*

Man Maker Project

Man Maker Project

Boys are Born.   Men are Made.

Chris Bruno

FOREWORD BY
Dan B. Allender

RESOURCE *Publications* · Eugene, Oregon

MAN MAKER PROJECT
Boys are Born. Men are Made.

Resource Publications
An Imprint of Wipf and Stock Publishers
199 W. 8th Ave., Suite 3
Eugene, OR 97401

www.wipfandstock.com

ISBN 13: 978-1-4982-0615-0

Manufactured in the U.S.A.   02/17/2015

To Aidan, my "Little Fire"
May you become a "Roaring Blaze"

Contents

Contents

Foreword

THANKSGIVING MORNING WAS CRISP and cool. My father had said we would go hunting early, and the sky was already light. I had not hunted before, but somehow I knew that hunters were supposed to go out early, before dawn. My father was a baker; Thanksgiving was the second-largest holiday for his goods. He had gotten up early the previous day and worked until evening. We had driven to my grandmother's farm late that night. I quivered with the desire to get my hands on a gun.

My father slept in on Thanksgiving morning. I don't blame him now, fifty years later. I know what it is to be bone-weary and forget promises made or merely postponed for a few hours, delays that feel like seconds to the exhausted and millennia to a twelve-year-old boy. That morning, I waited and waited. Finally he rose and began the process of firing up his body with coffee and a quick smoke.

After what felt like a lifetime, we were walking next to each other in a field where the cornstalks had been cut off at the knees. I begged for a shell, but he said it was not time yet. A rabbit ran in front of us, and I turned to look at my father disdainfully. I could have had my first kill. Instead, I watched the bunny bound off with utter abandon.

We arrived at a spot where my father put his gun up against a barbed-wire fence and sat on a log. I followed suit. He was a man of few words, but on this forty-five-minute walk he had been noticeably more quiet. Eventually, he began to speak. "Your mother asked me to talk with you about the birds and the bees."

I am not sure my brain has ever worked faster to figure out what was happening. My father had never intended to go hunting. No wonder I didn't have shells. This was the obligatory talk about sex that a few of my friends had had with their fathers, and I had been confident would never occur (*Thank God!*) with my dad. But here it was. The birds and the bees, all under the cover of a real, live, man-to-man hunting trip.

Foreword

My father couldn't look at me. He pawed the ground with his right foot, as if he could dig a hole to China and be swallowed up by his awkwardness. I felt fury at the bait and switch. I felt like such a fool, thinking my father had just wanted to be with me. All he was doing was my mother's bidding—again.

I stared at him until he met my eyes. "You mean how to f—?" I asked. I didn't say it politely. I spat the words out, intentionally communicating that I was not only cognizant but already more sexually active than he had ever been. He couldn't hold my gaze.

I must have felt some level of pity for him because I ended our "talk" by saying, "I know enough. Now give me a shell." He did. And that was the last major discussion about life that my father and I had until much later, when he was six weeks away from dying.

This is a generation-changing book. I can't find stronger superlatives. Chris is a friend, a colleague, and a man that I deeply respect. He is a superb writer. He has lived and suffered what he offers you. Let me state it forthrightly: there is no need to reinvent the wheel. You can take his wisdom, metabolize it for yourself, and wisely follow the plan he has set for you and your son. You will offer your son something that will fill his heart with joy fifty years later, rather than the tears I feel as I write about that Thanksgiving day so long ago.

My father was a man of his generation. His family survived the Great Depression and knew a level of financial fear and suffering beyond anything I have ever experienced. He was a sergeant in the Army who participated in early campaigns at Peleliu and Iwo Jima in the Pacific Theater. He witnessed his best friend's head being blown off and then falling into his lap. He suffered trauma that I will never know on this earth.

I can excuse my father in a thousand ways, but it is no more honorable than my efforts to excuse myself. I read about the gift Chris has given his son, and I feel sick. Sick in my heart for what I was not given; even sicker in my soul for what I did not provide my own son. But I do not write from regret or disillusionment; rather, from immense gratitude.

Regret is the province of a cowardly man. But if grief doesn't fill our hearts as we consider the failures of others—and even more our own— then we have written off the need for grace and forgiveness. There are three things I hope you will consider as you read this wise and freeing book.

Foreword

1. You will be asked to give what you likely have never received yourself. It is easy to resent or envy your son. He will be getting a gift from your poverty, not from what you have inherited. Bless your loss and his gain. Own the portions of your heart that feel envy. Honor the envy by letting it move your heart to grief and the desire to let our Father heal your un-fathered heart.

2. Seldom can we give what we don't have. As a result, you may be tempted to lead your son through this process out of your own anger or resentment, or you may anesthetize your feelings and simply go through the motions without truly investing your heart. In both cases you are asking your son to pay for that which your own father did not offer you. Don't do this. I encourage you to ask God through this process to awaken in you the parts of your heart that need his touch. It is a failure not to let God heal us in the very areas we are attempting to guide our sons in. You will be changed through this process as much as, if not more than, your son. Don't go into this process to earn a merit badge. This is a life-transforming journey for both of you.

3. Separate the process from your son's mother. Her boy is becoming a man. She may have a natural desire to hold on to what was rather than risking what is to come. Don't forget the power of her supportive heart to pray and cheer you on, but elements of this journey should be held just for the two of you. There are plenty of other dimensions that can engage her. Bless her struggle to let go and let it be a family process of blessing.

Most of all, don't fail to follow through. Many a venture has a good beginning, yet as it becomes more tedious or fails to satisfy your dreams, we can easily give up. Remember that you are taking your son on the hunt of his life. May you give him truth, kindness, honor, and your trust—and, in due season, shells and the promise that he will become a man.

I envy your journey.

—Dan B. Allender

A Word to Women

Mothers, Daughters, and Wives

If we have a crisis in this country, it's more than a fatherless crisis, though. It's a crisis of manhood, of masculinity. It's affecting our families, our schools, it's filling our prisons, and it's killing the hearts of our women.[1]

—DONALD MILLER

THE OTHER DAY, I visited one of the most amazing and odd environments I can imagine. The Alpha Center sits just off the campus of Colorado State University, in a quaintly remodeled bungalow. Jenny, the center's executive director, warmly and vivaciously welcomed me and ushered me into the depths of the building. Along the way, I passed brochures titled "Is it love?" and "How to Cope with STDs." I could hear raucous laughter coming from the larger staff room just off the hall and up the stairs, accompanied by the loud clicking of a spinning *Price Is Right*-style prize wheel. I would later see the wheel's bright, eye-catching words, "Got Sex? Get Tested!" The slogan boldly announces the Alpha Center's disruptive and redemptive work. As Jenny and I sat down, she joked, "I never thought I'd work at a place where we talk about sex every day."

The Alpha Center is a Christian medical clinic that provides free pregnancy and STD services, support groups, and post-abortion counseling, and assists the thirty thousand-plus sexually active college students at CSU in the area of sexual health. Their desire is to empower women and men with the right information about sex, healthy relationships, and right

---

1. Miller, *Father Fiction*, 3.

choices. It's not your average pregnancy center. There is hope and life and laughter and joking combined with concern, care, and nurture.

In a meeting with the staff team, I described my passion to help restore men to a godly understanding of masculinity. To my surprise, the *women* cheered. They literally shouted "Yes!" and applauded. At that time, eight of the nine staff members were women. And while centers such as Alpha typically service more young women than men, the staff fully recognize the role of men in the breakdown of wholeness and health. In sexuality, it takes two to tango. But most often women suffer the consequences.

As author Donald Miller talks about the growing epidemic of father-lessness in our nation, he identifies the ramifications on boys and young men, but also the impact these un-fathered men have on women. "It's killing the hearts of our women," he says. According to priest and author Richard Rohr, "The effects of this are lifelong for both genders, creating boys who never grow up and want to marry mothers instead of wives."[2] The poor or non-existent fathering of our boys wreaks havoc universally, and most profoundly on women. Centers such as Alpha would not exist if men would truly be men as God intended.

My hope in writing this book on the need for intentional fathering and rites of passage for boys has nothing to do with excluding or diminishing the value of mothers, daughters, or women in general. On the contrary, it is my belief that when fathers step into the fray with their sons and actively *make men* out of them, the world becomes a better place for all. Misogyny diminishes. Female objectification decreases. The passivity that haunts un-finished men ceases to force women to bear the brunt of their absences. Finished men turn lovingly toward their women, and the burden of society is lifted from the shoulders of our sisters and is mutually carried by all.

In the end, it is *because* of the high value of women, daughters, wives, and mothers that our boys need to become men.

My firstborn child is a boy, and God is leading me through the challenge and process of what it means to exceptionally father him to grow into an adult. I also have two beautiful, stunning, amazingly creative and daring daughters. Much of what I have to say about fathering boys also applies to fathering daughters. While there are some unique nuances to the father-daughter relationship, *my* journey takes me first to my son. Had God given me a daughter first, this book would be about girls.

2. Rohr, *Adam's Return*, 12.

I want to end this brief note to women with an earnest apology on behalf of all men. If I may be so bold—I am sincerely sorry. I am sorry for all the wrong that we men have done. I am sorry that we have not stepped up when you've needed us, that we have turned away into our own self-protective shells when you've longed for protection. I deeply apologize for the ways we have allowed our strength to turn into aggression and violence, how we have violated and harmed that which is most beautiful and precious. I am sorry that we have not led the charge to combat women-demeaning industries such as pornography and trafficking. We have failed you, and in humility and submission on behalf of mankind, I ask for your forgiveness and grace.

I also ask for your love, support, and patience as the men who read this book and endeavor to change the course of history take monumental and acutely personal risks in fathering the next generation. You are invaluable to this process.

If you are a mother raising a son without the support of his father, I want to encourage you with hope. Read through this book and take from it the basic principles of what a boy needs from a man. Then, boldly call on the church, your family, your neighbors, or your friends to come to your aid. Ask a group of godly men to gather around your son in order to answer his heart's deepest question: *Am I a man?*

Along with Jenny and the team at the Alpha Center, let us together pray for and applaud those men who courageously step into the ring and determine to make men out of boys.

Acknowledgements

OUR SON WAS A surprise—a welcome surprise, but a surprise nonetheless. After several months of thinking she had a mild case of the flu, my wife, Beth, finally decided to take a pregnancy test. Without planning or warning, I was thrown into the deep end of fathering with little sense of direction or preparation. I needed help.

Along the way, God has been gracious and good. He has provided me with a wealth of comrades and mentors who assisted my fathering attempts, picked up my fumbles, and corrected my blunders. The countless men and women who have surrounded me in this crazy venture called fathering are far too many to enumerate by name. Their influence and challenges fill the pages of this book and have become part of the fabric of my life. Thank you.

To my wordsmith-ninja editor, Dorcas Cheng-Tozun, I am deeply grateful. Somehow you took my meaning and made it understandable. Thank you for the long hours of deciphering, rewording, and clarifying. You are a patient, hopeful woman!

Throughout the last several years, as I have walked this journey with Aidan in his transition from boyhood to manhood, I have found hope and courage from the men involved in Restoration Project. These men have offered their voices, finances, thoughts, reflections, corrections, encouragement, and lives—believing along with me that fathers need resources to raise their sons well. To these men I say a profound thank you. I could not have done this without you: Shae McCowen, Jason Reid, J.Paul Fridenmaker, Bart Lillie, Brad Grammer, Robert Adolph, Nate Hershey, Bruce Stankavage, Jesse French, Craig Glass, Jase Smith, Brian Greiwe, Jeff Ammons, Zach Wear, and Justin Koehn. Thank you.

I do not have a biological brother, but God has seen fit to give me one anyway. I have grown closer to Greg Daley than any other man in my life. We have shared our stories, our victories, our failures, our hopes, our fears, and our lives. Our families have moved states together, we have served in the church together, and together we started a wild experiment called

Acknowledgements

Restoration Project. The Man Maker Project and this book would quite literally not exist if it weren't for Greg. I look forward to walking together through this life as we father our boys, our girls, and one another along the way. Thank you, brother.

I have been deeply influenced by the life, teaching, and friendship of Dr. Dan Allender. For the past twenty years, his work has been instrumental in the transformation of my heart, life, missiology, theology, and psychology. Dan's approach to God, the Scriptures, and the human heart regularly catch me off guard with his beautiful interplay of strength and tenderness. Dan's approach to story has blown my categories of what is possible as we live this journey. Having had the privilege of studying under and working with Dan at The Seattle School of Theology and Psychology, I consider myself honored and blessed to count him a friend. You are an everyday voice in my life and work. Thank you.

Finally, words cannot describe the depth of my gratitude and love for my amazing wife, Beth. She is my North Star, always reorienting me toward the truth and hope of God. Together we live a wild adventure, and I would have it no other way. Far more than any other person, Beth has influenced every word of this book through her advocacy, encouragement, and insight. She not only had the courage to birth our son, but continues to courageously parent him in every stage of life. We now venture together into the murky waters of helping our girls become women. I would not want any other partner ever, anywhere, at all, ever. I love you.

INTRODUCTION

The Man Maker Project
Rites for the Modern Age

If we don't initiate our boys, they will burn down the village to feel the heat.[3]

—AFRICAN PROVERB

I TALK WITH MEN all the time. It's what I do. My conversations have spanned a variety of topics and occurred in an even wider variety of locations—from the boardrooms of corporate America to back-alley cafes in Istanbul, from Skype calls to Afghanistan to the couch in my counseling office, from the backyard fire pit to high-country retreat centers tucked away in the Rocky Mountains. But none scare and thrill me more than the conversations I have with my own son, Aidan.

I spoke on the phone with him the other day. At least I *think* it was him. He's been visiting his grandparents for the past few weeks, and I barely recognize his increasingly deep voice. His vocabulary has taken a massive leap forward in the past year, and his humor and sarcasm have followed suit. About a month ago, his height surpassed his mother's, and his physical strength now rivals my own. My boy is growing up. I am in awe.

Every day I am challenged with the ever-changing boundaries around his heart, mind, and soul. When he was a child, I could protect him from the atrocities of the world by restricting his access and exposure to darkness. Early bedtimes, iPod and television monitoring, video game limitations, and even the choosing of his friends were all parenting tactics to protect and corral his heart.[4] But now, as he shifts and grows and becomes, those same

3. "Rites of Passage for Michael Milliken," line 1.
4. Don't tell me you haven't un-chosen certain friends for your children. It's not

boundaries don't make sense, and I am forced to re-evaluate almost daily. He is slowly becoming a man—a force with whom I must now reckon.

Many boys in this world today have little guidance, if any, from their parents. More particularly, they have little leadership from their fathers and are often left to wander into manhood alone. Boys are increasingly left to meander through puberty and early adulthood, all with the hope that they will *somehow* figure it out on their own. But the truth is, they can't. They won't.

From the moment of Aidan's birth, I knew that it fell to me, his father, to guide and teach him how to be a godly man. Something in me switched on, and I woke up. A deep place in me recognized how truly difficult modern-day manhood is, and how ill-equipped I myself had been to face the realities of life, home, work, church, marriage, and ministry. Add to this the utterly ridiculous challenge of pursuing godliness in the modern world. It's practically impossible. If Aidan is to succeed, he needs *me* to show him the way.

Few fathers actively seek to make men out of their boys. And it's killing us. Now more than ever, unfinished men confront us at every turn. Yes, fathers teach their sons how to read, throw a ball, ride a bike, and even stick to a budget. We take them to church and correct their table manners. While worthwhile endeavors, these skills are secondary to the deeper need for boys to grow into men—true men—who will stand up for honor, dignity, and justice. Boys who do not receive intentional affirmation and instruction in these foundational aspects of manhood often spend their lives living selfishly, seeking after their own gain, power, or reputation. They end up living lesser narratives, so far short of the epic tale God intended them to live. These boys grow into hollow men, and these men populate our neighborhoods, churches, and offices. While they may pursue "good" things, rarely do they become world-changers with a deep sense of purpose or impact.

As a counselor, I regularly work with men suffering from depression, anxiety, vocational concerns, addictions to alcohol or pornography, marital problems, fears, body image, and overall life confusion, to name a few. Yet, almost without fail, the moment I begin to poke around the stories of their fathers and their passages into manhood, their countenances change and their presenting problems fade into the distant background. The wounds that resulted from poor or insufficient fathering typically form the genesis of most other issues. In some way, they remain unfinished men.

---

malicious, just something like "Let's invite Johnny instead of Tommy."

Introduction

I recognize this is not the case for everyone, and I most certainly do not have a cookie-cutter approach to therapy. I do have enough data, however, to warrant the question: where was dad?

Masculinity by osmosis is a farce. Not all males become men. It doesn't just *happen*. Boys cannot enter manhood on their own. They may age into adult males, but they don't become men. Every boy must be led. Boys are born. Men are made.

Committed to this idea, I set out to create a modern-day rites of passage process for my son. I planned to intentionally usher him into a deeper understanding of godly manhood. As a fallen man myself, I recognized that I would fail and wound him. Yet my hope was to somehow lessen the impact of my failures and paint a picture of manhood that exceeded what I could model for him. I wanted to erect a mental scaffolding of manhood by which he could ascend and discover his own unique calling as a man. I knew the task fell to me to father him as best I could, and I wholeheartedly accepted the challenge.

As a minister to men, I spoke with men from all milieus of life, asking them for their stories and experiences of initiation and manhood. I spent months praying for insight and seeking godly counsel from older, wiser men. My bookshelf swelled with both secular and Christian titles from the past several generations of forerunners who have attempted to address this issue for men.

The result is the Man Maker Project, a yearlong initiation process facilitated by the father for his son. While a few other Christian authors have offered their own methodology and insight, little has been written about rites of passage since the 1990s. As a result, I felt compelled to expand and modify the work that has come before.

Throughout this process, as I have spoken with men around the world about the Man Maker Project, their eyes have lit up as they said, "I want to do that too! Can you help me with my son? I've wanted to do *something* with him, but I just don't know *what*." Even mothers who have heard of the Man Maker Project have asked me to help. They recognize in their sons the deep hunger for fathering, and tears betray their desperation as they see their husbands lying down on the job. It is to those hungry parents that I humbly offer this work.

As a father reading this book, you are likely committed to the idea that your son needs you to lead him into manhood. God intends every boy to enter the world equipped with a father who is committed to showing him how to be a man. For your son, you are that man. Regardless of your own past, good or bad, fathered or un-fathered, finished or unfinished, God gave you a son, and designed and called you to father him. I commend you for taking this step forward on his behalf. There is no greater legacy a father can give his son than a sure-footed foundation of true, godly masculinity. Generations later, boys and girls, husbands and wives, and even all of society will feel the effects of your bold move now.

You will find a major focus of this process also involves *your* heart and *your* story. I believe that your son's initiation into manhood also requires you to reflect and review your own narrative. Your son was born into an already-occurring story—yours—and for him to know himself, he will need you to know yourself. You can only take your son as far as you yourself have gone. Therefore, throughout this book, I encourage you to investigate the epic tale God is telling in *you* as you come alongside your son and help him discover his.

The reality is, we cannot do this alone. I encourage you to find a small brotherhood of men who share your desire to make men out of their boys. Read through this material together. Plot, plan, and pray with one another. Allow other men to sharpen you and be sharpened by you as God leads you forward in your intentional fathering. I have provided discussion questions at the end of each chapter as springboards to further conversation with other men. You can use these for personal reflection, but I encourage you to engage with other fathers, fully bringing yourself, your stories, your glories, and your fears to the table. You won't believe what results.

The Man Maker Project

I have laid out this book in four parts:

Part I: The Question and the Call describes the necessary background and need for modern-day rites of passage. In this section, I address the deeply hardwired question in the heart of every boy: *Am I a man?* I seek to create the context for how fathers, through an intentional rites of passage process, are called by God to respond.

Part II: The Atmosphere addresses the four atmospheric conditions I believe are necessary for a boy's passage into manhood. These include: *intention by the father; removal from the feminine; risk, pain, and danger;* and *fatherly blessing.* As you consider walking your son through his initiation, these four elements are crucial.

Part III: Restorative Manhood lays the foundation for godly manhood. If we are to initiate our boys into masculinity as God intended, we need to provide them specific categories of what that actually means. The world teaches our boys that "true manhood" involves a heightened sexuality, passivity, and machismo or violence. I have taken the long list of characteristics of a godly man and reduced it down to what I consider are six foundational qualities I want to bestow upon my son. These six are: *courage, integrity, excellent action, kingdom focus, protective leadership,* and *purity.*

Many authors in the modern-day men's movement represent manhood too narrowly. Not all boys love climbing mountains or hunting elk, and not all boys connect with knights and kings. Instead of an archetype of manhood, I focus on six primary qualities of manhood, asking fathers to consider how these characteristics apply to them and their sons uniquely in their settings and according to their interests, while still providing the mental file folders for God's intent for men.

Part IV: The Man Maker Project describes the practical process of creating a yearlong rite of passage. With a small group of other men, I designed a multi-stage process that spans the course of a year, culminating in an "examination" and ceremony. I provide specific plans and incorporate the six manhood qualities with sample questions, biblical stories, movies to watch, and conversations to have. I also describe the key elements of the final blessing and offer insights into how you can take my skeleton and customize it to your own unique story, situation, and son.

I conclude by addressing the need to return the new man to society, with new expectations and responsibilities. I also discuss the shift in relationship between the young man and his mother. Just as a baseball player or golfer knows the extreme value of following through on the swing for the ball to achieve its aim, so too must a father carry his son all the way through the initiation process to land him fully into manhood.

The Man Maker Project 101: A Father's Field Guide to Initiating His Son is also available as a supplement to this book. In it, you will find a step-by-step guide to help you plan and execute a yearlong rite of passage for your son. Worksheets, guiding questions, and supplemental material map out how to make the Man Maker Project your own. In addition, the field guide challenges you to consider your own life and story, asking you to *father yourself while you father your son.* This is available as a free digital download from restorationproject.net.

Ultimately, regardless of how you go about this process, my desire is that you will boldly and unequivocally step into your God-given role as the father to your son. There is no one else to lead your son into God's intended manhood. In the end, we must all draw our masculinity from him, our only hope.

PART I

The Makings of a Man

Becoming a Man in the Twenty-First Century

CHAPTER 1

The Question and the Call

In the Heart of Every Man

It is better to build boys than mend men.[1]

—S. TRUETT CATHY, FOUNDER OF CHICK-FIL-A

I WAS NOT SURE how he would respond. I only hoped that he would turn toward me and not laugh and run away. My heart pounded, and the anxiety of what I was about to do took the wind out of my sails. Had it not been for the loving eyes of my wife and the insistent nods of my best friend, I may have caved then and there.

On the eve of his twelfth birthday, during a camping trip in the Black Hills, I subtly beckoned my son, Aidan, to join me for a private walk in the woods. He agreed hesitantly, not knowing what was to come. The two of us set out for what would become a turning-point conversation for both of us. I had never done anything like this before, but I knew deep in my soul that it had to be done and I was the one who had to do it. There was no one else.

Aidan and I walked together for about an hour as I laid out my plans and dreams for what I termed his "Man Year." As he crossed a physical threshold at the age of twelve, I wanted to intentionally prepare him for the transition into manhood at the age of thirteen. I know boys don't become men at thirteen, but I also know they *start* becoming men then, and my role as his father was to prepare him to begin the journey.

Every male carries a deep, heart-level question: *Am I a man?* It is a haunting question that *must* be answered. Over the course of the next year, I

1. Cathy, *It's Better to Build Boys than Mend Men.*

designed Aidan's Man Year to unequivocally affirm him and usher him into manhood by answering, "Yes, Aidan, you have what it takes. You *are* a man."

I distinctly remember the day he was born. In the midst of all the wonder and beauty of his first moments of life, his very presence pushed on the edges of my soul. I had held many babies in my day, but he was mine. *Mine.* My son. My child. Something transcendent settled on me in that tiny corner of the world. As he lay innocently on my chest that first night in the hospital, I could feel the pounding question in his chest much like the desperate pounding of my heart in mine. *Will you father me?* he asked silently. *Will you love me* and *guide me into what it means to be a man on this earth? Will you?*

His questions intensified my own. As a grown male, I had created a child in union with my wife, and together we brought this boy into the world. But was I ready? Could I not only produce children, but truly *father* them? I knew he would look to me for guidance, and yet most of the time I only felt confusion. I knew he would ask me for purpose, and yet I often acted on whim and desire. I knew he would mimic me, follow me, find his strength in me, and ultimately bring his hardwired, God-given question to me for a clear answer. "Am I a man?" he would ask. To answer his question, I knew I had to wrestle with my own.

The Question in Every Man's Heart

I don't have a tremendous rites of passage story of my own. Most of my growing-up years were spent alone in the woods. Living on a small eight-acre horse ranch in the foothills of the Rocky Mountains, I found that the forty-five-minute drive to school, friends, or even the store significantly reduced the activities available to me. For the most part, I was stranded. I only have one older sister, who was born with a mental disability that has severely limited her involvement in normal society. Five years older than me, she is a mental three-year-old to this day. Her presence in my early life shaped my story in deeply meaningful and formative ways. With just the two of us in rural Colorado, I often found myself alone with the horses or ATVs on the backcountry logging roads. All the while, my own questions boomed in my ears. *What is a man? Am I a man? How will I know? How will I know?* And when I looked around for someone to answer, I found the elk, the dogs, and the silent breath of the wind. *Am I a man?*

My parents managed. After the birth of my sister, my mother quit her position as a teacher and has remained home as her primary caretaker for the past forty-five years. My father, the son of an Italian attorney in Denver, followed after his dad and soon became the senior partner in the family's law firm. While the financial rewards of his work offered provision and prestige, the demands of the firm removed him from home far too much. The typical story of the typical father in modern-day America.

One day, however, as I neared my sixteenth birthday, he told me to follow him outside. We had an old black Ford F-150 pickup, beaten up and scratched from the tons of hay and cords of wood we had hauled through the years. He threw me the keys, said, "Get in. I'm teaching you how to drive the clutch," and then proceeded to hop in the passenger seat. He told me to head toward the old Jacobs' road, one of the many unmaintained dirt roads that wound through the backcountry. Thrilled and extremely nervous, I got in and started the car. *Would I be able to do this? What will he think? Am I man enough to pass this test?* The vehicle lurched and stalled and lurched again, tempting my heart to shrivel in shame. My face flushed red, and rage rose in my soul. *I knew I couldn't. It's all over now.* Still, my father remained calm and kindly guided my movements until I successfully angled the truck down the road and up the next one.

After my success on the flat roads, he motioned for me to aim to the right, down a treacherous road I knew all too well. On the ATV, this road was challenging. In a truck, I knew it would be impossible. We stopped at the crest of the hill while he showed me how to lock in the 4WD hubs.[2] Then he got back in as if nothing extraordinary was about to occur. All he said was "Go." The pounding of my heart outpaced the RPM of the engine as we slowly edged down the rock-strewn road. Something in my heart began to shake loose. At one point, I high-centered the pickup and my father patiently got us out. But, the moment we were unstuck, he slid back to the passenger seat and put his arm out the window as if to enjoy the view.

That day, though it was never overtly spoken, my father began to answer my question. His confidence in me, his enjoyment of the process, his patience with my high-centering mistakes told me I was *on the road* to becoming a man. And while much more would need to occur in my life and my heart, both through him and a surrogate father figure who boldly rescued me from myself in later adolescence, the haunting question in my heart began to have a small glimmer of an answer that day. A father's intention toward his son is so potent and so powerful that a little goes a long,

2. For those of you who don't know what 4WD hubs are, switching to four-wheel drive back then required more than merely pushing a button on the dash.

long way. Now, twenty-five years later, I vividly remember that truck scene. It is emblazoned on my heart as a pivotal moment in my own masculine journey. My father's being there that day reassured my isolated soul that I had hope that, one day, I too could be a man. He offered me a morsel, and I gobbled it up.

As a boy grows and approaches adolescence, the haunting question increasingly reverberates in his soul: *Am I a man? Can I be a man? Will I be a man?* The closer the boy gets to the transformation of his body, the more urgent the question becomes. More powerful than his need to wrestle or his increasing curiosity about sex, this question becomes an unspoken yet compelling drive to know, to truly *know.* For girls, the onset of menstruation and the growth of breasts connect them soulfully to their answer: "Yes, I am a woman, a life-giver, a strong nurturer, and a beauty to behold." For many girls, the community of women artfully and delightfully journeys with them through these changes as they shop for starter bras and maxi pads. But for boys, puberty merely brings oddly placed crops of hair and uncomfortably swelling penises. Whereas a girl's body invites beauty, a boy's body makes no such invitation. The male body cannot provide answers.

In fact, the rush of hormones, muscles, and hair intensify the question. More than ever, the boy begins to recognize his strength and must now grapple with confusing urges and interests that are often hard to control. He is physically growing in power but has no idea how to wield it. Increasingly, he is equipped with the body of a man but continues to have the soul of a boy. His body outpaces his heart. He needs someone to teach him, lead him, and guide him. While he develops the steel-strong body of a man, his heart still feels weak, unsure, and untempered. *Am I a man?*

Other boys cannot answer, for they themselves do not know. Women cannot answer. Media cannot answer. Society cannot answer. Sports, work, gangs, cliques, video games, and academics cannot answer. The only one uniquely designed and equipped by God to offer a suitable reply is the *father.* It is the father who holds the key to the boy's masculine soul.

Very few boys can adequately articulate this question. In fact, most grown men only have a vague sense that the question exists. They know they long for *something,* they just don't quite know *what.* When the unspoken question remains unanswered, boys grow into unfinished men who spend their lives searching to fill the gaping holes in their hearts. What results are generations upon generations of men who desperately need dad.

Eric is one such man.[3] The youngest of three brothers, Eric lost contact with his father in early adolescence. After enduring years of her husband's yelling, fighting, and alcohol, his mother had enough, and his father fled into the night in a fit of rage and drunken self-absorption. Eric took on the mantle of spiritual leadership for his family, praying fervently for his older brothers and taking his mother to church. For many years he played the surrogate husband and father without even knowing what that meant.

Without a father to guide him, Eric faced the confusing teenage years alone, dabbling in the world of parties, drugs, and sex. He desperately longed for the strength of his father and yet came to view manhood as repulsive and violent. Struggling with his commitment to love and honor God, he found masculine comfort in sexual interludes, experimenting with both girls and boys. Recently, at the age of thirty-four, he came to me for help with his unmanageable lifestyle and distant relationships with his family.

As we talked through his story and he warmed to me as an older father figure, Eric began to recognize a subterranean longing in his heart. He recognized how much he longed for his father, *any* father, to honor him and bless him. Having given up hope on his own dad, he now looked to anyone who would boldly answer the question he didn't even know he had. During one of our conversations, I leaned forward in my chair and captured his eyes with my gaze. I asked, "Eric, has anyone ever told you that you have what it takes to be a true man?" His no was barely audible above the torrent of tears that ensued.

Over the next several weeks our talks shifted from family dynamics to manhood. He asked questions about love and sex. We talked about the difference between masculine power and masculine strength. He questioned me about my own life and family. Eric asked me about faith, doubt, and healing. Each week he came with a different curiosity, and each week I made it my goal to affirm and bless. He needed a model, a picture, a template of manhood. Though he was a thirty-four-year-old man, he still had the soul of a boy. The shame of his unfinished heart kept him from soul-healing relationships with other men. I cannot say that everything is fully healed in Eric's heart, but I do believe that the little fathering I offered him has fed an innate hunger he did not even know existed.

The way a father turns the masculine tide for his son and directly speaks to the aching in his soul is through an intentional initiation into manhood. More than simply offering a few words of encouragement here

3. Name and details of his story have been changed to protect his identity.

and there, the father's responsibility to his son, to God, and to society, is to capture the gaze and heart of the boy by intentionally teaching him about godly manhood, ushering him into the company of men, testing his grit, and then blessing him as a man. Only then will the pounding question be fully answered.

For the most part, boys only get morsels of masculinity. While good, these morsels leave them constantly hungering for more. The morsel I received in that F-150 off-road driving lesson fed a deep place in my heart. Having my father confidently sitting shotgun in my vehicle felt rich and overwhelming. I fed on that masculine food for days, weeks, and even months. But soon it dried up, the longing for his intention returned, and I spent many more years hoping for another few moments of fathering from him.

Too many fathers have abdicated their responsibility and left generations of boys unfinished and unanswered. The hunger for initiation plagues us and creates a maelstrom of woes in our world today. Just as the inevitability of puberty overcomes boys as they develop, so the deep need for initiation drives boys to find an answer to this question. If they do not receive this from the father, they look to false fathers such as gangs, drugs, workaholism, sex, pornography, sports, or anything that may come close to affirming their manhood. But the truth is, nothing ever does.

Our Masculine Mess

We find ourselves, our sons, and our society in a fantastic masculine mess. The epidemic of fatherlessness has spread far and wide, and the chasm between fathers and their children seems to be growing ever wider. Many in our generation seek answers—*how did we get here?* Some are quick to blame their fathers or their grandfathers for not being attentive to the needs of boys. Others run to their fathers' defense, saying, "They did the best they could." Regardless, the reality of our current situation demands action.

The fact is, for the several hundred years since the eighteenth-century Industrial Revolution, intentional fathering has been on the decline. Prior to this economic boom, fathers and sons often worked in intimate proximity to one another, whether in the field, the workshop, or the stable. The bestowing of masculinity occurred more naturally as father and son labored side by side. The opportunities for the father to affirm his son existed on a daily basis, and the steeling of the boy's masculine heart against his father's sharpening proved the boy was becoming a man. In the days of the apprentice, observation led to practice, and practice led to mastery. And somewhere in between, the newly developed master became a man.

Yet, with the dawn of the factory and the era of mechanization, fathers left home and headed off to work, leaving sons behind with mothers and female teachers. Industry swallowed men and separated fathers from their children. Without a man to guide them, boys were left to find their own way into manhood. The template of true manhood vanished, and men overwhelmingly became exhausted, distant, and inattentive. The definition of manhood switched from fathering to financial provision. Men lost sight of their impact on future generations. From the seeds of the Industrial Revolution, the landscape of masculinity took a dramatic turn.

Now in the twenty-first century, the cry for masculine clarity has reached a crescendo. We see the devastation such fatherlessness has wrought, and men across the nation have begun to recognize the importance of their fathering voices. More and more, fathers *want* to father, but we have lost the art of true masculine bestowal and fumble our way through our own brokenness as we attempt to redeem our children's futures. Fathers need help.

I believe fathers hold the key. Fathers who intentionally turn their hearts toward their children change the course of history, not only for that child, but for the world. Consider the final verse of the Old Testament in Malachi 4:6, God's last prophetic words about Christ before four hundred years of bleak silence:

> He will turn the hearts of the fathers to their children, and the hearts of the children to their fathers; or else I will come and strike the land with a curse.[4]

God indicates that the *turning toward* of the father's heart is directly connected to the welfare of the land.[5] The healing between fathers and children holds deep spiritual significance. More than a psychological experience, God's purposes on earth are directly tied to the reconciliation of fathers with their children. When they are reconciled, blessing is released. When estranged, the entire land suffers under the curse of destruction and brokenness. There is cosmic significance to fathering. Will you answer the call to father well?

4. New International Version (NIV).

5. I highly encourage you to review the statistics gathered by the National Fatherhood Initiative regarding the impact of father absence on our society. Visit http://www.fatherhood.org/media/consequences-of-father-absence-statistics. You will be astounded.

The Fatherlessness Epidemic

The very last words of the Old Testament echo for hundreds of years in the ears of the Israelites. God's final warning is serious and dire. In essence, the welfare of society rests on the intentions of fathers. "Father well," God says, "and the world is blessed. Father poorly, and the world crumbles. It's really that big."

Today in America we see the tragic results of the fatherlessness epidemic. The effects are so ubiquitous and far-reaching that it is nearly impossible to comprehend the depths we have fallen to. Here is a mere glimpse of the staggering statistics of fatherlessness. And, while I hesitate to reduce our country's fathering story to a listing of percentages and numbers, my hope is that they serve as warning signs and wake-up calls to fathers everywhere. Here are but a few startling facts:

- *Absence:* Twenty-four million children in America (1 out of 3) live in biological-father-absent homes.

  Lesson: Fathers are overwhelmingly absent.

- *Poverty:* In 2011, 12 percent of children in married-couple families were living in poverty, compared to 44 percent of children in mother-only families.

  Lesson: Children without fathers are more prone to living in poverty.

- *Incarceration:* Even after controlling for income, youth in father-absent households still had significantly higher odds of incarceration than those in mother-father families. Youths who never had a father in the household experienced the highest odds. A 2002 Department of Justice survey of seven thousand jail inmates revealed that 39 percent of them had lived in mother-only households.

  Lesson: Children without fathers are more likely to end up in prison.

- *Teenage Pregnancy:* Being raised by a single mother raises the risk of teen pregnancy, marrying with less than a high school degree, and forming a marriage where both partners have less than a high school degree.

  Lesson: Children without fathers are more likely to end up less educated and as teenage parents.

- *Child Abuse:* The absence of a biological father contributes to increased risk of child maltreatment.

  Lesson: Children without fathers are more likely to be abused.

- *Substance Abuse:* In a study of 6,500 children from the ADDHEALTH database, father closeness was negatively correlated with the number of a child's friends who smoke, drink, and smoke marijuana. Father closeness was also negatively correlated with a child's use of alcohol, cigarettes, and hard drugs.

  Lesson: Children without fathers are more likely to abuse substances and have friends who abuse substances.

- *Obesity:* The National Longitudinal Survey of Youth found that obese children are more likely to live in father-absent homes than are non-obese children.

  Lesson: Children without fathers are more likely to struggle with obesity.

- *Academics:* Father involvement in schools is associated with the higher likelihood of a student getting mostly As. This was true for fathers in biological-parent families, for stepfathers, and for fathers heading single-parent families.

  Lesson: Children without fathers are more prone to struggle academically.[6]

The Call of the Father

The day of my own son's birth, all my questions, fears, concerns, and failures came flooding over me. I knew that the one person designed by God to father this child now held him somewhat awkwardly in an uncomfortable hospital chair. I knew that I had the power to bless. I also knew that I had the power to crush. I had a choice to make, given that my son's greatest hope of living a true, godly life rested in my willingness to be his main man. Now, thirteen years later, the call to father comes full circle. More than

6. All statistics have been taken from research conducted by the National Fatherhood Initiative and can be found at http://www.fatherhood.org/media/consequences-of-father-absence-statistics. For more information on fantastic fathering programs, please visit www.fatherhood.org.

changing his diaper and teaching him to ride a bike and throw a football, it falls to me to step into the ring and actively answer his question. The time is now, and the man is me.

Through this process, I have come to realize that the call of fathering is just as much about *me* as it is about *him*. I have discovered, both in my own heart and in the hundreds of conversations I have had with men about fathering, that the masculine interchange between father and son is *mutually redemptive*. By God's great design, the call to intentionally father not only results in the monumental effect it will have on my son, but it also involves God's healing of my own heart. Fathering my son also heals *me*.

By holding this book in your hands, you recognize there is something within you that longs to answer the call. Perhaps you are motivated out of your own story of lack. Perhaps men you admire have challenged you to consider leading your son through a rites of passage process. Or perhaps your wife bought the book and told you to "do something." In the end, I don't really care why you are on this journey. The fact is, *you are.* That is to be commended, encouraged, and blessed.

At the same time, if you are honest, you are likely struggling with a deep sense of inadequacy. Do you have what your son needs? Do you even know *for yourself* what manhood and masculinity are? For many of us men, we have lived for so long with our own unanswered question that we fake our masculinity as we try to simply make it through. Without a clear sense of our own manhood, how are we to lead others? Many fathers today feel as though they operate from a place of weakness and vulnerability with regard to manhood, and cave at the prospect of offering it to someone else. Far too many men did not get enough fathering themselves and run away terrified when it comes to fathering someone else. They have fought so hard for the masculinity they have gained, they fear giving any of it away, even to their own sons. What if it is wrong? What if it is not enough?

To arrive at a place where you are reading these words and pondering a rites of passage process for your son, you have battled long and hard for an answer to your own question. In many ways, it may remain unanswered. Now, at the precipice of initiating someone else, are you willing to release the desperate stranglehold on your own question, open your hand, and offer yourself in faith, hope, and love to your son? I believe that, as Paul so eloquently admonishes us, we must rest in the faith we have that Christ is our redemptive Father. Our hope is set on the coming restoration of all things, and that deeply genuine love is found first in what we give up on behalf of another.[7]

God gave you a son. Answer the call to father him well. Both you and he will be restored through this process.

The Meaning of Father

For many men, the word *father* conjures a host of negative images, experiences, and emotions. I recently spoke with Rich, a man who grew up in a chaotic and abusive home.[8] When he was a boy, his father's beatings and verbal abuse crushed his soul. He often witnessed the drunken rage of his father against his mother, and bandaged the black-and-blue bruises of his younger brother. Determined to return the favor one day, Rich began lifting weights and consuming large amounts of protein in an attempt to out-muscle his abusive father. By the age of seventeen, he outgunned and outweighed him.

One day, when he arrived home from school, Rich found his mother crying and bleeding on the floor of the bathroom, and his father beating his brother and throwing him down the stairs. "At that moment, I knew that this was the end," he told me. "I picked up my mother and put her on the couch, then stood at the top of the stairs and yelled at my dad, 'Choose! Lay another hand on her or any of us, and I promise you I will kill you.' He looked at me with a defiant snarl and yanked my brother's hair. I leapt down the stairs and beat his ass. He never came back." For Rich, *father* meant abuse, hatred, and violence.

For other men, *father* means distance, absence, or apathy. Many men lost their fathers at an early age, whether to death, divorce, or abandonment. To them, *father* is a word of betrayal or loss. Still, to others, fathers may have been physically present but emotionally isolated and vacant. Yes, they may have played the "good guy," earning money for the family and taking them to church, but the gaze of the father never fell intentionally and lovingly on the son. For boys with such fathers, the hope of being adequately fathered rose and fell like the tide, ultimately to be squashed by disappointment. They have had to find their own way because their fathers would not or could not show them the path.

---

7. See 1 Corinthians 13.

8. Name and details changed to protect his identity.

For the fortunate few, *father* has meant goodness, strength, and blessing. He has been both physically *and* emotionally present. He may have had his failures, but he had enough of his own question answered to turn toward the son and battle on behalf of his soul. Those morsels of fathering, offered up by the imperfect man to the perfecting Creator, have been multiplied by Jesus into a banquet of goodness. By God's grace, these men have been fathered well.

Regardless of the genre of your story, it is vital that you honestly reflect on what *father* means to you. The actions and intentions you now take will radically change the trajectory of your family tree. You could be the one to lead the way toward wholeness and true masculinity for generations to come. I believe all of us would agree it is a risk worth taking.

Your Story

If I have any hope of ushering my son into his manhood, I must believe that God, by his restorative design, will also usher me into *my* manhood. The more I can engage my own story, my own journey, and my own masculine narrative, the more I can provide Aidan the freedom to discover his.

As a father considering a rites of passage process for your son, the most humble and manly place for you to begin is an honest review of your own passage and the state of your own question. Yes, your son has a question that must be answered. But so do you. In fact, those unfinished parts of your life and heart, even if hidden and tucked away, will inevitably surface and live on in your son. Just as biological DNA is passed from father to son, so too the unresolved and secret parts of our souls continue onward as a legacy to our progeny.[9] Father Richard Rohr says, "If we do not transform our pain, we will transmit it in some form. Take that as an absolute."[10] You do not need to be a perfect man to father well. But you do need to be an honest man who boldly and truthfully enters his own father-story, seeking restoration in your own soul as you seek to strengthen the soul of your son.

As a counselor, I see the worst in men. At this point in the game, there is not much that surprises me. The glory of my role, however, is not in exploring the darkness that shrouds the hearts of men, but in witnessing the

9. There are far too many passages to quote here with regard to the "sins of the father" and their effect on future generations. Do a quick search of the Bible, and you will find numerous examples of sin inheritance.

10. Rohr, *Adam's Return*, 37.

valiancy and courage with which they face their stories and boldly enter the grace and kindness of God's redemption. The more you seek the Lord for your own transformation, the more you will be able to offer transformation to your son. Transformed fathers transform sons.

In my counseling training, one of our guiding principles stated, "You can only take someone else as far as you yourself have gone." Beyond the classroom learning and academic rigor, we were required to engage our own lives, stories, and theologies, as well as learn how to honor and hold the stories of others. In the counseling room now, I am not surprised by the struggles of men because I have come to know those same struggles in myself. I have in no way arrived, but as I become more aware of my own journey toward restoration, I can offer hope to others.[11] Paul offers the same hope when he declares the patience of God and the power of the gospel enough to redeem even him, the chief of all sinners.[12]

As a father, the same must be true. If you are endeavoring to lead your son into the choppy waters of masculinity, few things are more vital than an intentional look at your own heart's depravity and glory. A bold reflection on your own story, and the healing of those places that remain unfinished or devastated, will launch you both toward the fullness of God's design for men. Simply put, have the guts to do your own work. Find a counselor, a mentor, or a spiritual director for yourself. Seek to discover all that God has for you. And, in turn, you will father your son well.

Questions for Your Journey

1. How did you get here? What has brought you to the point of considering a rites of passage process for your son?

2. In your own life and story, what does *fathering* mean to you?

3. How has the question "Am I a man?" resonated in your own heart?

4. How do you see that question in your son?

5. What are your hopes for your son as you embark on this endeavor?

6. What are your fears?

11. My email address is "I'm on the road" in Turkish. We are all on the way toward the Father.

12. See 1 Timothy 1:15–16.

CHAPTER 2

Boys Are Born, Men Are Made
The Journey of Becoming Men

People who grow up starved for a father's love become victims of an anonymous mugger or a faceless cancer.[1]

—ROBERT MCGEE

A FEW WEEKS AGO, my friend Ben hosted an unusual party. As he and his wife anticipated the birth of their first child, they invited friends and family to a "gender reveal party." I'd never heard of such a thing, but went with an acute sense of curiosity and interest. At the very least, Ben is a fun guy, and I knew he'd throw a tremendous party.

As guests arrived, he presented each one with a choice: pick either a blue or pink Mardi Gras-style necklace to wear throughout the afternoon to represent your guess of the baby's sex. Blue and pink cupcakes, cookies, M&M's, and lemonade also divided the crowd into the Girl Team and the Boy Team. A fantastic rivalry developed, and anticipation of the reveal increased as the sun set into evening. Sometime close to dusk, the crowd gathered around a small outdoor table as the expecting couple took a knife and ceremonially cut a cake, the color of which would reveal the baby's sex. The baker of the cake, the only one who knew the sex of the child, stood excitedly nearby. To capitalize on the anticipation, Ben slowly and methodically lifted the piece of blue cake for all to see. "It's a boy!" he exclaimed as he looked at me with both wonder and fear in his eyes.

A boy!

A boy?

Oh crap, a *boy*.

1. McGee, *Father Hunger*, 93

16

Boys Are Born

I believe it is the grace of God that gender determination occurs within the holy privacy of the womb. There, in the intimate place where husband and wife consummate their love in a divinely designed physical union, the beautiful presence of God fearfully and wonderfully knits together a child.[2] Not partial to male or female, but fantastically imaged equally in both, he lovingly determines the sex of the child.

"In the image of God He created them; male and female He created them."[3]

Every trip to the restroom reminds us that we are either one or the other. Male or female. Boy or girl. Man or woman. It's been that way from the beginning, and it will continue to be that way until the very end. It is the cosmic order that perpetuates creation and provides humanity with structure, identity, and purpose.

Yet this maleness and femaleness sits at center stage in the world today. Same-sex marriage. Gender identity. Transgender. LGBT. It is all getting so confusing. Recently, an online magazine posted a helpful list of appropriate language for the variety of gender-related descriptions. According to this, I am *cisgendered*. This refers to "someone whose gender matches up with the sex they were assigned at birth." In other words, a person is born and the doctor declares him male, and he identifies in adulthood as a man.[4] The level of complexity in our gender concepts has increased so dramatically that the evolution of language can barely keep pace.

A nurse at the Alpha Center, the Christian medical clinic specializing in sexual health in Northern Colorado, recently said that roughly 50 percent of women under the age of forty now identify as bisexual. This year, at the national staff conference for one of the world's largest Christian missions organizations, missionaries received specific training on how to engage the emerging language and culture of gender inclusion. Gender and sexuality are hot topics in the world today, and I am humbly aware of the cultural DMZ on which I tread. In every way, I attempt to do so gently and lovingly while holding out hope that God's original design remains his intention for us all.

2. See Psalm 139:13–14.

3. Genesis 1:27, NIV.

4. Kasulke, "Everything You Always Wanted to Know About Transgender People But Were Afraid to Ask."

PART I—The Makings of a Man

I believe that, after the fall of humanity in Genesis 2, *everything* fell. The effects of the devastation not only reach into the lives and hearts of people, but into the very natural order God so beautifully designed. Death entered, and along with death came brokenness on every level. This includes the sin of mankind, but it also includes decay, sickness, strife, loss, and even the marring of our very core, where maleness and femaleness dwell. And while "there is nothing new under the sun,"[5] we should not be shocked that the photocopy of the photocopy of the photocopy looks increasingly less like the original. In a decaying world, entropy reigns. Yet God has given us a hopeful indication of his original design in the clear delineation of man and woman. In the creation account of Genesis, no other created being received the bestowal of God's image in male *and* female. Other creatures received the necessary anatomy and even the command to multiply and fill the earth, but nowhere else did God clarify and emphasize gender. Human maleness and human femaleness are important to him.[6]

As a result, I do not condemn others for their journey and struggle to understand their gender identity. We all need compassion and grace as we attempt to understand our place in this world. At the same time, God's original design is both the beginning and the end, and I hold out hope,

> for the creation [that] was subjected to futility, not willingly, but because of Him who subjected it, in hope that the creation itself also will be set free from its slavery to corruption into the freedom of the glory of the children of God. For we know that the whole creation groans and suffers the pains of childbirth together until now. And not only this, but also we ourselves, having the first fruits of the Spirit, even we ourselves groan within ourselves, waiting eagerly for adoption as sons [and daughters], the redemption of our body.[7]

You may have noticed the use of the term *assigned* in the above definition of *cisgendered*. In my opinion, this is an interesting word, indicating that Someone did the assigning. For some, this may refer to the assumed randomness of nature or the fifty-fity statistical possibility of one or the other. As a believer, however, I have to believe that there is a God who

---

5. Ecclesiastes 1:9, NIV.

6. So important, in fact, that the author of Genesis *repeats* this important phrasing in Genesis 5:1. In Hebrew literature, repetition elevates importance. I am not totally sure what it all means, but I'm convinced it means *something*.

7. Romans 8:22–23, NIV.

weaves and forms people with purposeful intention, and that he is the great assigner of gender. He tells us that he has known and loved us from before the dawn of time, and it is in this hope and belief that I come to understand gender as purposeful to our intended identity.

This is a book about the rites of passage for *boys*. You likely knew your son was a boy from a fuzzy little knob protruding from between his legs on the image of the in-utero ultrasound. Or the doctor pronounced him "boy" at the moment of his birth. Your son was born a boy, and therefore will become an adult male. Gender identity issues aside, the biological imperative will grow an adult out of him.

Men Are Made

However, not every male transitions out of boyhood into manhood. Boys may be born of the womb, but men are born of *men*. It is a second birth—the birth borne of the masculine. Without the active intervention of older men, a boy simply does not make the shift. The womb of the woman miraculously weaves DNA and chromosomes together, yielding anatomies and bodies that turn one way or the other. Yet it is in the womb of masculine initiation that the boy's metamorphosis into manhood occurs.

Men, therefore, make other men. There simply is no other way. While puberty is an automatic response to hormonal changes in the boy's body, the process of change in the boy's soul must be *intended*. It does not happen by itself. Just as the infant boy roots and searches for sustenance from the mother's breast, every boy intuitively looks to other men for affirmation of his manhood. The echo of his question reaches sonic proportions, and the pressure to receive an adequate answer builds. The closer he gets to physical adulthood, the more intense the question becomes.

Rites of Passage: Initiating Boys to Manhood

Throughout history, the initiation of boys into manhood stood as a core element to many ancient cultures. Both women and men recognized the absolute necessity for such rituals, which often became the focus of the entire society. Mirroring the length, purpose, and intensity of the boy's physical birth, these rituals frequently spanned weeks or months, and had deeply meaningful, sacred symbols. These practices created a predictable passage that societies handed down from generation to generation, offering boys an undeniable place in the manhood community. In many cases, these rites of passage served to protect the society from the tragic results of unfinished men.

The goal of formalized initiation is to uncover and grow the seeds of manhood that God has placed in the depths of the boy's heart. The father and older men guide, direct, train, and complete that which God has already begun. It is the father's place to ally with God in the making and finishing of the boy's manhood. In essence, the question in the boy's soul stems from his manhood wanting to be set free, and the initiatory rites of the father catalyze his new birth.

When this occurs, the boy no longer strives for manhood but is set free to aim for *maturity*.[8] Manhood is what fathers offer their sons, and maturity is what boys-turned-men give back to the world. Not only does the boy transform into a man, but the question itself transitions into a different striving. The young man no longer needs to prove his manhood. Instead, he is liberated to strive for adulthood and become a positive force in the world. Without the father's intentional pursuit and initiation of the boy, he remains wounded and wandering, with a gaping hole in the center of his soul.

What was once an ancient, communal man-tradition has now become a source of angst, despair, and confusion for many boys in our Western American culture. Uninitiated boys grow into unfinished men, and the cycle repeats generation after generation. Though they continue to physically morph and change, they remain boys in men's bodies, with a man's responsibilities of work, finances, and family—but without a man's heart. Rites create the portal from boyhood to manhood. The father holds the key.

Today, many of these ancient rites may be viewed as primitive, harsh, or even sadistic. Indeed, some initiatory practices would be considered illegal today. But by declaring ritualized initiation rites "uncivilized," we have also lost the wisdom found in these processes and the importance these societies placed on the tempering of the masculine soul.

These ancient rites took a variety of forms but universally maintained the same core fundamentals. For example, in some tribes, the elders would whisk the boy away from the village unannounced and take him into the danger of the wild. There, he would be physically, emotionally, and spiritually tested, often at the risk of serious injury. He might be given hallucinogenic drugs, or sent to the sweat lodge for hours, or left for long periods

8. I credit Brian Molitor for this distinction. See Molitor, *Boy's Passage, Man's Journey.*

of time alone in the wilderness. Regardless of methodology, the purpose of the rite was to clearly mark the end of childhood and the beginning of manhood. [9] Even the apostle Paul refers to this process demarcation in his own life: "When I was a child, I talked like a child, I thought like a child, I reasoned like a child. When I became a man, I put the ways of childhood behind me." [10] [11] Just a few chapters later, he calls the Corinthians to follow his lead, to rise up out of their childishness and "act like men." [12] In ancient and biblical times, men knew what that meant.

But today, we have lost our way to the headwaters of masculinity, and our only hope of restoration is through the initiation of our sons. I believe the greatest and most long-lasting gift fathers can give to their sons is found not in wills, wealth, or inheritance, but in the intentional fathering and blessing of a father's true guidance from boyhood to manhood.

Boys are born. *But men are made.*

And so, I've set out to make my boy into a man.

Anatomy of Modern-Day Rites

As I began to scour the literature, the Scriptures, and my own life story, I wanted to create an epic passage process for my son. In the past, boys wholeheartedly anticipated their turn to submit to the initiatory rites from the moment they could understand language. It became the focus of their existence and the hinge-point transition for the rest of their lives. I wanted to be sure to create a rite of passage that Aidan would never forget.

At the same time, I live in suburban America, am self-employed, and have limited resources. I do not live in the wilderness, have no access to dangerous wild beasts, and I want to avoid trouble with the law for submitting my son to uncivilized or torturous abuse. The only "tribe" I have is a small group of friends who are also suburbanite fathers trying to make it in a struggling economy. My family is strewn across the United States, and

9. Other, more "humane," rites exist as well, including the Jewish Bar Mitzvah.

10. Keep in mind that Paul is likely referring to his own Jewish ritualistic transition from boyhood to manhood.

11. 1 Corinthians 13:11, NIV.

12. 1 Corinthians 16:13. Different translations render the Greek here differently. Some of the more literal translations, such as New American Standard Bible (NASB), actually use the phrase *act like men.*

my son is required to stay in school. And, truth be told, it's just easier for me to grab a beer and hit the couch. There are many barriers to creating an epic *anything*.

I began to wonder if there was some other way. Shouldn't it be easier to father our sons? The overwhelming difficulty of creating something out of nothing surely signified that a rite of passage was unnecessary, and trying to create one was ludicrous. But as I surveyed other potential options, I soon realized that nothing else would do. For too many generations, fathers have defaulted to the lowest common denominator when it comes to raising boys. I knew something had to change. I wanted and needed different results for my son. I could not offer him anything less. There was no other way.

I came to realize that I needed to work in three different areas of the initiation process. First, I needed to investigate the necessary elements to create the environment in which the man emerges from the boy. If this is to be a "second birth," what atmospheric conditions need to be in place for the delivery to occur? I knew that Aidan's current environments of home, school, and neighborhood provided him with a sense of safety and belonging, but they encouraged him to stay a boy. He needed to be put in new and difficult places for the boy to fade to the background and the man to be called out.

Second, I needed a new and clear definition of what godly manhood actually is. The world offers an anemic and insufficient (if not outright wrong) model of what true, God-focused masculinity is. Even the church proffers an inconsistent explanation of what "true men" look like. Most of the time, it involves either of these two words: *more* or *don't*. Modern-day Christianity tends to focus its man-message toward doing more, giving more, praying more, being more, serving more, journaling more, reading more—just plain *more*. Or the focus is on what men should avoid: don't leave, don't lust, don't swear, don't drink, don't spend, don't eat too much, and don't watch too much sports. What results is a long list of rules and regulations, expectations that no man can adequately reach. I wanted to redefine godly masculinity in such a way as to awaken Aidan's heart to a higher calling of manhood far above the depths to which it had fallen. *That* would be a lot of work.

And finally, without a handbook or manual to guide me, I had to create a passage process. I needed timelines, plans, resources, instructions, finances, and a logical progression toward an ultimate goal. Just as the ancient rites offered boys a sequence, I knew Aidan would need a plan. I also realized I could not do this alone, so I gathered up a small group of trusted men who know and love my son, and cast a vision for the audacious goal of initiating him into manhood. I asked for their participation and plotted the course for the year.

In all honesty, it was an ever-evolving process. There are many things that happened that I would repeat. There are some that were unnecessary or counterproductive. Yet what emerged from this work is my contribution to modern-day rites of passage for boys. It is what I call the Man Maker Project.

PART II

Atmosphere

The Environment of the Man Maker

Man Maker Atmospheric Conditions

IN THE ART OF making men, I have discovered that there are four primary atmospheric conditions that together create the environment for boys to emerge into manhood. Just as a plant requires soil, sun, water, and air, so the heart of a boy needs the proper conditions in order to make the transition from boy to man. The father holds the key to setting the stage, and it is through his purposeful action in creating the setting that his boy will respond.

The four primary atmospheric conditions for the Man Maker Project are:

1. Intention of the father
2. Removal from the feminine
3. Risk, struggle, and pain
4. The father's blessing

CHAPTER 3

Intention of the Father
Turning the Heart Toward the Son

*If you are a young man and you are not being
admired by an older man, you are being hurt.*[1]

—ROBERT MOORE

KARL STARTED COMING TO me at the age of fourteen, a gangly young man
who cowered in the corner of my office.[2] His eyes were surrounded by mas-
cara, and tattoos lined his forearms and fingers. Barely willing or able to
make eye contact, he spoke in such hushed tones that I often had to ask him
to repeat himself. Adopted at the age of five after a series of foster homes,
Karl still felt insecure as a teen. His anxious mother sat on the edge of the
couch, her eyes filled with tears of desperation and exasperation. Karl had
been threatening his siblings, torturing the pets, and getting in trouble with
the law. When he started cutting himself, his mother knew she needed help.

After our initial moments together, I asked mom to step into the lobby
and wait for us to emerge at the end of the session. I had no idea what to
do with this young man, but at the core of my being I knew that his heart
longed for a man to truly see him, to turn his face and heart toward him,
and to stay with him despite his attempts to resist, rebel, or defy.

Over the course of the next year, I learned from Karl about the worlds
of *Halo* and *Minecraft*,[3] the trends in marijuana usage amongst teens,

1. As quoted in Bly, *Iron John*, 31

2. Name and details of his story have been changed to protect his identity.

3. Both of these video games are the 2010 versions. The actual games are unimportant. What *is* important is that he was the expert and I was the learner. He had much to
say, if only someone would listen.

the language of cliques, and the confusion of popularity at the local high school. I learned about his art, his poems, his loves. The first of several to be adopted into his family, Karl experienced three years of love, adoration, and attention, only to be repetitively supplanted by the subsequent adoptees. His decline into disdain mirrored the increasing distance from the father he so desired to know, who was now too busy to give him more than five minutes a day. During our first few months together, Karl would regularly say, "When my dad has time, we're going to . . . " But dad never had time. Instead, when Karl misbehaved at home, he was sent to dad's real estate office and told to sit in the corner while dad worked. Time with dad became a punishment, not a place of healing, love, and restoration. Karl learned that he got more attention from his father if he misbehaved, pushed the limits, and wounded others. Any attention seemed better than none.

As I sat under his video-game tutelage, Karl slowly began to loosen and change. The Goth costume gave way to jeans and a T-shirt. I could finally see his bright blue eyes as he began to tuck his long blond hair behind his ears instead of using it to shroud his face. The leather journal I had given him arrived weekly with new drawings, sketches, and well-crafted fantasy story lines. The more I asked about him, the more he desired to show me. Like a parched plant's response to a few drops of water, Karl's soul slowly came alive. I am not so bold as to say this transformation happened solely because of me. But I know I had turned my eyes and heart toward Karl with *intention*. And even though we only had one hour a week, I discovered that a little indeed goes a long, long way.

The Eyes of the Father

Several years ago I caught a small glimpse of how important the gaze of the father is to a son. At the final football game of the season, my son's coach instructed the quarterback to launch the ball downfield, into the hands of the waiting tight end—Aidan. There, just yards from the end zone, my boy jumped up with puma-like agility, twisted his torso just right to snatch the ball from the air, tucked it under his arm, and landed on his feet. A few steps later, he danced in for a touchdown. It was epic. He had made *the* play of the game. We won the game and completed the season on a high.

Despite the exaltation of the win, my most significant memory of that last game was not the touchdown itself. It was Aidan's eyes. At the moment he realized he had successfully caught and carried the ball into the goal, his head snapped up and his eyes searched the crowd. Though we locked gazes only for a moment, I knew he was looking for me. Something innate in him wanted to know that his father had seen him in his moment of glory, and approved.

That same need dwells deep within me. Although I am a grown man, my heart still longs to be seen, noticed, and reveled in by my father and my Father. The connection between a father and his children is utterly other-worldly. There is a substance that passes from father to child, especially from father to son. It is something special, something substantial. It is like spiritual soul-food that feeds a deep hunger. Just as mothers feed their children with the physical sustenance of breast milk, fathers are called to feed their children with the masculine food of their intentional, loving eyes of blessing. It can happen with a look, a smile, a wink, or a single word. While so difficult to explain, most men have a sense of what I'm talking about. It just *is*.

I know deep within me that my children long for my heart, my attention, and my devotion. Whether on the football field or not, they hunger for me as their father. I cringe at the notion that my children need me so deeply. I cringe because I know I fail constantly and will continue to fail for the rest of my life. I wonder constantly whether I have what is needed to even begin to bless my children in the ways they so desire. And no matter how much I give today, the well inevitably seems to run dry again tomorrow. Their hunger is insatiable, and I constantly wonder if I have enough to give.

I believe this is the question of every father. Somehow, in God's ultimate grace in the creation of humanity, he designed the hearts of children to want and need this substance from their fathers just as naturally as they need their mothers' milk. Can I then trust and believe that I, as a man, am *equipped* by God to offer my children the soul-sustenance they so need? That is my only hope.

And it is a strong hope.

I have committed to being there on the sidelines—watching and waiting not for the touchdown, the goal, or the home run, but for the eyes that search for mine, looking to see if I am watching and reveling in the knowledge that I see.

That day in the Black Hills, I invited my son to walk with me in the woods and turned my gaze fully toward him with intensity and intention. I could see his heart melting with appreciation and relief. Instinctively, he flung himself into my arms and wept, saying, "Thank you! Thank you!" To be honest, it was the response I least expected. Instead of gratitude, I had anticipated his typical middle school sarcastic scoff.

Boys know the power of the father's gaze. They wait for it. They seek it. Such intentional, purposeful, thoughtful movements by fathers toward their sons is what frees them to relax into the process. When they know a bigger, stronger, wiser, and kinder man is at the helm and they do not have to find their own way toward manhood, they discover the freedom to settle in and accept the growth that God designed. When no such fatherly gaze exists, their hearts turn toward panic. They do whatever is necessary to capture the attention of their fathers. Of anyone.

Fathers must set their gaze on their sons, and sons must *know* that dad is watching, planning, creating. Like the heat and light from the sun, the intentionality of the father warms the heart and illumines the way. It is truly a mystery.

Boys who do not receive the intention of their father find alternative ways to acquire it. Just as Karl escalated his demands for his father's gaze through alternative clothing, lifestyle choices, and ultimately through self-harm, boys go to great lengths to know that their fathers see them and care. Their fathers are their primary audience for most anything they do. Unfortunately, all too often dad has forgotten all about his son and has busied himself with other things. Every boy longs to know that his father sees him and approves. In fact, the lack of a father's intentionality in a boy's life has the same emotional, psychological, and spiritual effect as abuse.[4] The most damaging wound in most men's lives is the absence of the father's intention. It's that serious. And I see it all the time.

It's so serious that even God the Father gives us a window into his intimacy and intention with the Son. At the inauguration of Jesus' ministry, before he enters the wilderness to be tried and tempted (Christ's own version of a passage sequence), Matthew 3:16–17 tells us, "After being baptized, Jesus came up immediately from the water; and behold, the heavens were opened, and he *saw* the Spirit of God descending as a dove and lighting on Him, and behold, a voice out of the heavens said, 'This is My beloved Son, in whom I am well-pleased.'"[5] The Father rips open the heavens, turns his face and heart clearly toward the Son, and in essence says, "I *see* you, I have plans for you, and I love you." What an example of fatherly intention.

4. Bruno, *Unintentional Abuse: Rites of Non-Passage,* unpublished manuscript.

5. NASB, italics added.

Immediately following this blessed interchange, the very next verse says, "Then Jesus was led up by the Spirit into the wilderness to be tempted by the devil."[6] God first turns toward Jesus, and then leads him into the process of becoming.

Attention Versus Intention

When my kids were toddlers, rather than holding their hands and pulling (i.e. dragging) them through the store, church, or parking lot, I frequently hoisted them up on my hip or shoulders and carried them. It was just more efficient and secure, and I had more control. As a type-A, driven sort of person, I easily slip into "make it happen" mode, and my mind goes blank except for a narrow focus on accomplishing my goal. People can talk to me, phones might ring, children can cry or make requests, I may even need to go to the bathroom—but once the "go" switch is turned on, there is little that can deter me from my aim.

To rouse me from the stupor of my determination, my children often resorted to placing both hands firmly on my cheeks and wrangling my face toward them. They would push and pull and prod until my eyes met theirs. At times they would pull my nose, cover my eyes, or stick their fingers in my ears.

"Dad, Dad, Dad!" they would plea.

"What?!" came my short reply.

"I need your *eyes*."

Our children need our eyes. They need our *attention*. They need to know that we have turned our face toward them and are giving them our mindful consideration.

Attention means turning *our face* toward our children.

In a world that demands our attention, our children often receive the short end of the stick. They compete with our work, our meetings, our bills, our hobbies, and our television. Our sons and daughters not only need our undivided attention, they deserve it.

But *intention* takes it one step further. Intention includes attention, but it also involves a turning of the heart. Intention demands a deeper level of commitment on behalf of the other. It involves a heart-level orientation toward the child and communicates not only delight or attention, but a plan. It says, "For I know the plans I have for you. Plans to prosper you and

6. Matthew 4:1, NASB.

not to harm you, plans to give you hope and a future."[7] Attention says, "I see you." Intention says, "I have good plans for you."

Consider again the passage from Malachi 4:6: "He will restore the *hearts* of the fathers to their children and the *hearts* of the children toward their fathers."[8] Intention demands more than attention. Something more than physical is required here. It's an internal shift of a father's heart, soul, mind, and strength.

Intention means turning *our hearts* toward our children.

The first atmospheric condition necessary for a boy to become a man is the *active intention* of the father. Turn your gaze, yes, but turn your heart also. This far exceeds any other atmospheric condition, for it means that the father must purposefully turn his face and his entire being.

As I began the process of creating a rites of passage process for Aidan, I made sure he knew what I was up to. I did not share the details, but I ensured he knew that the pile of books on my nightstand, the hours of conversations I had with other fathers, and the massive amount of notes strewn across my desk were *for him*. I told him his time was coming and I was devising a process to prepare him for manhood. He began to ask questions and even told his close friends and family members, "Dad is doing something for me. Next year, I'm becoming a man." I wanted the mystery of the experience to heighten his anticipation. Throughout the planning and preparation, I wanted him to know that my sights were fixed on him.

Your Story

Take a few moments and think about your father's eyes. What do they look like? What color are they? What shape? But more importantly, what do his eyes *say*? Do they communicate kindness and joy, or distance and passivity? Do they say harshly, "I'm watching you"? Or do they say, "I see you"?

In our Italian family, my paternal grandmother had "the look." If you did anything distasteful, such as whisper in church or arrive late to a meal, she would narrow her eyes and lock onto your face. Then, with the slightest of motions, her left top lip would arc into a snarl. Now, mind you, she was most often a playful and kind woman. But our family still jokes about "the Bruno look." My father inherited it from his mother, and I have apparently inherited it from my father.

7. Jeremiah 29:11, NIV.

8. NASB, italics added.

Intention of the Father

In all honesty, I can't remember much about my father's gaze other than "the look." I'm sure he looked at me often, and I do not think he has any difficulty holding eye contact during conversations. But I don't remember an eye-lock or gaze that communicated a *turning toward* me with purpose or intention. In fact, I came to fear his gaze, knowing the times he let it linger meant disapproval.

Turning your heart toward your son is one of the most powerful actions you could ever make on his behalf. But if you carry deep wounds in your own heart as a result of your father's absence or disdain, you must face that loss and grieve what has been denied. As you likely know, these hurts run deep, and your call to step into the life of your son could be God's way of also calling you to healing in your own life.

The *intention of the father* is the first and most essential atmospheric condition for male initiation. Without it, nothing can grow.

Questions for Your Journey

1. Read Matthew 3:1—4:1 and Luke 3:21–22. What elements of the Father's gaze strike you? What importance might there be in the Father's declaration of affirmation and intention toward Jesus?

2. What are one or two stories from your own life in which you sought your father's gaze but found emptiness or disapproval instead? How has this shaped you?

3. What is the story of your own ache for fatherly intention? How does that feel? How are you still seeking it? Where are you seeking it?

4. How do you look at your children? What do they see in your eyes?

5. Attention requires you to look. Intention requires you to plan. What excites you about this process? What scares you?

6. As you continue investigating this initiation process for your son, what will you need in order to follow through with your intentions?

CHAPTER 4

Removal from the Feminine

Ushering the Boy into the World of Men

[During the ancient initiation rites] the absence of women and young boys is apparently critical, for it is strictly and universally enforced. During this time the mysteries of manhood—anything from tribal lore to hunting skills to sex education—are revealed to the boys; these are the carefully guarded secrets which serve to separate the initiated from the uninitiated.[1]

—RAY RAPHAEL

EVERY YEAR, TWELVE MEN descend on an unsuspecting remote home somewhere in the United States. Flying in from all corners of the country, these men each contribute and participate in the ministry of Restoration Project. Some are board members, some are advisers, and others act as advocates and fellow journeymen. Our simple gathering involves three essential elements: sharing our stories and personal experience of the masculine journey; man-focused play, including jet skis, snow mobiles, guns, poker, ATVs, fly-fishing, card games, fire pits, and late-evening, honest conversations; and finally, *no women.*

At the risk of offending our female counterparts, this final rule has less to do with them and far more to do with us. There is an atmospheric shift in a group of men when women do not grace our presence. Men are more focused. Men are more free. Men are less concerned with what or how they eat, look, or sound. In the space that is solely masculine, something spiritual occurs. Men simply *change.*

---

1. Raphael, *The Men from the Boys,* 5.

Removal from the Feminine

Without fail, all ancient male rites of passage included this key element: the older men removed the boy from the presence of women and took him, sometimes even kidnapped him, to a strictly men-only space. This separation from the feminine world wrestles the boy from the spiritual and psychological arms of his mother, removes him from the comforts of boyhood, and delivers him—wide-eyed with fear and anticipation—to the company of men. While some cultures simply invited the boy on a sacred journey, other cultures dramatized this separation.

> A typical initiation rite in a primal society might have occurred something like this. On a prearranged but secret day, masked village male elders appeared at the homes of young boys, aged about ten or twelve years, and seized them. Feigning surprise, their mothers put up a symbolic fight, only to lose the child to the male elders, who spirited them away to a secret location accessible only to men. The stage of *departure* was a vivid and decisive one; the tribal ceremony told the boys with shocking and unmistakable clarity that they could neither remain children for the rest of their lives, nor could they live in the feminine, domestic world of mother any longer. They had to leave. They had to become men.[2]

The primary underlying theme of any male initiation rites is a change in identity, in which the boy fades away and the man emerges. Everything that has come to represent boyhood, childhood, youth, or innocence must be symbolically put behind him, and he must be intentionally ushered into the world of men. As the father and older men whisk the boy away, they call him to leave his infancy and enter the father's world.

Boys live in the comfort and nurturing environment of the mother from birth. Especially in today's society, in which few boys enter their fathers' environments except on the occasional, school-endorsed "take your child to work day," boys have little idea of the world of men. The most likely places men congregate—the office, the gym, the bar, or the field—do not actively welcome children. Most men don't have playdates with other dads and their kids. According to a recent report, the average amount of time a father spends talking with his children is a mere *seven minutes a day*. Seven.[3]

Girls who grow up in this feminine environment naturally come to understand what it means to be a woman. They watch their mothers, interact with them, learn to talk like them, and live their lives like them. Boys,

2. Arnold, *Wildmen, Warriors and Kings*, 42.
3. Chadwick, "Seven Minutes a Day: The Modern Excuse for a Parent."

however, have no such model. Most boys spend the majority of their childhood devoid of men. And while both girls and boys need their father, the boy ends up wondering what to do with his masculinity. Likely, it gets him in trouble, is stifled and corrected, and ends up becoming a source of shame.

Just as the initiation is a shift from one emotional, spiritual, and psychological place to another, the physical separation of the boy from the feminine punctuates the process and says to him, "You are one of *us* now."

The World of Women

About a block away from our house is a fantastic elementary school. In fact, it is ranked second in the entire state. When we made the move to northern Colorado, we focused our house search around the best schools we could find. Once we landed on this particular school, we narrowed our search to the surrounding neighborhood. Attending this school has been a tremendous experience for all our children.

There is, however, only one male teacher in the entire school. The entire teaching staff, from principal to part-time paraprofessionals, are all female. These stellar women have made the school what it is. I owe them an enormous debt of gratitude and commend them heartily for their work. I could not—would not—be able to do what they do. They are veritable superstars.

For my two daughters, this female-focused environment has excited their creativity, developed their love for the world, and cast a tremendous vision for fully alive femininity. For Aidan, however, the vast majority of his interactions with adults during his growing-up years have been with women. At school, Sunday school, even the doctor's office, women inhabit the adult world of children.[4] Some research estimates that children have a greater than 98 percent chance of having all their primary-school teachers, babysitters, and day-care providers be women.[5] Astounding, but not surprising.

---

4. One great pet peeve of mine: If you did a comprehensive review of the churches in your area, how many of the children's ministries positions would be occupied by women? I estimate that it's about 80–90 percent. Praise God that these valiant women have stepped in to lead the charge in the spiritual education of our children. But I'm left with the haunting question: where are all men? Guys, it is *not* the sole responsibility of women to serve in Sunday school. It's the responsibility of *both* men and women. Get off your duff and get into the kids' ministry at your church.

5. Lee and Wolinski, "Male Teachers of Young Children," 343.

To a great degree, men work outside the home in places inaccessible to children. Whether in office buildings, factories, sales meetings, mechanics' pits, or on the road, the last two hundred years have shown an increasing separation of men from their children. From the man's perspective, *going to work* means providing, laboring, and making his way in the world. From the perspective of the child, "Daddy's going to work" simply means "Daddy's going away." The where, when, how, and why remain mysterious.

Consider your own life and ask the question, "How much interaction do I have during the day with children—any children?" My guess is that, for the vast majority of men, the answer is alarmingly little.

As boys, especially pre-pubescent boys on the threshold of physical change, attempt to understand themselves and their masculinity, the world of women rarely offers them a clear answer. The masculine influencers of young boys typically come from movies, sitcoms, video games, or other boys their own age. They have nowhere else to turn. It is into this feminine world that men must step to remove the boys and transfer them to a place where they can learn true godly masculinity. Every boy needs a father to break in and steal him away. But, to a great extent, this is not happening.

Women are not doing something wrong. In fact, women are doing more than their fair share. I believe the root of the issue is that men are abdicating their responsibilities and not doing their God-given job. In order for boys to become men, they need a clean break from the world of women. They cannot wrestle themselves free. Someone has to step in and do it for them. And that someone is *you*.

Peter Pan Syndrome

The moment Samuel walked into my counseling office, I knew. His beard hung below his chin, full and unkempt, the kind of beard that makes you wonder, *How do you eat?*[6] He had a gut that hung over his un-pressed pants, and the style of his white socks and loafers took me back a couple of decades. Samuel worked for a local software design company, attended church sporadically, and indicated that most of his "friends" communicated with him online. He seemed to be having relational problems—with his parents. You see, he had moved back in with them after college and had continued living rent-free in their basement for the past seven years. They wanted him out,

6. Name and story details changed.

and he didn't understand why. It took five minutes for me to determine what had to be done. This man needed to be initiated—and fast.

Samuel is one of a host of men who, to varying degrees, have never been removed from the feminine world of their childhood and ushered in to the realities of the world where men must rise up, lead, fight, and protect. This refusal to grow up finds its archetype in the famous Peter Pan, who says to Wendy, "No one is going to catch me, lady, and make me a man. I want always to be a little boy and have fun."[7] It is far easier and more comfortable to deny passage than to face it. Without the active intervention of the father (or another older man) to take the boy out, he will remain stuck in childhood indefinitely. The Peter Pan man remains consumed by his own self-centeredness and cannot break free of his mother's influence. Even if she pushes him from the nest, he remains trapped in the Neverland of unending childhood. Something must be done, and it is up the father to do it.

As I worked with Samuel, we began to talk about the places where grown men congregate. We found a men-only small group at his church and sent him on a men-only retreat in the mountains. He signed himself up for an overseas missions trip and found a friend with whom to work out at the gym. Slowly, as he absorbed masculinity from these other men, his commitment to passivity and childishness began to fade, and his masculine confidence grew. After three months of living more fully in the masculine world, he moved out of his parents' basement and joined two other solid Christian men in his very first bachelor pad.

Masculine Space

Masculine space looks different depending on the location. When I was a college student in urban Chicago, my friends and I would retreat to the cramped home of our small group leader. He made sure we knew and cherished his wife, while still keeping our gathering spaces strictly male. I recently hosted the six men with whom I have journeyed this past year, exploring our stories and perspectives on manhood around my fire pit. As a missionary in the Middle East, I gathered with the men on our team, who lived strewn across the country, for a camping weekend in the mountains each year.

7. Kiley, *The Peter Pan Syndrome*, 22.

In the end, the *where* is secondary to the *who*. Almost any environment can be transformed into masculine space.[8] Where there are men, masculinity typically follows. It is vital for boys to increasingly experience these places to gain a sense of what it feels like to be in the company of men. During one of my last camping trips in the Middle East, my team members and I invited our sons to join us. Doing so added bit of discomfort, complaining, and a few of those annoying midnight peeing trips, but it welcomed our sons into the mystery of masculine space. Watching those boys climb trees, wrestle, and play swords with the other men in our group made my heart sing. I know Aidan gained much from those times with only men.

As part of this rites of passage process, it is important for you to consider how you invite your son to be with you, separate from women. He needs to know he is welcomed and expected, and he is safe to explore your environment. Throughout Aidan's Man Year, I increasingly invited him to join me in my world, from asking him to join me on a run to the store to having him come along to hang out with my adult friends. Are you one of those "average" fathers who gets little more than seven minutes a day with your son? You simply cannot initiate him into manhood if he is not *with* you in the process.

What masculine spaces are available to you? Consider mountains, beaches, boulders, rivers, man-caves, trucks, high-rises, deserts, historical buildings, or billiards tables. Even your office will do. Take stock of the places you like to go, and invite your son to go there with you.

As you develop your plan for his Man Maker Project experience, you will want to intentionally and regularly take him away from the feminine and welcome him to the world of men.

Your Story

On every Monday night and Wednesday night throughout high school, I stopped at the small 7-Eleven at the bottom of a windy mountain road, bought three medium-sized coffees, and stuffed hazelnut or French-vanilla creamers into my pockets. I gently maneuvered the coffees into the cup

8. I have written about the importance of space in *Brotherhood Project*. While I believe that any space can be made masculine simply by the people who populate it, I also hold to the notion that intentionality with space can have a massive impact on how men experience one another. Imagine a men's Bible study in your mother's craft room versus around the fire pit in the backyard with a dram of Scotch in your hand. Space mostly depends on the who. But a bit of ruggedness helps too.

holders of my car, and set out up the steep, hairpin turns toward "Manure Ranch."[9] I always timed the drive so I would arrive about fifteen minutes early, just so I could meet Ben at the fence. One coffee for him, one for his wife, and one for me. You see, Ben saved my life.

I've already mentioned that I grew up in a home of only two children—myself and my older, mentally handicapped sister. My father worked at a law firm in downtown Denver, and my mother, sister, and grandmother created a very feminine environment at home. Without a brother or close neighbors, I often found myself alone in the woods with little masculine influence to guide me. Until Ben.

Ben was the fifty-year-old Young Life leader in our small mountain town. His trickster smile and quick wit always kept me guessing, yet his wholehearted laugh reassured me that his humor was filled with love. At times, he'd make jokes about body functions and awkward moments in his life.[10] At other times, his eyes would narrow as he asked a question that inspired hope and faith.

Ben became a masculine lifeline for me. During those fifteen minutes before the Young Life meetings at his home began, we would stand with coffee in hand and one leg up on the split-rail fence. We'd watch his few buffalo graze on the mountaintop meadow while his horses whinnied and danced in the wind. Our conversations rarely had a point or specific topic. In fact, I don't remember a single thing Ben said at that fence. But, to this day, I would do almost anything to deliver him a coffee one more time.

Ben would gather up all the high school boys, and we'd head off on a hike, hang out late at night, or find ways to serve our community. Sometimes he'd arrange a white-water rafting trip down the Arkansas River or serve as our cabin counselor at camp. Ben knew the value of men-only time and intentionally offered me the very masculine space my young man's heart needed.

9. Manure Ranch is indeed what it was called. Knowing that middle and high schoolers can't but laugh at anything having to do with excrement, Ben intentionally incited jokes and hilarity. He even offered clothespins to newcomers—for their noses—as a gesture of welcome. In fact, the ranch did not stink of manure at all.

10. I have to forever memorialize this story. Once, Ben told the story of a bathroom experience he had as a counselor at a Young Life camp. Doing his business on the toilet, he heard the grunting and groaning of the camper in the next stall. After a few minutes, the camper exclaimed aloud, "Corn?! When did I eat corn?" That phrase became *the* phrase for an entire year.

I never had an intentional rite of passage as a boy. I wish I had. But the time and space I spent with Ben offered me the lifeline I needed.

When you were growing up, did you have places that, by an older man's design and intention, were men-only? Which men, if any, stepped into your life and whisked you away to masculine spaces? In what ways do you still struggle with the ties to your mother? What resentments might you hold against your father for *not* rescuing you out of the world of women?

As you consider this aspect of the Man Maker Project for your son, be sure to spend some time reflecting on your own story. Did you get what you needed as a boy from the world of men? Men who were never ushered away from the feminine may react against the feminine to the extreme with their sons, not allowing their sons *any* nurture from their mothers. You will want to take stock of your own life, heart, and narrative before you begin to plan this aspect of his journey.

Remember, the first essential element to ushering your son from boyhood to manhood is your intentional heart-turn toward him. The second is to ensure that he finds himself in increasingly *male-focused environments* in order to sever his ties from the feminine and forge his way forward toward the masculine. In so doing, he can bless and thank his mother for the life she has granted, and turn his face forward to what is to come.

Questions for Your Journey

1. How present was your father in your childhood? If he was physically present, was he emotionally available? If he was physically absent, to whom did you look?

2. What stories do you have about your father taking you away from the world of women into a solely masculine space?

3. If he did so, what did your conversations look like? What did you do together?

4. In what ways have you suffered from the "Peter Pan Syndrome"? Have you?

5. Describe your current relationship with your mother. Anything to notice there?

CHAPTER 5

Risk, Danger, and Pain
Death and Resurrection

Since it was absolutely central that a man die before he dies, every initiation rite I studied had created some ritual and even theatrical way in which a man could walk through that scary threshold in some form. They could not experience rebirth, being born again, without experiencing some real form of death first. The old self always has to die before the new self can be born.[1]

—RICHARD ROHR

AT 5:30 A.M. ON July 15, 1982, twenty-nine million gallons of water broke through the naturally formed moraine at Lawn Lake in Rocky Mountain National Park. Sweeping massive trees and car-sized boulders four miles down the valley, the wall of water scarred the landscape, took two lives, and flooded the nearby town of Estes Park, Colorado, to a depth of six feet. Now, over thirty years later, the devastation's remains have become a bouldering playground.

We had visited the Alluvial Fan valley numerous times as a family. The visit we made during Aidan's Man Year, however, was different. Swift water still flows over and around the rocks, creating a large and beautiful cascade of waterfalls. But, for Aidan, the water was irrelevant. The sweet aroma of the peat and the mesmerizing roar of the falls meant nothing to him. All he wanted to do was climb. The bigger the boulder, the higher the vista, the greater the challenge.

I had taken him alone on a camping trip to the national park in order to create some masculine space for us to continue our Man Maker Project

1. Rohr, *Adam's Return*, 101.

conversations. After pitching the tent, he knew exactly where he wanted to go—to the top. As we left the trail and the out-of-state, out-of-breath flatlanders, we navigated our way through the boulder fields and ascended the steep valley gouged into the mountainside by the flood. Aidan hopped and climbed, twisted and parkoured his way through the granite minefield.[2] I struggled to keep up.

At every turn, with every victory and with every conquered boulder, he yelled, "Dad! Look!" or "Mom would never let me do this!" At the core of his young masculine heart resides a deep need to push the limits, take risks, and go higher and farther and bigger and stronger than ever before. For a boy—and a man, for that matter—the physical world dramatizes the internal world. "If I can master *that*, then surely I am a man."

We ventured up the ravine as far as we could go. On top of the most massive boulder we could find (which *had* to be in the middle of the raging water), we sat together in silent awe of the majestic landscape. Little was said. Little needed to be said. In those fifteen minutes of rest, the only words that escaped my mouth were, "You came. You saw. You conquered." He smiled a wry smile, stood up, and said, "Bet you can't keep up!"

Facing Death

I had dinner alone with my parents recently. My wife and children were visiting family in Florida, and I had the house to myself. Naturally, questions like "How are the children doing?" arose, and we began talking about my son's newfound interest in the Navy. Inspired by his Navy Lieutenant uncle to pursue a career in aeronautical engineering, Aidan has developed a desire to build airplanes and travel the world. He's still young, and this interest may go the way of all adolescent inclinations. As my mother asked more about this, she said, "Oh, I wouldn't want him to do *that*. That's too dangerous. Maybe he could work for Boeing or something." My wife's sentiments exactly.

The natural inclination of a woman's heart is to nurture and protect her children. Just the other day, a female moose, in an attempt to protect her young, mauled a woman walking her dog in a nearby mountain town. Most of us would not be alive today if we did not have the tender shielding of our mothers. Bless them. Bless them.

2. If you don't know what parkour is, you should check it out. It's a form of urban gymnastics goes ninja.

Yet true male initiation only occurs when the young man faces death. In the process of entering manhood, God has ordained a *death* and a *resurrection*. The appearance of a finished man only occurs as he emerges from the grave. The child must die so the man may live. Once the boy has been removed from the protection of the mother, he must test his manhood against risk, danger, and death in order to prove to himself and his mentors that he is indeed a true man. The mountain must be conquered, the giant vanquished, the enemy routed, and the beast killed. Every great story of valiancy and masculine honor involves the hero risking his life to slay the dragon.

Almost without fail, the men in the Bible whom we consider true men all entered a season of suffering, pain, and death. Interestingly, most of their affliction occurred in the wilderness away from women. Moses spent forty years, disillusioned, in the lonely desert. Jacob wrestled with the Angel of the Lord throughout the night, and was left wounded yet renamed. The brothers of Joseph threw him in a well and sold him into slavery, after which he was falsely accused and imprisoned in Egypt. David, taunted by the uncircumcised Philistine Goliath, threw a few stones and cut off his head. Jonah became intimately acquainted with a large fish's innards. Peter denied Christ and suffered deeply for his betrayal of his best friend. Paul did a face-plant in the dirt after a bright light blinded him and threw him from his horse. And, ultimately, we are reminded of the model of Christ himself, who faced death on the cross as the perfect human sacrifice for our sins, and was raised three days later as our conquering King.

Unless a boy proves the depth and breadth of his true masculine strength in a rites of passage process, he will be forever tempted to follow the waywardness of his own sinful heart and seek false power. An uninitiated boy is prone to spend the majority of his life seeking a sense of strength from possessions, power, and prestige.[3] Purposeful initiation forces a boy to face the reality that God's purposes for his life far exceed his own naturally self-centered inclinations. It begins to break the idols of his rebellious heart and point him toward true masculinity. The boy must come face-to-face with death and survive in order to know that his life is not his own. Without the struggle of initiation, a man is tempted devote his time on earth to consuming things and people (possessions), creating a pseudo-empire for himself and his own self-protection (power), and building a reputation for

---

3. I am grateful to Richard Rohr for providing the basis for this language in *Adam's Return*, 17. I have taken his foundational thinking here and modified it a bit in view of the temptations of Christ.

his own fame rather than setting his eyes on Jesus (prestige). Masculine initiation has the power to lead the boy through the grave of self-death and into the newness and hope of a God-oriented life.

Indeed, Christ himself faced these same temptations in the wilderness. In Matthew 4 and Luke 4, we find Satan tempting Jesus to *possess* food not offered to him by the Father. He then tempts Christ by offering him *power* to command armies of angels. And finally, the devil attempts to seduce the heart of Jesus by presenting him *prestige* over the kingdoms of the earth. Three times Jesus rebuts the temptations with true strength and reliance on the Father. He never lost sight of the greater narrative. Men who do not face an intentional season of danger or hardship maintain a focus on lesser stories, resulting in self-centered living. Paul, having given up everything for the sake of Christ, talks boldly and plainly about his suffering and his desire to further partake in the sufferings of Christ.[4] This is a man who has suffered much and has come to know what life is truly about.

Stop for a moment and consider the most recent television ads you have seen. Every single marketing effort, especially those directed at men, is an attempt to ignite in his heart an unfinished need to gain possessions, power, or prestige. Fathers who intentionally create environments that test their sons offer them a perspective on life that can be gained nowhere else but in the furnace of suffering.

There is something about true manhood that requires a boy to face risk, suffering, and pain—and win.

Ancient Ways

Just as the ancient rites of passage always included the active intervention of older men and removal of the boy from the world of women, so too they involved some element of prescribed or ritualistic struggle and pain. These often involved some form of difficult task, physical challenge, or even corporal wounding. Brutal cultures would brand, cut, or mutilate the boys as an everlasting sign of their manhood. This often included tattooing, piercing, or scarring in a ritualistic way to symbolize the boy's passage to

---

4. See Philippians 3. Interestingly, most modern-English versions tame the language Paul uses in this passage. Paul says that he considers all things "rubbish." In fact, the Greek word there means "crap or dung." Paul is verging on the edge of ancient Greek cuss words here, folks. He wants to load the word up with punch in order to make his point that the suffering and loss he endured matters little compared to what he has gained.

manhood and his citizenship with a specific tribe. Boys were given the task of surviving in the woods alone, killing their first wild animal, or surviving the sweat lodge for an extended ritual cleansing. In the Algonquin tribe of Quebec, for example, boys were given a toxin called *wysoccan*, a hallucinogenic drug said to be one hundred times more potent than LSD. The drug would induce a trance-like state in which they lost all memory of childhood and discovered their spirit guides.

Other cultures focused their wounding on the genitals, as a constant reminder of the difference between a boy phallus and a man's. This included such practices as circumcision, superincision, and subincision. One Aboriginal tribe even makes the boy eat his own foreskin. Still other rituals forced boys to eat certain roots or body fluids rumored to invigorate their manhood.

Regardless of means, ancient elders recognized the need in a young man's heart to face death and emerge the victor. These practices, while extremely brutal, accomplished the purposes of boldly signifying and sealing the transition from boyhood to manhood. Naturally, I do not advocate any of these physical woundings, and the Department of Child Services would not be too keen either. Fathers can accomplish much the same effect through symbols and thoughtful effort.

One key element to the initiatory rites was the older men's careful planning for danger and risk. It was not brutality for the sake of brutality, but it always involved a greater narrative into which the boy now fit. Every aspect of the ritualistic wounding had a symbolic meaning that reminded the boy and his society that he had passed through the fire of initiation. Those who come through the painful rites could then be considered trustworthy, other-centered, and strong enough to take on the mantle of masculinity.

Thrill Seeking and Death Defying

This hardwired need for risk in young men is so compelling that, if they are not led into it by an intentional father, they will inevitably seek it on their own. I have a friend in Seattle who works with men in gangs and prisons. As a thirty-year-old white guy, he has come to be known as "Pastor Chris" amongst the homeys in jail. He has the unique ability to hold his own with their banter and foul language, while still maintaining a laser-like focus on their hearts. Chris recently told me, "These guys never knew what it was like to have a father. One hundred percent of them are fatherless. All of their antics, all of their violence, all of their crime and gang activity and craziness stems from the need to show other men how dangerous they are." Most gang violence, especially random shootings or stabbings, reflects a gang's unique "rites" for the new initiate. Young, unconnected, and typically fatherless men commit heinous acts of violence to prove themselves worthy of acceptance into the group. Perhaps more familiar to most, college fraternity hazing and high school bullies reflect the young man's need to show the world that he is indeed "a man." If these boys had a father to walk them through a season of death and resurrection, they would not continually need to prove themselves. The question would be answered.

According to Pastor Chris, the most effective way of reducing gang and prison violence is to offer men the opportunity to prove themselves without bloodshed. Involving at-risk youth in pseudo risk-taking rite of passage experiences significantly reduces their need to act out violently later. Many community-based organizations have discovered the power of such rites of passage processes in the lives of young people, and employ them regularly as part of their social services.

The next time you witness a death-defying act by a young man, consider what his heart truly needs.

Risk and Danger in the Sight of Other Men

Last year I had the opportunity to gather at a Minnesota lake house for a weekend retreat with a small number of other men. The house came equipped with a speedboat, a pontoon, and two Jet Skis. Having never truly ridden a Jet Ski before, I leapt at the chance to take it out on the water. For roughly forty minutes, I darted and twisted, sped and slowed, jumped the wake and laughed at the wonder of God. But, after a while, I returned to the dock in search of someone to join me. Another man hopped on the other machine, and the two of us sped off across the lake in a Jet Ski feud. We raced, sprayed, flipped, and literally flew through the air as we risked—together.

The greatest joy I experienced was not during our time on the water. The most enjoyable time for me came *after* we returned to the house, dried off, and lay exhausted on the living room couches.

"When you launched it off that wake, I couldn't believe my eyes!"

"Yeah, well, when you played chicken with me, I thought for sure you were insane."

"You *are* insane!"

Doing daring things alone can be fun. I enjoyed my time alone on the Jet Ski just fine. But doing dangerous things in the company of another man takes it to a whole new level. There is something magical in the heart of a man that needs to both hear and offer accolades of masculinity. We all long for another man to affirm us, praise us, and validate our manhood. We Tweet about our bowling scores and post updates about our marathons on Facebook. We take pictures of our elk-kill and immortalize our "big kahuna" with a plaque on the wall. Men long for other men to say, "Nice one!"

Your boy may already climb trees, jump off the roof, or launch his bike off the homemade ramp in the driveway. But what his heart truly needs is for *you* to see it.

The day I took Aidan up the Alluvial Fan ravine, he continually looked back and called for my affirmation.

"Did you see that?" he asked.

"Yes, son, I did. You are Spiderman!"

Some boys, however, are not naturally geared toward physical trials. Their interests lie in art, creativity, music, science, or academics. Or maybe it's animals or a foreign language. Risk does not necessarily mean bodily risk. The essential element is that the father leads the boy to push the limits and stretch the boundaries of what he has already accepted for himself. He must break through conventionality and conquer an impossible task. Some aspect of healthy fear needs to be present in order for the young man to be challenged to push through. For example, if your son is a musician, risk may mean playing in front of a crowd, or recording and releasing a single. If he's an artist, it may mean working on a piece and submitting it to a local gallery or art show. If he prefers science, perhaps a father-son trip to NORAD would open up his soul.

Regardless, the death-resurrection aspect of male rites of passage is a vital element to his process. I consider it a pilgrimage, a physical journey, with a spiritual goal.[5]

Man Maker Project Death and Resurrection

Obviously, feeding toxins to your son or mutilating his body is not what I'm talking about here. We must, however, actively and purposefully create

5. I credit my friend Craig Glass, founder of Peregrine Ministries, for this definition of pilgrimage. Learn more about Craig at http://peregrineministries.org/.

an environment where the boy faces a difficult task and does so in the company of other men. The affirmation of his manhood comes when he succeeds in doing something dangerous *and* older men acknowledge and accept his bravery.

As you begin to plan and create a Man Maker Project for your son, consider the resources God has already provided you. You may choose to have multiple excursions throughout the year, or your plan may culminate in a highly symbolic physical test at the end. The most important aspect of the experience is to intentionally create a place where your son is tested and affirmed.

Throughout Aidan's year, he experienced a variety of risks and faced numerous environments that stretched his limits and thrilled his soul. He climbed mountains and sailed the ocean. He learned how to play golf and how to gut a fish. He even had the opportunity to fly in a Cessna and visit a foreign land. The greatest test of his grit came on the day of his final Man Maker Project ceremony, where I required him to face a significant physical challenge—alone. Not every father needs to provide this sort of variety in the risk, danger, and struggle portion of your son's experience. Yet the space where the boy must face a significant and meaningful challenge is the space where boyhood dies and manhood comes to life.

Your Story

As a father, consider your own experience of danger and risk. Your body is likely covered in scars, each a narrative of daring, stupidity, or an accident. Every once in a while, my children ask me to tell them "the stories of the scars." They want to know how I was wounded and how I survived.

How do you engage danger? Are you overly reckless? Overly cautious? How did this come to be? What times do you remember facing a fear or doing something on the edge? What sorts of masculine affirmation did you receive, if any? Take stock of your current behavior. What does it tell you about your heart? What are you still longing to hear from your own father with regard to your manhood?

Many times, the activities we pursue as adults received their shape in our hearts as boys. Many men with woodworking fathers become wood-workers themselves. Outdoorsmen create other outdoorsmen. Authors beget authors, and ministers create more ministers. Boys naturally fol-low their fathers' lead and go to the places their fathers are, because that is where that they will most likely be seen and affirmed. Even if a child does not like the activity, he often follows his father in hopes that dad will see him succeed.

On the flip side, some men eschew their fathers' activities because the importance of the activity exceeded the importance of the son. For example, my father loves fishing. Every year our family made a journey to several mountain lakes, into which we threw our lines from the shore and waited. Some days, we caught massive amounts of rainbow trout. Other days, not even a bite. As a young boy, I indulged my father's passions and learned the ins and outs of lake fishing. I learned how to cast, bait the hook, reel the fish in, and clean them for cooking. I became an expert. But, throughout the process, I rarely felt the delight of my father. His focus was often on my sister or mother, and, proficient as I was, I was left to my own devices. I grew to hate fishing as a result, for it came to symbolize how my deep need to be seen and affirmed was all too often met with absence or inattention. By middle school, I still joined the family fishing trips but took a book and a chair instead of a rod. I simply gave up.

What are your stories of masculine affirmation or denial? How do they shape you today? In what ways are you engaging your son around activities? Are these activities *he* enjoys?

After the heart of the father has been intentionally turned toward the son, and after he has been actively removed from the world of women and ushered into danger and risk, the boy now needs to hear the powerful words of the father's blessing. This intentional and verbal approval of the son provides the everlasting seal to the rites of passage process.

Questions for Your Journey

1. Why do you think most ancient rites of passage included a dangerous element to their process? What does it do in the soul of the boy?

2. What do you think about the notion of risk and danger as part of the effective rites of passage process?

3. What stories do you have in which you looked death in the face, and won?

4. For some men and boys, risk and danger has less to do with the physical and more to do with the emotional or social. Men who are not "outdoorsy" may be compelled to risk in other areas. What might some of these be?

5. How important was it for you as a boy (or even now as a man) to have someone else watching you as you face risk?

CHAPTER 6

Father's Blessing

Masculine Substance

The blessing serves as a "send-off," an empowering release that encourages a young man to rise up and take his place, contributing to the larger world.[1]

—JOHN SOWERS

THE OTHER DAY, I sat for a few hours with my friend Craig at Equinox Brewing Company. Twenty years my senior, Craig also directs a ministry to men, and over the past few years our involvement with one another has grown as we have become better friends. He has served as mentor, adviser, and friend, continually filling my sails as I endeavor to bring life and restoration to men through the ministry of Restoration Project. That day, we drained a pint together and talked about the work of God in our lives. Toward the end of our time, Craig said something that stopped me in my tracks, brought tears to my eyes, and fed my soul. "Chris, I think so highly of you. Let that sink in for a moment." After a brief pause, he continued, "There is medicine in you. Deep medicine that brings restoration." I sat stunned and silent as I allowed his words to nourish my soul. Hearing those words *at all* brought life, but hearing them from this man who knows me and loves me filled me with the courage, energy, hope, and humility to press forward on my own journey of manhood. I left that pub full. Soul-full.

Craig offered me a blessing. They were not just words of encouragement, though they encouraged me deeply. They were intentionally chosen words of covering and approval. Even now, as a man in my forties, I desperately long to hear these words. I imagine you do too.

1. Sowers, *Fatherless Generation*, 118

Father's Blessing

As a culture, we have lost the art of blessing others. All men are hungry for blessing. God designed it as *the* way for our heart-level manhood question to find an answer. When a man like Craig looks into my soul and says, "Yes, you *are* a man. You have what it takes. I see it, and approve," something shifts, releases, and grows. Every boy needs to hear clear words of blessing in order to emerge as a man. And every man needs to continue hearing blessing from other men as fuel for the onward journey. As fathers and men, we must recover this ancient and powerful art, for in it is life and masculine substance found nowhere else.

Masculine Substance

There is no other place on earth like a mountain stream that makes my heart come alive. The bubbling and glistening of the water, the fierceness of imposing boulders with the delicacy of smooth pebbles, and the never-ending flow of current that rushes to meet me and then tumbles onward beyond me. I am undone by streams.

Yet the most amazing aspect of these high-country wonders, or any miracle of creation, is that they all find their origin in words. *Words.* Simple words spoken millennia ago continue to create every new moment of the seasons, the skies, and the streams. "And God *said* . . . " set everything we know, and so much more, in motion. God spoke the world into existence, and the effect of those spoken words will ripple until he speaks again at our full and final restoration.

There is great power in words.

Women have been given the beautiful and miraculous privilege of the womb, in which life is formed and woven together in intimate detail. Within the holiness of this place, a child is created, taking nurture and sustenance from the mother's body as it grows and develops and becomes. At birth, this offering of her body to the child continues through the life-giving sustenance of her breast. Mother provides the nutritional building blocks for the child, and they come from her body. In those intimate moments as she holds her baby and rocks and sings and nurses, the mental and emotional aspects of the child's psyche also form, paving the way for all future interactions and relationships.[2] The sheer physicality of this exchange is a stunning reminder of the gracious gift of God's physical sacrifice for us all.

2. In attachment theory, this initial intimate connection between mother and child is vital. The attunement of emotions, the mirroring of affect and face, and the bond that

But what about the father? From his seed, the child grows. Once the miracle of conception takes place, however, the father has no physical role in the development of that child. He has offered what he can, and must wait for Eve (which means "giver of life") to bring the child into the world and suckle him or her to life. And yet, by God's design, there is a different hunger in the heart of every child that the mother can never fulfill. Beyond the physical, God weaves together in the heart of every child a hunger for the father that can only be fed by his words. Where the mother gives life, the father gives shape by what he says.

The woman mirrors the Creator in her miraculous ability to bring forth life. But the father reflects the awesomeness of God in his life-giving words of blessing. The most amazing experience of any father can also be found in the simple phrase "And he *said . . .* " What passes from mother to child through the womb or through the breast is physical sustenance. What passes from father to child through words is spiritual food. There is no greater way for a man to give life to another than to speak intentional words of blessing. Likewise, there is no greater way for a man to crush a child's soul than to speak words of death or criticism—or to not speak at all.

From Words to Messages

Stanley grew up in a contemptuous and emotionally vacant home.[3] From the age of two, his parents would leave him unattended in his room to play by himself for hours at a time. If he wandered away from his virtual prison, he received a harsh punishment and hateful words, and was brought back to face the lonely isolation once again. As he grew and his boy-heart continued to long for the love of his father, Stanley attempted to please his father through service, often finding himself at the bottom of a ladder, holding a hammer or fetching a wrench. Yet if he handed up the wrong tool, a torrent of demeaning words crashed down on him like an anvil. His father even renamed him Stupid. "Hey, Stupid, come here" or "Stupid, get in the car. You're late."

As I worked with Stanley and we became familiar with the landscape of his life and story, he admitted, "Shame surrounds me. Everywhere I go,

---

forms create an "attachment" that serves as a foundation for that child in the future. It is really quite stunning how God built the body/brain/soul connection. To learn more, search for attachment theory.

3. Name changed to protect his identity.

everything I do, I only know shame. Self-contempt has become so familiar, I actually find comfort in how much I can hate myself. I cannot imagine a life free from shame and contempt." The harsh and cutting words of Stanley's father shaped the depths of his identity. He filtered every future relationship through the core beliefs that he had nothing to offer, amounted to nothing, and was just plain stupid. Active and destructive words shape a child's soul.

Another man named Jacob recently told me that his father abandoned the family when Jacob was five years old.[4] One day dad was there, the next day he didn't come home from work. Over the course of the next several years, Jacob discovered that his father had started a new family a mere two miles away. His other children had all they needed, both physically and emotionally. In the meantime, Jacob and his mother languished in poverty, struggling to feed themselves and keep the lights on. Over time, in the absence of his father and the emptiness of his words, Jacob began to believe "I'm not worth staying for" and "There must be something wrong with me." These messages shaped his actions as a teen and eventually as an adult. His vigilance to never again be abandoned created intense anxiety and bouts of depression, and led him to always feel on edge in even the most comforting environments.

For Stanley, the harsh words of his father devastated his soul.

For Jacob, the absence of words created a black hole in his heart.

Fathers have been given the power of words. They can annihilate or haunt, or they can be used to bring life, wholeness, and shape. Proverbs 18:21 speaks to the power of our words to bring life or mete out death: "The tongue has the power of life and death, and those who love it will eat its fruit."[5] Fathers wield the power of words, and we must thoughtfully and intentionally use them to imbue life in our children, our families, and other men.

From Encouragement to Blessing

That day at the pub, Craig encouraged me. He listened to my many overachiever endeavors and gave me the opportunity to ask his advice. He heard my heart for this writing project, said, "You can do it!" and sent me on my way with a firm man-hug and a pat on the back. All of us need encouragement to press onward in this life.

4. Again, name changed.
5. Proverbs 18:21, NIV.

The word encouragement stems from the French word *couer*, meaning "heart." At the core, *to encourage* means "to give heart" or "to enliven the heart." Paul seeks to encourage the Galatians when he says, "Let us not *lose heart* in doing good, for in due time we will reap if we do not grow weary."[6] To the church in Thessalonica he says, "We urge you, brethren, admonish the unruly, *encourage the fainthearted*, help the weak, be patient with everyone."[7] When we find ourselves empty and in need of heart, encouragement is the key.

A man needs encouragement when he is about to ask a woman to marry him. We need encouragement just before heading into a job interview or a football team tryout. A young mother needs encouragement to make it through the "witching hour," that late-afternoon window when all her resources are spent and her husband has yet to leave the office. A student needs encouragement for the SAT, and a teacher needs encouragement during the final days before summer vacation. To encourage others is to be their cheerleader. Encouragement says, "You can do it!" or "You got this!"

Blessing, while similar to encouragement, acts more like a covering and a vision than a shot in the arm. The Hebrew word for blessing is *barak*, and literally means "to kneel." To bless others is to kneel before them in honor and awe as we speak words of insight and prophecy over their lives. To bless requires that we know the landscape of their souls and envision a future that is made better by their active participation in it. Whereas encouragement supports by coming up underneath, blessing seeks to cover and release goodness from above. It casts a vision and offers a trajectory into which the person can step with faith and hope. Encouragement gives strength, while blessing gives shape and a future.

Craig *encouraged* me by cheering me on in my ministry projects. But he *blessed* me by saying, "There is medicine in you." From now onward, I can live into the vision of offering life-giving medicinal healing to others, regardless of what my occupation or current projects may be. He has covered me with his words of blessing.

Knowing before Blessing

The pub where we met pushed capacity on that hot Saturday afternoon. It was full with other patrons seeking refreshment from some of Colorado's

6. Galatians 6:9, NASB, italics added.

7. 1 Thessalonians 5:14, NASB, italics added.

best brews. During my conversation with Craig, had any other person randomly leaned over and said to me, "There is medicine in you," I would have looked at him oddly, thanked him for his kind words, and resumed my conversation with Craig. Either that, or I would have ignored him altogether.

But when Craig, a man who knows me and loves me and is committed to my best, said that, things changed. His words were intentional and knowing, calculated and delivered with intensity. I knew he meant what he said, and he had data to back it up. A blessing is truly powerful when the speaker has insight into and deep familiarity with the inner workings of the life he desires to bless. This man-to-man affinity and awareness is earned by long hours of sharing, togetherness, and vulnerability. It doesn't happen in a few moments. It happens over the course of a lifetime. Those who know us most deeply bless us most profoundly.

The Christian world has neutered the word *blessing* by using it to describe any sort of prayer or good thing. Something is a "blessing" if it feels good or meets a need, as in, "It was such a blessing to have an extra hour of sleep last night" or "Honey, would you say a blessing for our meal?" Blessings today come in the form of good grades or unexpected gifts. In the Bible, however, *to bless* has a far deeper meaning. I've already mentioned that the Old Testament meaning of blessing is "to kneel." In the New Testament, the word *blessing* is directly tied to the notion of *blood*. To bless means to anoint or cover, to make holy and set apart, or to separate and safeguard.[8] In the blessing, there is sacred and sanctifying power, not just goodness.

In order for the true impact of blessing to be felt, a father must first truly know his son as God created him, and seek to honor and cover him for the future God has intended. This is not a father's "wish" for his son, but a true understanding of who the son is designed to be and a release for him to become that man. Proverbs 22:6 encourages fathers to discover our children's "bent" and clear the path for them to live fully into their God-given nature: "Train up the child *according to the tenor of his way*, and when he is old he will not depart from it."[9] Fathers who help their sons discover

8. For more on this concept, see Molitor, *Boy's Passage, Man's Journey.*

9. Darby Bible Translation, italics added. There is sufficient controversy around this verse. Many readers assume this instructs fathers to raise a child *in the way he should go*, i.e. in the paths of God. Indeed, other verses clearly indicate that fathers have the responsibility to instruct their children with regard to faith and godliness. However, this passage in Proverbs, when translated literally, states that the training of the father *is in the direction and way of the child's bent*. When fathers spend the time to discover and bless the people God created their children to be, they live free and fully. Otherwise, they spend

God's design for them, and then bless them to fully become that man, offer life and vision and hope.

In the past, Aidan has gravitated more toward athletics than academics or other extracurricular activities. To be honest, he is pretty good at sports. He has played several seasons of football, basketball, soccer, and baseball. His passion is tackle football.

So, last year, when he came home and announced that he wanted to try out for the school musical, I was floored. I myself performed in a musical in sixth grade. It was the last time I ever sang in public. As Aidan told us about the upcoming play and his desire to audition, my wife and I looked at each other quizzically, but naturally offered our blessing. Turns out, he loves musical theater. And though he still has the gangly-boy-teenager look and is in the throes of a changing voice, he is pretty good. My football-playing son is also a Broadway star in the making.

As his father, I have a choice. I can simply offer my support and show up at the show. Or I can intentionally approve of him by fanning this new-found passion and blessing him with words of life, covering, and vision.

Blessing Touch

Last year, at a men's retreat I facilitated on a small Christian ranch in the backcountry of northern Colorado, Mike changed everything. I had divided the larger group of men into smaller clans. Throughout the weekend, each group reflected and talked together about the content of the retreat, but they also worked as teams in the burn zone that resulted from the devastating High Park Fire in 2012.[10] Laboring together on the mountainside, fifty-plus men would descend from an afternoon of erosion control and tree felling, looking like chimney sweeps from London. We had a marvelously exhausting time.

On our last evening, as the culmination of our experience together, I led the groups into a time of mutual blessing. Each man received words of blessing from the other men in his team, while one of them recorded the blessings for him to keep. It was a rich time that lasted hours, and it brought these men, many of whom had known each other at church for

---

their time attempting to please the father rather than live according to their design.

10. The High Park Fire of 2012 burned more than 87,000 acres over the course of three weeks. It is the third largest fire in Colorado history.

years, into more intentional and intimate relationships with one another. It was powerful.

But Mike did more than speak. He knelt (remember that blessing involves kneeling?) on the ground before each man and placed his hands on the man's chest. In that posture, he looked directly into the man's eyes and spoke words of blessing. As you can imagine, the recipient squirmed and fidgeted, not used to being touched so deliberately and tenderly by another man. But, within a few moments, the power of Mike's words and touch combined to bring every man to tears. The eyes, the words, and the hands created a trinity of blessing that altered the entire atmosphere of that team, and every man walked away changed.

Men these days don't touch one another. If we do, it's a jostle or a punch. Even our hugs are shake-hands-and-bump-shoulders kinds of embraces. Just as there is power in the words of the blessing, so too is there incredible impact from touch. In biblical times, when a father blessed his child, he would reach out his hand and place it on his son's head as a physical representation of covering. James talks about the spirituality of touch as he encourages elders to lay hands on the sick.[11] Moses blessed Joshua by placing his hands on him.[12] Paul blessed and commissioned Timothy through touch.[13] The church at Antioch sent out Barnabas and Paul by blessing them through the laying on of hands.[14] Jesus himself touched those he healed and blessed.[15]

As part of the Man Maker Project, I knew intentional words of blessing needed to be spoken over the life of my son. I knew that the clear words of blessing would answer the booming question in his heart and feed his deep-seated hunger. I have already made a point of being verbal with my children, seeking out ways to encourage and support them in their lives and endeavors. But I knew that—for Aidan to unequivocally *know* that he is indeed a man, and that I see him and approve—I would need to intentionally and intensely lock eyes with him, touch him, and bless him.

In the final stages of his passage year, I spent significant time writing a blessing that walked through the various aspects of manhood he had encountered in the experience, and then spoke words of affirmation and

11. See James 5:14.

12. See Numbers 27:18 and Deuteronomy 34:9.

13. See 2 Timothy 1:6.

14. See Acts 13:3.

15. Verses about the blessing and healing touch of Christ are too numerous to count.

approval of how I had seen them at work in his life. During our final ceremony (which I will describe in more detail in Part IV), in the presence of other men, I spoke these words over him as my hand rested on his shoulder. While my hope is that my words echo in his heart even now, I know that the offering of that blessing over his life changed *me*. When fathers bless their children, God has designed the gift to go both ways. The healing power of a father's words is so potent it cannot but affect everyone involved.

Your Story

In all unfortunate likelihood, you have only a few stories of blessing in your life, if any at all. If you do have moments of blessing, they are likely seared into your heart forever. Who has offered you intentional words of blessing? Maybe your father, maybe an uncle or a grandfather. Maybe a coach, a teacher, or a youth pastor. What did he say? What were his exact words? Where did he speak it? How?

For most men, however, words of blessing have never been offered. Our hearts remain parched for these words of life from another man. In that desert, what have you done? Where have you gone to find the spiritual sustenance your father's blessing *should* have offered? Is it to work? Women? Apathy? Church?

In what ways has your hope for blessing been so disappointed that you would not be able to accept it even if it *were* to come? And in what ways is God calling you to be a masculine agent of life through offering words of blessing?

Jesse, a twenty-six-year-old man who attended the same retreat at which Mike knelt and blessed others, shared this about his experience of blessing that weekend:[16] "It was a profound and really rich experience to offer that to these five other guys. But, more for me, it was to receive their words of blessing. That was something that at the time I didn't realize how much I needed, but as I heard these honest words of blessing to me and for me, their words just felt like rain on dry ground, and I realized how much I had longed to hear those words from men I respected."

We all long for a father's intentional words of blessing. What is your story, and how will you engage that in the process of blessing your son?

16. That is his *actual* name.

Questions for Your Journey

1. Have you ever experienced an intentional blessing from another man? What happened? How did it feel?

2. What words do you long to hear from other men, especially your father?

3. In what ways have you given up hope of receiving such an intentional blessing?

4. What challenges you when you consider offering these words to your son?

5. How would you respond to an older man who knelt before you, placed his hands on your chest, and spoke intensely into your eyes?

6. Who are men in your life whom you can bless even now?

There are four primary atmospheric conditions necessary for male initiation. These include first the *intention* of the father as he turns his heart toward his son with the goal of making him a man. Second, the boy needs to be *removed from the world of women*, ushered away from boyhood and drawn purposefully into the company of men. Third, the young man must face some element of *risk, danger, or struggle*, entering into the symbolic death of the boy and resurrection as a man. And, finally, as a seal and permanent signifier of his affirmed manhood, the father offers a *blessing* to his son that unequivocally and undeniably states, "I hereby deem you a man!"

With these four elements in mind, we now turn our attention to redefining for our boys what true, godly manhood means. Part III explores the six categories I chose as foundational to modern-day manhood. While other aspects of masculinity are equally valid, these six created the structure around which I built the Man Maker Project.

PART III

Restorative Manhood
Redefining Masculinity for Our Sons

The Meaning of Manhood

If we are called to usher our boys into true, godly manhood, we need to clarify for them just what "being a man" means. Messages about manhood, gender, and masculinity abound, and yet most of them fall far short of the true calling of God for men. Over the course of several months, I scoured the Scriptures, literature, and ancient rites of passage material to determine the core aspects of manhood according to God's design. Naturally, I found many—so many, in fact, that I myself became overwhelmed. With the help of a friend, I narrowed down the list to what I believe are the six main categories that provide the foundation for all others. Other men may arrive at an equally valid list, but for my purposes and the Man Maker Project, I decided on these six:

1. Courage
2. Integrity
3. Excellent action
4. Kingdom focus
5. Protective leadership
6. Purity

I believe that God designed men to ally with him in his restorative purposes. Men are intended to bring restoration, and each of these qualities of manhood seeks to release strength, blessing, and hope to himself and the world. When men live according to these principles, individually and communally, they find their restorative place and literally change the world. When men are men, the kingdom comes a little closer.

Naturally, much can be said about each of these qualities. They each deserve an entire book, and the treatment of them here feels cursory and limited. I encourage you to research, pray, read, and investigate beyond what I am able to offer you now. God has not left us without wisdom or godly instruction, and he promises to lead you according to his ways. It merely requires your initiative as a father to determine the right path for your son.

Prior to describing these biblical qualities of a man, we must first wrestle with the reality of how modern-day society treats and defines manhood. The messages and meanings of masculinity have become garbled and empty. In order to return to true manhood, we must start with an acute knowledge of the current situation. From there, we can more effectively provide definitions of godly masculinity.

We will then move forward in the exploration of each foundational man-quality, its meaning, and God's purposes. I have attempted to create a simple definition, one that both you and your son can easily remember. Later, in Part IV, I offer a cheat sheet for each quality with a few biblical examples of men who either displayed or struggled with the characteristic, as well as modern-day models found in film. My hope is to not just talk about the man-quality, but show what it looks like through story. Few things stick in the mind longer than a well-told story, and the medium of film is our modern-day storyteller. You may not remember Balaam from the Bible, but I'm sure you remember Luke Skywalker. And, finally, each section includes questions for you to consider in your own life with regard to the issue at hand, as well as questions designed to explore the landscape of your son's life and heart.

For now, let us dive into God's design for men.

CHAPTER 7

Fallen Manhood

Men in the Eyes of the World

There has been a veritable blitzkrieg on the male gender, what amounts to an outright demonization of men and a slander against masculinity.[1]

—ROBERT MOORE AND DOUGLAS GILLETTE

GREEK RUSH WEEK AT most colleges happens just before classes begin each year. Every fraternity and sorority gears up for their new potential recruits, creating elaborate parties that showcase their house, ethos, history, and membership privileges. It is a time of intrigue and debauchery, in which glassy-eyed freshmen make a lifelong decision to belong to a certain brotherhood or sisterhood. It's really quite a fascinating process.

As a college freshman, I showed up on campus, ready for the excitement and freedom of college life. I quickly made friends in my dorm and got involved in several campus groups with interests similar to my own. One evening in early September, my roommate invited me to go to a rush party at one of the fraternities on the north side of campus. We joined hundreds of other new students on the dance floor of the trashed frat house, witnessed the consumption of massive amounts of alcohol and the resulting drunkenness, and eventually walked home after campus police dissipated the crowd for noise disturbance and underage drinking. It ended up being a horrible evening, one that I vowed never to repeat.

I recognize that not all rush experiences mirror this one. In fact, many of my friends have had tremendous experiences of brotherhood or sisterhood as a result of their involvement with the Greek system in America.

---

1. Moore and Gillette, *King, Warrior, Magician, Lover*, 156.

However, for me, I distinctly remember going home that night and saying to myself, "If being Greek is like *that*, I want nothing to do with it."

Manhood today suffers the same fate. We live in a world where true manhood and masculinity are barely known, and we have settled for a pseudo-masculinity that debases the intention of God in men by reducing us down to the lowest common denominator. As the world attempts to understand and accept fallen masculinity, it glorifies certain common aspects of manhood that fall far from the mark. When we consider raising our boys and initiating them into the fellowship of men, we must ask ourselves, "If this is what being a man is like, do our sons even *want* to be men?"

Negative masculine messages abound. Wading our way through them can prove challenging at best, impossible at worst. Over the past several years, I have made a point of noticing and cataloguing how our world defines manhood. It is clear that three main categories continually rise to the top of the list.

According to modern-day definitions of manhood, we are first and foremost rabidly sex-crazed, unemotional, and vacant beings whose daily life is driven by an overwhelming pressure in our shorts. Second, men are seen as stupid buffoons. We are often characterized as non-thinking idiots who sit idly on the couch in our underwear while the world pulls the wool over our eyes. Third, men are violent and have a fascination with gore and a need to harm.

Watch almost any television show or movie. Ask "What do men want?" of any crowd of people—men or women, boys or girls—and I can almost guarantee that the results will reflect a common societal understanding of what defines men. According to today's society, the glory of masculinity has been reduced to sex, idiocy, and violence.

And what boy wants to be inducted into *that*?

Sex-Crazed Fiends

My wife and I recently watched the first episode of *The Secret Life of the American Teenager*. The story is set in a "typical" high school in America. You've got jocks and nerds, football players dating cheerleaders, band camp and church-gym dances. The parents are doing their best to raise the kids while missing most of their lives and most of the point. There's nothing extraordinary about the plot. In fact, it is rather ordinary. The main character, Amy, is a sophomore who gets pregnant after a one-night, not-so-good sex experience at band camp. She wasn't even sure she had sex. How's that for a compelling story?

Throughout the forty-three minutes of the show, I marveled at how the producers and screenwriters portrayed high school boys. Actually, I was furious. If we are truly attentive to the media's representation of men and boys, we might assume that they (we) are nothing but sex-crazed animals, with nothing else between our ears than thoughts on how to score. Now, I am fully aware that teenage boys are at a heightened level of sexual awareness. I also know that sexual activity among high schoolers is at a historic peak. But there is far more to a young man than his sex drive.

What infuriates me is that sex has come to *define* men. Whether it is the high school boys in *Glee,* James Bond, Jason Bourne, the male characters in *Arrested Development,* or even Tony Stark in *Iron Man,* is there nothing more to men than sex? Is the definition of manhood to be reduced to unbridled sex drives? Has sexuality become such an idol that it overrides any other potential in whom these men might become? Is there more to a man than what hangs between his legs? It seems that the answer society offers is an authoritative no. And while a powerful libido does exist in the lives of many men, so too does the instinctive desire for love, connection, affection, and mutuality. The act of intercourse has been removed from the greater narrative of life and love, and has been tattooed on the hearts of men as if it were the ultimate ingredient to happiness and fulfillment.

I've been working with a young, college-aged client who began seeing me for depression and anxiety. As we investigated the greater story of his life, he revealed an enormous catalogue of sexual relationships that have defined his every waking hour. He constantly texts women, looking for a hook-up or a party to attend. His drinking leads to unhindered behavior, which in turn leads to bed. When he is not actively engaged with a real woman, he often finds himself home alone with some lubrication and an X-rated video. Rather than attack the sexual addiction head-on, we began to explore his definitions of what it means to be a man. At one point he looked at me with shock and hope in his eyes, saying, "You mean I can be a man and *not* have sex?" Somewhere along the way, the wires got crossed in his body and soul, and he lost his way to true intimacy.

Idiots and Passive Buffoons

In addition to sex-crazed, men are often viewed as vacant idiots. Men are stupid, simple creatures who sit passively on the sidelines of life, are easily manipulated, and have very little of importance to say. Men have become *irrelevant*.

Last night, at the dinner table, one of Aidan's younger sisters made an interesting comment about her brother. Though not intended to harm, this comment indicated a culturally informed understanding of what it means to be male. When my son didn't quite catch something that had been said, she blurted out, "It's okay. He won't get it. He's a boy." There exists a deeply rooted, media-informed perspective on masculinity that I find both extremely offensive and terribly detrimental: men simply do not have the personal or social competence to matter.

Prior to this dinner-table conversation, I had joined my kids in watching a Disney Channel show called *Good Luck, Charlie,* a seemingly harmless sitcom about the hilarity of family antics. During this episode, the teenage daughter conspires with the mother to get the dad into a good mood. The goal? To buy the daughter a new car. The entire episode is about how they manipulate, connive, and undercut him for their own gain. At one point, the mother even says, "He's a simple man." In essence she is saying, "We know how to get what we want from this irrelevant man." The father, in turn, plays the part. He does not notice the subtleties of their game and walks around in a vacant, unknowing cloud. Even in the opening credits, the family is pictured as fun-loving and engaging, while the father sits in the background with a befuddled look on his face. Needless to say, I was appalled.

I knew we had a problem when that statement escaped the innocent lips of my daughter. We later had a family discussion about the stereotypes of both men and women, as understood in our world and culture today. We discovered that our kids had a multifaceted, yet still not fully formed, opinion about women— ranging from the traditional "stay-at-home-and-cook" stereotype to the "she-can-conquer-the-world" belief. We found that our daughters believe they can go anywhere and be anything, but also have a high value on motherhood, nurture, and caring for others. In my book, a success.

For boys, however, we uncovered one incredibly disturbing stereotype: guys are dumb. They meander aimlessly through life without point or purpose, and can be easily manipulated for anyone's selfish gain. Their needs are simple, and their perspectives are often uninformed and irrelevant. Idioms like "The way to a man's heart is through his stomach" indicate an assumption of simple thinking overshadowed by physical need.

Often, when I am counseling a married couple, I focus much of my attention on the man. Why? Because, more often than not, he has succumbed to the idea that it is the wife's role to talk about the relationship, make the appointments, and arrange for the growth to happen. He often allows himself to be overshadowed when it comes to relationship and emotions because, he says, "I'm not good at this stuff." As I work with these men, one of my first efforts is to give them permission to speak. "Yes," I tell them, "your thoughts and feelings and perspectives are important. Tell us what they are." Many times, he has no idea what they are at first, but through coaching and encouragement, he begins to uncover a self that has long gone unnoticed, unknown, and dismissed as mostly irrelevant.

What boy wants to grow into *that?*

Violence Obsessed

There is no doubt that our prisons are full of men. It is estimated that about 83 percent of all crime in the United States is committed by males.[2] And while there are many hypotheses for *why* men are violent, there is little said about what to do about it.

When it comes to violence, I will be the first to admit that I prefer blow-them-up kinds of movies. I thrill at the battle scenes in epic movies such as *The Lord of the Rings, Gladiator,* or *Last of the Mohicans.* My son and I enjoy films such as *X-Men, Bourne Supremacy,* and *Avengers.* There is something warrior-like in the heart of men.[3] Yet there is a grand chasm between violence that seeks to destroy, and violence that seeks to protect. They are of a completely different essence.

In our home, my wife and I have made the decision to monitor the types of video games Aidan plays on his X-Box. Over the past decade, modern advances in technology have catapulted gaming graphics into completely new territory. Only a few decades ago, *Pac-Man* and *Centipede* thrilled young players. Now, it's *Call of Duty, Mortal Kombat,* and *Halo.* These games include an increasing amount of violence and are now rated

2. Krienert, *Masculinity and Crime.*

3. Much can be said about this statement, yet I will save that for another work on the phases of a man's life.

like motion pictures. As we have wrestled with what games to allow him to play and which ones to avoid, we have attempted to draw a line between games that ingratiate violence and those that don't. If I am honest, this boundary is very hard to manage, and we have not succeeded on every level. However, the more exposure to violence a boy has, the more immune he becomes to the devastation it can bring.

God designed the male structure, both in mind and body, to fight. Musculature, bone density, stature, digestive systems, and adrenal glands all contribute to a man's ability to battle well. God himself is called a warrior, and he has commanded men to join him in protecting the innocent.[4] [5] Fighting is part of God's intention for men, and needs to be allowed and encouraged while maintaining instruction and direction. At times, Aidan will still join his younger sisters in make-believe games with stuffed animals. The girls create elaborate scenes with relational drama, parties, families, and games. Often, after only a few minutes, they expel Aidan from the room, complaining, "All he wants to do is attack the farm and blow things up." Boys naturally gravitate toward fighting.

But boys do not need to be defined by violence. Men may tend to play rough, but the heart of a man is far deeper than a need to shed blood. Men who battle on behalf of another are far more masculine than those who kill without thought. No one would argue with that. Just as God has given men the innate drive for intimacy and connection *along with* a drive for sexual intercourse, so he has also give men the passion to protect and safeguard *along with* the strength to do so.

In my work with men, I find that many do not have the vocabulary to adequately express their inner worlds. To assist, I often begin by offering them four of the most common top-level experiences men have.

1. *Happy:* Good things are happening in life, and a man is pleased, excited, celebrating, anticipating, grateful, at rest, or satisfied.

2. *Hungry:* A man feels the need for something, whether it is physical sustenance, emotional fulfillment, spiritual nourishment, or mental rest.

3. *Horny:* Many men confuse their sexual desire for their desire to be connected, close, nurtured, cared for, or comforted.

4. See Exodus 15:3.
5. See Isaiah 61.

4. *Hostile:* A man may feel agitated, frustrated, alone, confused, pressured, betrayed, abandoned, impotent, futile, overlooked, demeaned, anxious, depressed, overwhelmed, empty, frightened, missed, unknown, unblessed or stuck.

As we drill down into the depths of these words and begin to truly understand what is going on in the man's heart, the most difficult and broad catchall category is *hostility*. More often than not, when a man has a negative experience of any kind, it leads him toward a hostile response. The most common experience of mankind is frustration, and it rears its head in the area of violence.

Frustration and futility lie at the core of the Genesis man-curse. After the fall of Adam, God solemnly tells him that the consequence of his sin will be the frustration of his work. That which was designed to be good, rewarding, and life giving will now be difficult, hard, and futile. Under the curse of Adam, all men engage in a battle with futility. We are never enough. We cannot do enough, be enough, or provide enough. Under the curse, we are destined to a life of futility.

The glory of the gospel and the beautiful trajectory of all history is that the abundance of the restored earth breaks through the curse and provides for all without cost, pain, or labor.[6] It is a glorious end to a woefully tragic story.

For now, however, we are frustrated. This includes, unfortunately, the journey of masculinity from boy to man. In our world today, where boys so desperately need access to their fathers in order to fulfill their God-given masculine destinies, they are more often than not met with barriers, frustration, lack, or neglect. In many cases, their hunger for their father is rewarded with disdain. As the hope in a boy's heart shuts down with the loss of not receiving what he needs from the father, he internalizes it into something that will make him feel powerful, accepted, and manly: rage. I believe that most acts of violence perpetrated by men, especially young men, is in fact a soul-level cry for dad. Violent behavior becomes an outlet for father-frustration.

Not all violence is vicious and criminal, however. Good, upstanding, well-adapted men may have episodes of culturally acceptable violence. This may include self-sabotaging violence in the form of having a few too many drinks, thrill-seeking motorcycle rides on the highway, or excessive

---

6. See Revelation 21–22 for a fantastic picture of what restored life will look like.

workouts at the gym. Recklessness has come to be a measure of a man. The more he can push the boundaries, the more manly he becomes. When a man's core question (*Am I a man?*) remains inadequately answered, he turns to recklessness to prove himself, hoping that somehow his risk will silence the hunger in his heart.

Or a man may engage in violence against another in an attempt to reduce him and take his place: over-the-top competition on the court, ruthless trading on the floor, or keeping-up-with-the-Joneses behavior with regard to cars, TV size, or lawn manicures. Our hunger to be affirmed drives us more than we know.

At the core, violent men, both those in prison and those in the boardroom, are simply offering their temper-tantrum cries for *someone* to take notice and bless.

Returning to an Ancient Definition

I believe that, in order for boys to be made into men, we must recover and redefine what godly masculinity truly is. If we are to usher our boys into genuine manhood, we are compelled to provide them with a vision of manhood restored. We must have a vision of where we will take them. Otherwise,

> men go through life struggling with what they *believe* to be the demands of their masculinity. They try to be what they think a man *would be*, and they make a tolerable approximation of masculinity. They may compare themselves to the myths of masculine heroes, and find themselves lacking, and give up on the struggle to be masculine. They may run from masculinity and become feminine instead, or just go through life as a boy, terrified of becoming a man. Or they may exaggerate *whatever they think men are or should be*.[7]

Therefore, the task is greater than we imagined. Not only do we as fathers need to step onto the field and begin moving our sons intentionally toward manhood, but we also must redefine for them what manhood truly is.

Fortunately, in his mercy and goodness, God has provided us with clear scriptural principles that act as guardrails for both our definition and experience as men. When Paul says to "act like men,"[8] he has specific

7. Frank Pittman, *Man Enough*, 4, italics added.

8. See 1 Corinthians 16:13, especially the NASB version.

characteristics and responsibilities in mind. It is our role as fathers to mine the Scriptures for those eternal truths, digest them in light of our current culture and time, and deliver them to the next generation of men.

It is not enough to say, "Yes, you are a man." We must also help our sons know what a man truly is. As a culture, we need a masculine language that builds hope, identity, and direction. We cannot settle for what society offers us. We must look to the Creator's design to know whom he made us to be as men. Only then can we step into true manhood.

The next several chapters address six specific manhood qualities I wanted to address with my son during his Man Year. While they may not paint a complete picture of godly manhood, they provided significant scaffolding for him to begin to understand the heart and direction of God's design and intention. I believe these qualities are ubiquitous across all men regardless of geography, ethnicity, economic status, age, or denomination. As an intentional father, you will need to adapt their application to the uniqueness of your situation and your son.

Questions for Your Journey

1. How would you describe the modern-day definition of manhood?

2. How do you see men portrayed in media today?

3. In what ways do you agree or disagree with this understanding of masculinity?

4. Consider the three categories I've proposed: sex-crazed, idiot, and violent-obsessed. How do you fit?

5. How do you think the church defines masculinity? Do you agree?

6. What are your hopes for manhood in future generations?

CHAPTER 8

Courage
Having Heart

Above all else, guard your heart, for everything you do flows from it.[1]

—PROVERBS 4:23

Have I not commanded you? Be strong and courageous. Do not be afraid; do not be discouraged, for the Lord will be with you wherever you go.[2]

—JOSHUA 1:9

Courage is the most important of all virtues, because without courage you can't practice any other virtue consistently. You can practice any virtue erratically, but nothing consistently without courage.[3]

—MAYA ANGELOU

MOST EVERYTHING IN A man's life requires courage, because most everything in a man's life requires heart. The wise sage of Proverbs tells us, "everything you do flows from the heart."[4] *Everything.* The heart is the core, the center, *the* totality of the inner man. I have already mentioned that the root of courage is *couer*, meaning "heart." Every other aspect of a man's life

1. NIV.
2. Ibid.
3. As quoted in Graham, *Diversity*, 224.
4. See Proverbs 4:23.

involves how he interacts with the world, focusing on his external relationships and actions. Courage, on the other hand, involves a deep internal
reservoir of a godly blend of strength and tenderness. Courage calls a man
to be both bold and gentle. The way a man is inwardly in his heart determines who he is externally.

Courage represents an inner strength that decides to enter in rather
than wimp out. It is the core of the man that chooses to stand up for what
is right rather than stand back and allow injustice to flourish. It is the conviction to live well and rightly and with purpose rather than to passively
watch life go by. A man with courage is an unstoppable force, facing life's
challenges with boldness and despite fear.

Yet we live in a world of masculine cowardice. We are a paradox. We
love to watch movies with those quintessential moments where the protagonist must make the courageous choice to save the world as he sacrifices
himself. Our hearts swell as he steps into the role of hero, believing that we
too, if put in the same position, would make the same courageous choice.
We live vicariously through the courage of these fictional characters while
we sit comfortably on our man-chairs in a world light years removed from
true epic adventures. Far too many men cave at the mere hint that something sacrificial might be required of them. Instead of rising in courage, too
many men cower.

Courage just takes too much effort. And who has time for it anyway?
It's just easier to . . . Insert your own sentence here. *It's just easier to roll over
and go to sleep. It's just easier to wait and see what happens. It's just easier to
focus on the 401k than to focus on today. It's just easier to watch a show. It's
just easier to masturbate than engage her right now. It's just easier to let the
high school teachers deal with him than for me to bring it up. It's just easier
for the youth pastor to teach them about God.*

Some segments of our culture require more courage than others.
Daily, our soldiers and police forces, our fire fighters and wilderness first
responders, our inner-city social workers and international justice seekers
lead us through valiant examples of bravery in the face of danger. These
men (and women) should be commended and highly honored.

But is it *heart*? I know many men who face physical danger daily
because the job requires it. Danger on the job is their duty. But when it
comes to facing their wives or being present for their children, when the
rubber meets the road and their hearts are required, many of these men of

"courage" tuck tail and run to the shadows. They can take a jaw-crushing blow to the face, but they cannot stand the sight of a desperate wife.

In structuring the Man Year for Aidan, I knew that courage must create the foundation for all other masculine qualities. A man cannot and will not be pure, for example, if he does not have the courage to stand up against the forces of impurity in the world. He will not be a protective leader if he does not have the courage to step into harm's way on behalf of another. A man cannot display integrity if he does not have the courage to speak the truth. He will not engage the world as a kingdom citizen if he does not have the courage to represent the King. A godly heart, therefore, is the foundation of masculinity. No wonder Paul admonishes us to "not lose heart."[5]

Courage is the first gate through which all boys must pass if they are to truly become men. Ask any guy (and ask yourself) if there is any word more demoralizing or degrading for a man to be called than *coward*. It cuts to the core. I would rather be an idiot, a loser, a poser, a trickster, a failure, or a liar than a coward. Our language is rife with euphemisms connecting courage and cowardice with male genitalia. "He's got balls" or "You need to grow a pair" or "Don't be so limp" or "That was ballsy." Being emasculated means that a man's courage has been surgically removed. Even the phrase "Man up!" means "have courage." To be a true man means to have courage.

I love Aidan's honesty when I first presented the Man Year to him. There among the pines in the South Dakotan Black Hills, he absorbed all I presented and the plan I had for his rites of passage process. First, he looked at me with tears and thanked me. I melted. But then, almost within the same breath, he said, "I'm not sure I can do it." Somehow he knew that true heart would be required, and he wasn't convinced he had enough. Then, he said the four words I long to hear most out of the mouths of men. "I'll do my best."

God deposed King Saul from the Israelite throne because of his lack of courage. In 1 Samuel 13, we find a frightened Saul who, upon seeing the amassing Philistine army, became afraid and acted rashly. In his fear that led to cowardice, he took matters into his own hands and disobeyed the command of God. Later, Samuel corrects Saul and tells him that the man God has chosen to replace him is "a man after the *heart* of God."[6] For a man of God, courage is required.

5. See 2 Corinthians 4:1,16.
6. See 1 Samuel 13:1–15, italics added.

Courage: having the guts to do hard things despite your fears

The opposite of courage is to be "heart*less*." A heartless man is overcome by his fears, paralyzed to move, and tempted to withdraw. He lacks conviction, direction, passion, and purpose, and stays on the sidelines while life passes him by. He is the Lion in *The Wizard of Oz*, who trembles at the sight of danger and runs for cover. In addition, heartless also means callous, cruel, or unfeeling. A heartless man has well-constructed self-defensive mechanisms that deny access to his internal world. Interestingly, a heartless man in our society may be viewed as macho, manly, or unmoved by emotion, when in fact he lacks access to the true life God intended him to enjoy.

Heartless men abound. Recently I spoke to a married couple on the cusp of their fifteenth anniversary.[7] The husband, a military man, sat before me with a flat expression and folded arms, waiting for me to "fix" their relationship. His double-barrel biceps bulged beneath his sleeves and his chest stretched his shirt. Though almost a foot shorter than I, he could definitely take me. He was the epitome of physical masculinity, but he pouted like a boy as he huffed and puffed about his wife's faults and demands. She, on the other hand, sat longingly on the other end of the couch. She had almost given up on him—almost. At one point he asked her, "What do you want from me, anyway? I give you everything you need. What else do you want?"

Her reply: "I want your heart."

At that moment, he broke. Through the first tears she had ever witnessed on his face, he said, "I'm afraid I don't have one. It got lost. My dad took it from me as a boy and locked it up. My mom threw away the key when she called me a coward. All my work, all my fighting, all my anger toward you has been aimed at keeping you away because I don't have the courage to face you. I'm just a coward." It was the most courageous moment I've witnessed in a decade.

To be a coward is to be overcome by fear, to *not* have the internal strength of heart to face adversity, difficulty, or danger. Cowardice leads to apathy and withdrawal, and keeps men from engaging the world in restorative ways. Cowards resort to using rage, power, and authority to accomplish their wants without the thought of serving others. They become high-chair tyrants who make temper-tantrum demands.

Cowardly men consent to evil's assault on their hearts. From the moment of a boy's birth, the intent of darkness is to annihilate or anesthetize

7. Details have been changed to protect their privacy.

his heart, for evil knows that a man with a heart of courage cannot be stopped. Evil seeks to destroy that which is most threatening to its advance in the world—a true heart for God. Men who succumb to cowardice or heartless vacancy have come to believe that their hearts are not needed, necessary, or even wanted.

No man is born a coward. He becomes one through evil's elaborate strategy of heart-targeted brainwashing. He stays one by agreeing with evil: "You are right. I'm not needed."

All Men Have Fear, But Not All Men Are Cowards

Cowardice is vastly different from fear. All men have fear. Experiencing fear is a normal human response to a threatening stimulus. Fear is not the issue. According to the definition I've proposed, courageous men act "despite our fears." Cowardice occurs when a man gives in to fear and allows it to become the ruling narrative. Cowardice is when he tucks tail and runs. Men who embody courage recognize their fears, often openly and vulnerably, and still find the strength of heart to move in.

Every man who has seen the movie *Braveheart* remembers the scene in which William Wallace rallies his ragamuffin collection of freedom fighters to stay their ground against the English:

> I am William Wallace. And I see a whole army of my countrymen, here in defiance of tyranny! You have come to fight as free men. And free men you are. What will you do without freedom? Will you fight? Yes, fight and you may die. Run and you will live, at least for a while. And, dying in your bed many years from now, would you be willing to trade all the days from this day to that for one chance, just one chance, to come back here as young men and tell our enemies that they may take our lives but they will never take our freedom?[8]

Outnumbered and exhausted, Wallace's men shook with fear. In all likelihood, this would be the day of their deaths. But rather than shame them for their fear, Wallace called them to courage, to fight on behalf of a bigger story, and to stand their ground in the face of danger. He asked them to have heart, to stand in the gap, *despite their fear*. He did not demean them for being afraid, but challenged them to consider the death their cowardice

8. *Braveheart*, 1995. What man-book would be complete without a reference to *Braveheart*?

would produce. In the end, they fought their enemy, and, though many died that day, they won the war.

We must build into the hearts of our boys a commitment to courage. We must remind them of the heart with which they were born, and call them to remember the greater story. Too many boys enter manhood without developing a core of courage. They live as empty, frightened, passive men who squander their manly responsibilities to step in as an ally of the King and push back the darkness.

Every father must help his son find his heart and live heart-fully. Only then will he know his true manhood.

God's With-ness

Courage asks a man to step up and face his fears—to look them in the eye and find the strength to move forward in faith. God never asks a man to stand alone, but consistently offers courage to the man who locks into the strength of God's presence with him. A true man's courage must be based in his faith and love of God. Otherwise, his strength inevitably fails and he finds himself in too deep without a rope. Self-reliant men come quickly to the end of themselves.

The core of courage must be bound to the strong presence of God, that is, in remembering his presence, his *with-ness*. A truly courageous man knows his place in service of the King, and rests in the strength of God rather than his own. As believers, we are freed to experience courage because we are in intimate relationship with the One who never fears. Indeed, "there is no fear in love. But perfect love drives out fear."[9]

Almost every time a human encounters an angel in the Scriptures, the first words of the angel are "Do not be afraid. The Lord is with you." Consider Gideon, the fearful Israelite hiding in a hole from the oppressive Midianite army: "When the angel of the Lord appeared to Gideon, he said, 'The Lord is with you, mighty warrior.'"[10] Or when Gabriel talks to Mary, he says, "Do not be afraid, Mary, you have found favor with God."[11] And remember when Jesus walks on the water in the middle of the night? The disciples think he's a ghost. He says, "Take courage! It is I. Don't be afraid."[12]

9. 1 John 4:18, NIV.
10. Judges 6:12, NIV.
11. Luke 1:30, NIV.
12. Matthew 14:27, NIV.

When left to ourselves, we are an unsure people. In the face of the unknown, we default to fear. But with the presence of God, we have the freedom to take heart. Our fear is relieved by the with-ness of God. Courage comes from a transcendent understanding of the greater narrative—a story where God *is*, and that is enough. It is this courage that allows the imprisoned and chained apostle Paul, knowing that his life rests in the hands of a cruel despot, to sing.[13] His courage joins with the presence of God and stands in outright defiance of evil, saying, "You shall not pass!"[14]

In this way, courage joins God in the battle against evil and pushes it back in a defiant assault. Whereas cowardice joins evil in agreement, courage defies evil in attack. To have godly courage is to stand with God as he stands with us and says, "No. As far as it depends on me, I will not allow the enemy to steal, kill, and destroy any longer. And while I may lose my life in the process, I am convinced that, in the end, I will find it."

In the ultimate act of courage, Jesus himself walked through several agonizing hours of fear and despair. He begged his friends to be with him through the darkest night in the history of the world. While they slept, he entered the overwhelming agony of betrayal, powerlessness, and ambivalence as he faced the dawn of his death. Too much cannot be said of these moments where the depth of his humanity came crashing into the reality of his divinity. He begs the Father for a different way. In the end, no other avenue is found. And so, despite his fears and for the sake of the entire world, he steps into courage and says, "Not my will, but yours be done."[15] True courage is an intentional entrance into potential pain rather than a reckless leap into the unknown. There is no recklessness in the cross.

Recklessness

Where is the line between stupidity and bravery? The same act can, at different times, have vastly different motivations. Recently I saw a GoPro video clip of a young man jumping from a high, fenced-off cliff into deep water below. Along with his smiling friends, he thrilled and cheered as he leapt from the fifty-foot-high rock and splashed effortlessly into the waves. His waterproof video camera caught everything, from his skirting the fence to his feet leaving the edge to his plummet beneath the water's surface. It also

13. Acts 16:25.

14. An obvious reference to my hero, Gandalf, from *The Lord of the Rings*.

15. Luke 22:42, NIV.

caught his slow ascent to the surface again, and the ten-foot shark whose attention he accidentally captured. In a flurry of bubbles and panic, he swims quickly to shore, checking again and again for the underwater predator. With a flurry of profanity, the video abruptly ends.[16]

This man's jump was indeed brave. Leaping from that height took guts. But it was not courageous. Courage demands an engagement with the heart-desire to see goodness and restoration. While we never see the young man's friends in the video again, courage would have meant one of *them* leaping into the same water in the same way to rescue their now shark-bait friend. Same act—leaping from the cliff into the water—and yet one is reckless, the other courageous.

As fathers, we must help our sons navigate the enormous differences between courage and recklessness, which are divided by a very thin line. Without guidance, boys will tend toward recklessness and call it courage, when in fact they have missed the mark by a mile and a half. All boys are caught in the bind of their core question: *Am I a man?* But the drive to have this question answered will lead them to leap off cliffs into shark-infested waters with a GoPro camera on their heads. It is our calling as dads to help them adequately find their heart of courage, to know when it is needed and right and good, and to understand when their actions are stupid rather than courageous.

Courage forms the foundation for all other manly qualities. Without courage, without a true heart, no man can live life without defaulting to emptiness, autopilot, or violence. For this reason, God's preparatory words for Joshua prior to his entrance into the land of promise gently resonate: "Be strong and courageous. Do not be terrified, do not be discouraged, for the Lord your God will be with you wherever you go."[17]

Your Story

There are few things more powerful for a boy than to hear the courageous stories of his father. Our narratives offer our sons a real-life experience that they can relate to, remember, and incorporate into their own lives. Too often fathers withhold their stories, fearing that the listener will be

16. Interestingly, upon further investigation of this video, I discovered many objections to its authenticity. Regardless, it's an interesting clip.

17. Joshua 1:9, NIV. Note God's words include, once again, a call to courage in the face of fear in light of God's promise of with-ness.

uninterested or offended. When we tell our children how we have struggled and succeeded, they come to realize that they too can overcome: "If Dad did it, I can too."

Be sure to tell your own stories of being challenged to have courage. These can be stories in which you won or lost, as both courage and cowardice give windows into your life and heart, and normalizes your son's experience. Think about things you did well, such as when you asked your wife to marry you, when you made a decision to change career paths, or when you became a Christian. Also tell stories of times you regret, such as not having enough courage to take a good opportunity, losing a relationship because of fear, or not standing up for what is right. Tell him about the courage it requires to daily pursue your wife's heart, and the courage you have struggled to find to step into this process with him. Also tell him how you handle your fears, and how you rely on the Lord for strength in the face of fear.

At this juncture the initiation process of your son also becomes a healing process for you. The more you engage your own life and stories in relation to your boy, the more you will be able to free yourself and even "father" yourself through those areas that remain unfinished and hungry. Just as the Scriptures give us a multitude of stories that orient us toward the King, give your son stories from your life that will stand as beacons of courage to be remembered in times of trouble.

His Story

Young men also need to tell their stories of courage and valor. Ask your son to reflect on his life and identify times when he had courage to face a fear or difficult situation. You may need to prompt him with specific questions to spur a memory or to get him to talk. As you know all too well, boys don't talk about these things without significant prompting. While you listen, be mindful to tell him, "Wow, now *that* took courage." What his heart most needs from you is the affirmation and acknowledgement of his courage.

Be very careful not to incite shame. There are fewer things more emasculating than the implication of cowardice. Help your son navigate those stories in his life in which he failed to find courage, and gently provide him categories to understand the difference between fear and the actions of a coward. Identify with him his own desire to be courageous "next time," and be intentional to offer him an inordinate number of high-fives, fist bumps, and celebratory words when he has indeed been both strong and courageous.

Questions for Your Journey

1. What comes to mind when you think of the word *courage*? What about the word *heart*?

2. What aspect of "having heart" challenges you the most? In what area of life do you struggle to have courage?

3. If God is big, good, and in control, why do you think he calls us to have courage?

4. How was courage modeled for you? Was it?

5. What does the word *coward* evoke in you? What would happen in your soul if your wife, your father, or your son called you a coward?

6. In what ways have you been reckless in your life, with the mistaken belief that you were showing courage? What do you see as the main differences between the two?

7. As you lead your son through this process, what do you want to be sure to tell him about courage?

8. Turn now to Chapter 15, where I have provided you with a summary for each characteristic of manhood, along with a list of suggested movies, biblical characters, conversation starters, etc. Consider this a sort of cheat sheet for you and any other men you involve in this process for your son. Photocopy it, take a picture of it, rip it out. Whatever you do, enter the conversation intentionally and create space for you and your son to talk about and experience these topics together.

CHAPTER 9

Integrity

Whole and True

Whoever walks in integrity walks securely,
but whoever takes crooked paths will be found out.[1]

—PROVERBS 10:9

Truthful witness by a good person clears the air,
but liars lay down a smoke screen of deceit.[2]

—PROVERBS 12:17

Integrity characterizes the entire person, not just part of him.
He is righteous and honest through and through.
He is not only that inside, but also in outer action.[3]

—R. KENT HUGHES

LET'S BE HONEST. LYING is at the core of every person's heart. From the very beginning, deception has been a central part of the human condition. In our attempts to self-protect, to seem bigger and better, and to outdo our fellow man, we resort to all sorts of deceptions to throw others off the trail of our true selves.

1. NIV.
2. The Message.
3. Hughes, *Disciplines of a Godly Man,* 128.

Integrity

I lie every day. I hide the truth from others for my own gain. I say things that are not true and omit things that are. I have a variety of reasons for this, and some might be noble but most are not. In the end, I just do not want to deal with the weight of integrity. I try hard not to lie big, but I am a liar nonetheless.

To be clear, I don't have a second secret family tucked away in the Kentucky Mountains. I don't have bank accounts my wife does not know about. I don't cheat on my taxes or take "business" trips to Vegas.

But I do tell my kids that I don't have any gum when there is a new pack in the glove compartment. When the crossing guard in front of the elementary school asks how I'm doing, I smile and answer with a cheery "Fine," when in reality I'd prefer to hide under the covers of the bed I rarely see. I nod at the dental hygienist, indicating that I value flossing and commit to do so regularly from here on out.

I am not a big liar, but a liar nonetheless.

As I've approached this topic of integrity for the Man Maker Project, I have had to take a deep and honest look at my own heart. I would much rather teach integrity to my son than live it myself. Yet I know that, as the Proverbs promise, those who choose the crooked paths of deception will be found out.[4] And no one wants to be found out.

Lies are like bunnies. Though seemingly small, innocent, and sometimes even "white" at the start, they multiply and multiply in exponential explosions until the cute little "wabbit" becomes a host of pesky pests. In my work as a counselor, I often deal with the devastation that results from one little lie that has mushroomed into a family-, marriage- and career-killer.

If you took a moment to survey your world, your life, and your heart, you would likely find a multitude of examples of such devastation. You know this destruction firsthand and have suffered as a result. Yet, despite our own pain at the hands of the dishonest, we daily find ourselves in the very place of the liar. In many ways, we cannot escape our own lying lips.

For months, I counseled Tina and Jim.[5] They came to me for help with their failing marriage. Together for over fifteen years, they found themselves in a place of hatred and hopelessness. We had made no headway after several sessions, and I began to wonder what force prevented our movement forward. Jim was obviously straddling the fence. Each week he brought up his unwillingness to commit to either staying in the marriage

4. Proverbs 10:9.

5. Names and details changed to protect their identities.

or getting out. At one point I even called him "slippery" and likened my conversations with him to how ineffective it must feel to punch a wall of Jell-O. Probably not the best admission of a therapist to a client.

As time passed, we uncovered a horrible truth. For fifteen years, Jim had not been honest. No, he had not hidden a secret life or had a multitude of affairs. No, he did not have a shameful addiction, and, no, he was not struggling with his sexuality. The fact was that he had never loved Tina, and he had remained woefully dishonest for a decade and a half. The seeds of his displeasure had been sown years and years ago, and now we were walking in a forest of his lies, wondering why we kept bumping into trees.

Jim's lack of integrity ruined their marriage in subtle and quiet ways. Nothing overt, nothing clearly "sinful," but devastating nonetheless. As a young man, Jim not only became committed to dishonesty, he became a man not truly himself. He was *dis*integrated.

Honesty and Integrity

There is a small but vital difference between honesty and integrity. Being honest simply requires telling the truth. Often, one of my first suggestions for my clients is to start an "honesty journal," in which they are to write the truth—the naked truth—about what they think, feel, believe, and hope. It should be raw, unfiltered honesty about all that they desperately seek to conceal. The daring souls who begin to write soon discover that their deception goes far deeper than they realized—they are not even honest with themselves. By practicing honesty, they unblock the dam of true emotion, and the intense pressure to contain and conceal the nakedness of their true selves is relieved. I tell them that honesty builds our self-esteem.[6] Much more than self-talk and motivational speaking, truly being honest frees our souls from the prisons of our own deceit. If we cannot esteem our own selves enough to be honest, we cannot imagine others would respect us either. The more free we are to tell the truth, the more we build our sense of agency and place in the world.

Honesty has the same root as *honor*—honor of another, honor of God, and honor of the self.[7] Honesty is *inter*personal. Being honest with your

---

6. I first heard this concept from Dr. O'Donnell Day. Ever since, I have tested this theory with myself and my clients, and I have found that she is right. Honesty holds the key to being, as she always put it, "Just as I am."

7. Consider the tri-fold relationships in the great commandment to love God, your

wife, friends, neighbor, pastor, boss, kids, or the IRS requires you to honor them enough to tell the truth. We honor others by being honest. I don't know about you, but when I discover that one of my children has been less than truthful, I consider it an act of disrespect. They have dishonored me by not telling me the truth. More than the lie itself, the lack of honor in the interchange is the greater offense.

Integrity, however, takes honesty to an uncomfortably high level. Integrity comes from the word *integer*, meaning "whole," the antonym of *divided*. Integrity refers to being full, complete, unbroken. Having integrity means that you are the same person on the inside as you are on the outside. While honesty is interpersonal, integrity is interpersonal and *intra*personal. It requires not only that I not lie to another, but also that I do not lie to myself. Being a man of godly integrity—that is, being integrated—means being whole. Our words and actions match our attitudes and motivations. Our interactions with people correspond with our feelings toward them.

We all know the difference between simply saying "I'm sorry" and a true, heartfelt apology. For many years, after our children committed some offense, my wife and I required them to approach the victim and "say you're sorry." They soon learned that, when they promptly said these simple words, they would be released and allowed to move on to other things. Over time, my wife and I realized that their hearts were disconnected from their mouths. Though they went through the motions of apology, they were not truly repentant or remorseful for the harm they had caused. Integrity requires outward actions to match inward motivations. It demands integration.

A man of integrity is true to who he is. He strives to be the person he was created to be in his most true and authentic form. He is whole and complete, not divided. Living without integrity is the same as being a hypocrite who pretends to be something in his heart and soul that he is not. Another perfect word for this is *poser*.[8]

Nothing so incensed the heart of Jesus than a poser. Nowhere else in Scripture do we experience the wrath of Christ as fiercely as we do against the disintegrated. In Matthew 23, Jesus reserves special punishment for the Pharisees and the teachers of the law. He says, "Do not do what they do, for they do not practice what they preach. They tie up heavy, cumbersome

neighbor, and yourself.

8. John Eldredge has popularized this term as it relates to a man's self-protective mechanisms designed to keep others at a safe distance from his true heart.

loads and put them on other people's shoulders, but they themselves are not willing to lift a finger to move them."[9] He continues with one of his most blasting sermons. Seven times he says, "Woe to you, teachers of the law," and calls them hypocrites, children of hell, blind guides, fools, dirty dishes, whitewashed tombs, and snakes who are unable to enter heaven and are responsible for death.[10] In other words, Jesus is not happy with two-faced, dishonest men.

Living with integrity requires much more than honesty. It demands that we know our inner man as God designed him to be.

As a result, teaching your son about integrity involves instructing him in the essentials of telling the truth *and* teaching him how critical it is to know, explore, discover, and love the man God made him to be. Only then can he have integrity. C.S. Lewis says, "The question is not what we intended ourselves to be, but what He intended us to be when He made us."[11]

In a world where reputation and personas are paramount, we grow up believing that what is inside is less valuable than who we think we *should* be on the outside. Conformity is the antithesis of integrity, for it asks us to sacrifice our true selves on the altar of society's notions of who we all should be. In this way, façades, smoke screens, reputations, and fads are weapons of disintegration. When we are not our true selves as image-bearers of God, when we do not know or boldly proclaim his magnificent and unique fingerprint on our hearts, we dishonor ourselves and mock the Creator.

The devastation in Jim's life and marriage came as a result of his dishonest and disintegrated heart. What might have happened if, fifteen years ago, he knew his own heart well enough to be honest about his displeasure and did something about it?

It is often said that truth is like a compass that will guide us through life. Stay as close to truth as we can, and we will navigate our existence well. Anyone who has flown a plane or captained a ship knows the supreme value of course settings. In the short term, a one- to two-degree variance makes little difference. But, over the length of the journey, a small alteration in bearing will bring us to a completely different destination.

Integrity: honoring yourself and others by being
wholly *you*, even when it hurts

9. Matthew 23:3–4, NIV.

10. Matthew 23:13–39, NIV. Quite an interesting read.

11. Lewis, *Mere Christianity,* 202.

Freedom and Truth

For almost forty years, my father served the Denver community as a freedom fighter. I prefer that name to *attorney*, as I hope to inspire images of justice and goodness instead of greedy tort lawyers or slimy ambulance chasers. Following in the footsteps of his father, my dad defended our city's civil servants in their moments of crisis. Our house hosted a steady flow of police officers, sheriffs, firefighters, and rangers, all hoping that he would help them tell their stories well in the pursuit of justice and freedom.

My father was no stranger to the nuances of law, the intensity of trial, and the glories and failures when verdicts are read and sentences meted. At all hours of the night, he was called out to crime scenes gone bad, where cops had shot robbers, and BB guns in the hands of youth had been mistaken for assault rifles in the hands of assailants. It was grueling work.

As a result, our home was inundated with discussions about ethics, truth, and law. Our vacations involved long walks through our country's historic districts, stopping at almost every plaque to ingest the stories of how our nation's system of truth came to be. My father is a man who stands for justice and truth, knowing that, in the government of God, "truth will set you free."[12] Even when some of his clients told the truth and received the appropriate punishment for their crimes, they remained inwardly free from the gnawing soul-erosion that occurs when lives are based on lies.

There is always a correlation between truth and freedom. Where there is truth, there is freedom. Where there is freedom, there is truth. They are mutual and together. In the same way, untruth is always connected to captivity. Where there are lies, there is slavery. Where there is slavery, there are lies.

Consider for a moment the modern-day epidemic of slavery, commonly known as human trafficking. Instead of the forced abductions common to the slave trade centuries ago, traffickers today use deception and manipulation to seduce their victims. Those struggling with poverty are told grandiose stories of money and jobs awaiting them in city centers across foreign borders. They hear tales of women who make enough money waitressing in one weekend to support themselves and their destitute families back home. Captured by the lie, they end up captured by the pimp, only to discover that they have fallen into a trap of deception with no way out.

Is it any wonder then, that the grand seduction of humanity in Genesis 3 involved an untruth from the Father of Lies? From the beginning,

12. John 8:32, NIV.

Snake-Tongue wove his deceit into shackles for humankind, resulting in our bondage to sin and death that only Christ himself could break. The fall of our race hung on the lie that we too could be like God. John 8:44 tells us, "He was a murderer from the beginning, not holding onto the truth, for there is no truth in him. When he lies, he speaks his native language, for he is a liar and the father of lies."[13] And how did Jesus shatter our enslavement to death? The one who said, "I am the way, the truth, the life. No one comes to the Father except through me" comes to rescue his long-lost sons and daughters from captivity.[14]

To be dishonest is to join Satan. To "speak the truth in love" is to decisively stand with the King in defiance against the evil one.[15]

The Truth Hurts

"You can't handle the truth!" screams Jack Nicholson as he plays Colonel Nathan R. Jessup in the 1992 blockbuster *A Few Good Men*.[16] In one of the most well-recited monologues of the early nineties, Jessup blasts Tom Cruise's character in a vehement battle over responsibility and truth. In the end, Jessup is found guilty of a heinous crime, but he also brilliantly exposes one of the most difficult realities of truth: it is often extremely painful.

In many ways, we prefer our well-crafted alternate realities to the truth of our existence. We'd rather watch a sitcom or a ballgame than hear on-the-ground reports of devastation in remote villages in Syria or Iraq. We'd prefer to think about the fuel efficiency of our new vehicle than about the ozone destruction already occurring as a result of our old car. We put our unopened credit card bills on the desk, hoping that our debt is not as bad as we assume. We avoid the annual checkup and find excuses to dodge the annual tooth cleaning. When asked how our marriage is, we smile and nod and say, "Oh, it's just fine." We minimize our struggle to sin, our captivity to addiction, our distance from God, and our anemic relationships, all with the pleasant lamination of platitudes. "It's fine. Just fine. All fine," we say. In reality, we can't handle the truth.

Unfortunately, there is a deeper truth we most certainly can't handle. One that so unnerves us and makes us squirm that we rarely hear it, let

13. John 8:44, NIV.

14. John 14:6, NIV.

15. Ephesians 4:15, NIV.

16. *A Few Good Men*, 1992.

alone believe it. Dan Allender recently said, "When you look at the nature and state of your soul, it is really much, much worse than you ever thought. But the more devastating and stunning reality, and the one at which we can only ever so briefly glance, is the truth that you are more deeply loved and cherished and delighted in than you can imagine. *That* is a truth you most certainly cannot bear."[17] In the end, it is this truth, this devastatingly beautiful truth, that will set us free.

In order to live as men with integrity, and to raise a generation of men who know how to hold their integrity with determination and grit, we must call our boys to not only stand for what is right and true, but to know their deepest heart—and love it.

Your Story

As the father, it is important for you to take the lead in telling stories of integrity from your own life. These are murky waters, and your son needs to know that he can have a safe conversation with you without feeling ashamed or condemned. He needs to know that you struggle with integrity every day, sometimes succeeding, sometimes failing. Tell him stories in which you were stretched and had to make difficult decisions. Share stories in which you don't know if you made the right choice. Many of our stories of integrity involve pain. Invite your son into the dilemmas you've faced, and help him understand why and how you made the decisions you did.

Beyond conversations about honesty and truthfulness, also share how you have continued to understand more of who you are on the inside, and how you are trying to live from that place. What stories can you share with him about how God has been leading you to be more true to yourself? Do you have those experiences? The more you give him a window into the internal world of your heart, the more free he will be to explore his own. Remember, you are ushering his heart into the deeper waters of manhood. He will need encouragement and love to dive in.

His Story

More than you may care to know, your son has already been deeply challenged in the area of integrity. He has had to make choices, some good and

17. Allender, a lecture given at The Seattle School of Theology and Psychology.

some bad. In all likelihood, he has lied to you directly and manipulated you subversively. As he wrestles with the topic of integrity, he will need to know that you love him, regardless of what he reveals. The grace and kindness of the father invites openness and confession in the son. At the same time, try not to create a space where he feels like he needs to confess his deep, dark sins. You will want to ask about stories of success as well as stories of failure. He needs to hear words of affirmation and approval from you.

Questions for Your Journey

1. The topics of honesty and integrity automatically invoke shame in most people. We immediately have the fear that we will be found out and exposed. As you were reading this chapter, on what areas of your life did God press? Where is he calling you to step further into integrity?

2. How have lies and *dis*integration marred your life (whether your own lies or those of someone else)?

3. When in your life have you stood at the crossroads of truth and lies, and had to make a choice? What did you choose? What was the result of your choice?

4. What internal work do you need to do before you lead your son into the category of integrity?

CHAPTER 10

Excellent Action

Extraordinary Impact

The test of the artist does not lie in the will with which he goes to work, but in the excellence of the work he produces.[1]

—THOMAS AQUINAS

Whatever you do, work at it with all your heart, as working for the Lord, not for human masters . . . It is the Lord Christ you are serving.[2]

—COLOSSIANS 3:23–24

Whatever your hand finds to do, do it with all your might . . .[3]

—ECCLESIASTES 9:10

I CAN'T TELL YOU how incredibly frustrating it is to open the door to my son's room and find mounds and mounds of laundry impeding my entry. The bed remains unmade, the room smells of pungent nastiness, and football pads, his helmet, socks, and underwear lie where they were thrown the night before. I know for a fact that there is no chance they will make it into the washing machine before the next game. I suspect that many ado-

---

1. "St. Thomas Aquinas Quotes," quote 8.
2. NIV.
3. Ibid.

lescent boys produce similar squalor, much to the chagrin and disgust of their parents.

But, more than the mess, I am particularly frustrated by the lack of excellence. I find within most men a strong temptation to shoot for the status quo. "Good enough" seems to be the mantra of our masculine society today. In so many ways and in so many things we lose sight of what could be because we are not willing to put in the extra effort to make it great. Do it with excellence? No, thanks. That takes too much work. I'd rather slide by with minimum effort.

I woke up to this reality in Aidan's life when, in response to a request to pick his underwear up off the bathroom floor, he said, "Why? Is the president coming over or something?"

Ouch. Fail. Anger.

And then I realized my boxers hadn't made it to the hamper either.

Convenience and Entitlement

Over the last several hundred years, since the advent of electricity, indoor plumbing, and especially the internal combustion engine, much of the focus in the West has been to increase efficiency and convenience. We no longer hunt for our own food, but rely on freshly delivered produce and meat from the refrigerated grocery store. We no longer carry our water from the stream or well, but bathe in hot water at the flip of a nozzle. We no longer walk to work or school, and have begun traveling fifty to one hundred miles a day for the sheer enjoyment of the ride. We are committed to creating a comfortable world for ourselves, and modern-era conveniences have exponentially increased our luxury.

At the same time, we have inadvertently stripped ourselves and our children of the responsibility to be active participants in the pursuit of life, creativity, and work. In our innovation, we have found ways to automate life and provide comfort to such a high degree that the need for an active pursuit of excellence has been deeply diminished. Rather than calling our sons to action, we have instead found ways to give them more time on more screens. We see the erosion of excellence because we no longer expect it.

Yet we are fascinated by end-of-the-world stories in which apocalyptic events strip society of these modern conveniences and reduce humanity to primitive survival. When food, water, safety, hygiene, and medicine become scarce, what will we do? When electricity fails and our conveniences disappear, what happens to our well-constructed entitlements? Those who step up and embrace excellence and hard work survive. Those who throw childish temper tantrums tend to meet a vicious end.[4]

I am certainly not against progress or technology. I have the freedom to write this book because I have the convenience of a refrigerator full of food, an air conditioner cooling my room, and a computer that auto-spell-checks my typing. At the same time, many—not all, but many—youth today believe they are entitled to comfort and convenience without having to put forth any effort to achieve it. One poster, satirizing the inspirational posters so often seen in workplaces, sarcastically states: "Entitlement: You deserve life, liberty and the pursuit of happiness, a college education, a house, new clothes, a big-screen TV, an X-Box, Wi-Fi, and a foreign-built car." Fortunately, social justice advocates are pushing back on this epidemic of entitlement with television and print ads about "first-world problems." This generation faces a battle against privilege and prosperity, having lost what it truly means to work hard.

Passivity

On top of this is the innate struggle with passivity in every man's heart. From the dawn of mankind, passivity has haunted us with its temptation to withdraw and hang back while the world passes us by. Our father Adam succumbed to passivity when he stood by and witnessed Eve's fatal conversation with the Tempter. The Scripture is clear: Adam "was with her" and did nothing.[5] His inaction led to the downfall of all humanity. Passivity is bred into our hearts.[6]

As a marriage counselor, I see an increasing number of couples made up of what I call "the passive man and the over-functioning woman." In the relationship, he has found ways to pull back, pull out, and pull away, leaving her to hold it all together. Sure, he may work and bring home a check, but in all other areas of life he is woefully absent, and she is desperately trying to keep the marriage and family afloat. The fact is, he's capable of greatness and has usually won her heart through an intentional and intense pursuit.

4. My current favorite apocalyptic series is *Walking Dead*. Though gruesome, I find the reduction to tribal survivalism and forged allegiances fascinating.

5. See Genesis 3:6.

6. I highly recommend *Silence of Adam: Becoming Men of Courage in a World of Chaos* by Larry Crabb, Don Hudson, and Al Andrews.

But something switches shortly after the honeymoon. Far too often, he settles into the anemic routine of life and loses his mojo, leaving her with a ring but no relationship. From the outside he may appear to be a "nice" man, but behind closed doors, he is vacant, distant, and downright passive.

Author John Lee explains, "Passivity is a compulsion or learned tendency to live at half-speed, which ultimately leaves many men feeling their glass is half-empty and thus they half-heartedly commit to projects, plans, and goals. Passive men are half in and half out of relationships. Passive men are more attached to not having what they think they want or desire, even though they protest loudly this is not so."[7] In other words, passivity in men means half-living, where a man's heart may beat, but his heart is not truly in anything.

Many men tell me, "But I'm not passive. I work eighty hours a week, I volunteer at church, and I've built a successful business. How can you call me passive?" I find that passive men often have an unusual imbalance between their personal and professional lives. The world of work offers men a great place to hide from their hearts.

For example, a man named Simon recently sought my help for an addiction to pornography.[8] He had served decades in the military, often going to global hot spots as an intelligence agent for months at a time. Now, he over-works for a private firm as a software engineer specializing in foreign languages and cross-cultural partnerships. In the course of our work together, we uncovered a long-term absence from his wife (a common symptom in men who struggle with porn), and subsequently shifted into marriage counseling. At the end of our first couples session, I made the simple suggestion that they sit for twenty minutes a day, knee-to-knee and eye-to-eye, and just *talk*. Simon looked at me as if I my skin had turned green and I had grown a second nose. "What?" he inquired. "We've been married for thirty years, and that's the strangest thing I've ever heard!" She, on the other hand, turned to him and said, "And I've been waiting for thirty years for you to even look me in the eye."

Simon had lived an unbalanced life. In the world of work, he gave his all. Yet in his own home, he became consumed by passivity and the status quo to the extent that he did not even know his wife's eye color. Passivity emasculates men in the areas of life where they are needed most.

7. Lee, "Passivity and the Male Psyche," lines 6–10.
8. Name and details changed to protect his identity.

While passivity is as ancient as Adam, I believe it is an increasing epidemic, especially in the convenient West. Psychotherapist Peter Michaelson tells us, "It's a leftover mental-emotional residue from the stages of helplessness and dependence we experience through our childhood years. When we're not aware of inner passivity, we can fall prey to its influence and become weak, ineffective, and prone to self-defeat. Instead of possessing true power, we're likely to react unresponsively, passive-aggressively, or with belligerent, self-defeating aggression."[9] As children, extended helplessness and dependence create in us an expectation that things will magically appear with no effort. In our pursuit of convenience, we create in our children an inability to imagine or experience the beautiful results of true, hard work. Indeed, a recent cover story in *Time* magazine was "How to Eat Now: The Truth about Home Cooking," which featured the unusual notion that food can be prepared from scratch in one's very own kitchen.

Filled with such overwhelming conveniences, the Western world increasingly raises young men who are further and further away from the active pursuit of quality. I believe that, for men to truly be men, we need to resurrect for our sons the importance of excellent action.

Excellent Action: making an extraordinary impact

Excellent

My brother-in-law Chris is a model of excellence. As a middle- and high-school student, he trained vigorously and was recruited to play catcher on some of Virginia's finest baseball teams. Traveling with author John Grisham's team, he caught the attention of several scouts and received an invitation to play on the Navy team at the Naval Academy in Annapolis, Maryland. During the same time, he completed a degree in some sort of engineering that I can't even pronounce, and went on to court and marry a beautiful Honduran woman he met through a friend. After graduating from the Academy, he served several tours, patrolling the coast in anti-drug-trafficking stings, and later did a tour with NATO in Afghanistan. Now a lieutenant, he recently completed a master's degree in a brainy rocket-propulsion engineering program at the Naval Post-Graduate School in California. He currently lives in northern Virginia and serves as one of

9. Michaelson, "How Inner Passivity Robs Men of Power," lines 16–20.

the top advisers to the Navy in satellite and rocket technology. He has top-secret clearance, so none of us knows what he does exactly.

Needless to say, *slacker* is not in his vocabulary.

Some may read about Chris and focus on his athleticism or academic success. Indeed, these are commendable. Yet I am interested less in his success and more in the excellence with which he has pursued every aspect of his life. His most amazing excellence, in fact, is found in how present he is with his children and how attentive he is to his wife. Excellence surrounds him on every side. I am sure there were moments when he handed in sub-par homework or complained of an injury to get out of baseball practice. But his overall commitment to surpassing the status quo in the pursuit of the extraordinary is a model I hope Aidan will follow.

I believe that God calls all men to make a significant impact in the world. How will the world be different, better, and closer to the kingdom as a result of your existence in it? What change will you effect, and what influence will you have? Too often we are tempted to sink to the most comfortable, convenient, and passable option in order to avoid the hard work excellence requires.

The apostle Paul calls us to view our work and labor in the world as service to the King: "Whatever you do, work at it with all your heart, as working for the Lord . . . It is the Lord Christ you are serving."[10] As we run this race on earth, our focus must be on the eternal purposes of God. Excellence, therefore, is required not because the president is coming over, but because the King is on his way.

Action

It has often been said, "All that is necessary for evil to triumph is for good men to do nothing."[11] How many innocent lives were lost during the Holocaust due to the inaction of the world? How many displaced people suffer in Africa and the Middle East because on-lookers can't seem to do more than tsk-tsk at the evening news? How many women and children are sexually abused each night around the world because good men choose to turn a blind eye to the horrors of modern-day slavery? Death wins almost every day because good men to nothing.

10. Colossians 3:23–24, NIV.

11. The origin of this quote is unclear. It has been attributed to Edmund Burke, John F. Kennedy, and Charles F. Aked, among others.

Excellent Action

On September 11, 2001, hijackers took control of United Airlines Flight 93 a short forty-six minutes after it had departed Newark on the way to San Francisco. After realizing the plane had been seized, a few passengers were able to make phone calls and soon discovered that other planes had already crashed into the World Trade Center Towers and the Pentagon. At that point, several courageous passengers revolted against their attackers, resulting in the plane's crash in a field near Shanksville, Pennsylvania, instead of at its intended target, the US Capitol Building. That day, the actions of good men and women foiled evil's attempt to destroy and triumph. But when we do nothing to fight it, death wins.

Not all action needs to be of this magnitude. Many small actions can multiply into significantly meaningful events. Consider the millions of small active interventions of elementary school teachers in the lives of their students. Over the course of a few years, children learn how to read, write, and add. In the same way, every word on this page required the action of thought-turned-finger stroke to create the larger manuscript. Whether big or small, the butterfly effect of our actions can carry meaningful results.

The greatest enemy of action is not inaction, but apathy. *Inaction* implies a choice to *not* act. Indeed, I choose to *not* act several times a day. But I still choose, and I do so for a reason. Far more dangerous than inactive men are those who are inured to need, unaware of pain, anesthetized to their potential, and numb to the encroaching darkness that surrounds their lives and families. When men are lulled to sleep by comfort, convenience, and carelessness, they give the illusion that they are present when, in reality, they are light years away. They may be in church, but their minds are on the game. They may be at the dinner table, but their ears don't hear the tremor in their children's voices. They may be in bed with their wives, but the movie screens in their minds are full of fantasies of other women. Numb men create incredible confusion for others because their butts may be in the seats, but no one can rely on them to show up when they're needed. They are there but not really there. They give up on being the stallion and settle for being mere cattle.

In C.S. Lewis's famous book *The Screwtape Letters*, a fictional demon named Screwtape is teaching his protégé how to win and manipulate the hearts of men. "We want cattle who can eventually become food; He [God] wants servants who can finally become sons."[12] He later continues, "[God] wants men to be concerned with what they do; our business is to keep them

12. Lewis, *The Screwtape Letters*, 38.

thinking about what will happen to them."[13] The plan of the enemy is to keep mankind distracted from active involvement in the important things of the world, and focused on our own comfort and destinies. Action, therefore, is at the core of a man's ability to influence the world, bring about change, and live on behalf of another. Numbness and passivity cut him off at the legs and render him unimportant and irrelevant. It is far easier to play a video game than it is to fight a real battle.[14]

God did not make men to be adequate. He made men to act excellently—but he does not expect perfection. Thank God! If that were the case, we'd all be sunk. His desire is for us to do things well, not perfectly. In Matthew 25:21, Jesus says to his people, "Well done, good and faithful servant!"[15] Ultimately, his heart for us is to *try*.

As we seek to teach our sons the value of excellent action, my hope is that they will be inspired to move boldly forward to restore themselves and the world.

Action Toward Restoration

Every action has a direction. Recently I spoke with an East Coast executive who repeatedly said, "Our goal is to move the ball forward." The aim of every football offense is to take the pigskin toward the goal line in order to score. Every play, every decision, every action is aimed in a goal-focused direction. The defense, on the other hand, works in the opposite direction—to keep the ball from advancing. Every defensive strategy seeks to stop the offensive advance and turn the direction of the game.

When men act, they act in a direction. Any action that sets an object in motion sends it *toward* something and *away* from something else. Every excellent action has an aim. As representatives of God on earth, we are most satisfied when our direction aligns with his and seeks to bring restoration to all things. Men who actively engage in bringing about kingdom restoration find within themselves a true, deep, divinely inspired purpose.

13. Ibid., 28.

14. I am not fundamentally against video games. However, I often wonder what would happen in our world if we collectively fasted from our electronics for a week. Just a week without distractions, where the screen could not capture our attention and we instead turned our gaze toward those around us—our wives, children, neighbors, communities, and churches. It would be an awesome experiment, but one I'm sure would get very little buy-in.

15. Matthew 25:21, NIV.

Consider Isaiah 58:9–12:

> If you do away with the yoke of oppression,
>
> with the pointing finger and malicious talk,
>
> and if you spend yourselves in behalf of the hungry
>
> and satisfy the needs of the oppressed,
>
> then your light will rise in the darkness,
>
> and your night will become like the noonday.
>
> The Lord will guide you always;
>
> he will satisfy your needs in a sun-scorched land
>
> and will strengthen your frame.
>
> You will be like a well-watered garden,
>
> like a spring whose waters never fail.
>
> Your people will rebuild the ancient ruins
>
> and will raise up the age-old foundations;
>
> you will be called Repairer of Broken Walls,
>
> Restorer of Streets with Dwellings.[16]

Excellent action aims at full and complete restoration. Rebuild. Repair. Re-story. Renew. Return. Renovate. Refurbish. Restore. When men show up and join God's purposes for the world, they act in the direction of restoration. They are not satisfied with the status quo. They do not settle for darkness and decay. They cannot live with ruins, desert, famine, oppression, emptiness, or brokenness. Men who act excellently co-labor with God to bring about the restoration of the world.

Sadly, this is a far cry from what we see in our society today. As fathers, we must raise the bar and refocus our sons to embrace a vision that offers a hope worthy of their lives. Excellent action involves far more than picking up one's room or showing up at dinnertime. The kingdom of God is at stake.

Your Story

Discussing with our sons the ways in which we have succeeded and failed in pursuing excellent action may be extremely difficult, for in so doing we must confront the fact that we fall into passivity all the time. I recently

16. Isaiah 58:9b-12, NIV.

spoke with a man whose wife wanted him to move a medium-sized piece of furniture. It sat on his living room floor for weeks. Eventually, he found it at the bottom of the stairs, where his fed-up wife had muscled it on her own. Then, it sat *there* for an additional month until he finally moved it the last few feet into the storage room.

Our sons need to hear our stories of passivity, as well as hear how we have gained our key victories. Most young men do not truly know how difficult it is to make it as a man in the world today. Tell him.

When anyone seeks counsel from me with regard to vocation or profession, my first question is "What breaks your heart?" I want to know what aspect of this broken, fallen world most troubles them. Nine times out of ten, I am met with blank stares or anemic answers. The reality is that most men do not live fully and with purpose for the kingdom. Excellent action requires a heartfelt pursuit of goodness on behalf of the King.

As you consider teaching your son about the importance of excellent action, first begin with some serious self-reflection. Where is your impact felt? Is it? In what areas of life have you settled for the status quo because true excellence requires just a little too much? Evaluate those places in your own life and story where you struggle to put your shoulder down and push into places of the kingdom. Check in with your wife, with your closest friends, and with God, and allow him to restore your own heart as you seek to teach your son's.

His Story

Of course, your son needs to tell you stories of his greatness and success. He likely has trophies, ribbons, A+ papers, or other celebratory items that long to be noticed. Go with him to his room and ask him to show you all the memorabilia that has come to represent him. Ask him about how hard he had to work for these things. What did he have to do? When did he feel like giving up? What new challenges is he facing?

Additionally, as you give him the language of excellent action, you can now interact with him in times where you find him sloughing off his responsibilities or not truly trying hard enough. Be careful to allow for failure. It is not about success but effort and determination. One billboard on the way to my office says, "*Triumph* results when you put *try* and *umph* in the same breath."

Excellent Action

Questions for Your Journey

1. In what areas of your own life are you most tempted to settle for the status quo?

2. What did your father teach you about excellence? Did he?

3. How have entitlement and modern-day conveniences lulled you to sleep?

4. What breaks your heart? Does this motivate your daily action?

5. How would your wife and family evaluate you in the area of showing up when needed?

6. In what direction is your action aimed?

7. When you consider the unique character of your son, what do you think will be his biggest struggle in the area of excellent action?

CHAPTER 11

Kingdom Focus

Living in Light of the Greater Narrative

A life without purpose is a languid, drifting thing. Every day we ought to renew our purpose, saying to ourselves, "This day, let us make a sound beginning, for what we have hitherto done is naught."[1]

—THOMAS A'KEMPIS

But seek first his kingdom and his righteousness,
and all these things will be given to you as well.[2]

—MATTHEW 6:33

All these people were still living by faith when they died. They did not receive the things promised; they only saw them and welcomed them from a distance, admitting that they were foreigners and strangers on earth. People who say such things show that they are looking for country of their own . . . . they were longing for a better country—a heavenly one. Therefore God is not ashamed to be called their God, for he has prepared a city for them.[3]

—HEBREWS 11:13–16

1. a'Kempis, *Record of Christian Work*, 711.
2. NIV.
3. NIV.

"CLASSICAL CHILL" IS THE name of an iTunes radio station I listen to regularly. Nothing quite beats an early morning cello duel while I journal before sunrise, or the rise and fall of Rachmaninoff's piano concertos as the day begins, or the powerful yet supple invitations of Gregorian chant as I consider the upcoming events of the day. I am taken to another place.

Yet something different happens when the broadcast sneaks in a soundtrack from an epic movie or play. I can tell the difference, even when I can't place the music. I hear the build from gentle to powerful; the crescendo of battle between good and evil; and the resolution and harmonious rhythms that bring the piece full circle, letting me know that all is well and life has been restored—at least for now. Something happens in my soul, and I am caught up in the drama of the music as I join characters unknown in a story greater than my own.

One of the great things about this Man Maker Project process is that I get to watch all the epic man-movies again. I have a righteous excuse to immerse myself once again in stories that inspire me and call out all that is manly about my own heart. I have introduced Aidan to some of the classics, including *Cinderella Man, Braveheart, Les Misérables* (some of you may not count this as a man-movie, but I do), *Gladiator, The Chronicles of Narnia*, and *The Lord of the Rings*, to name a few.

All of these films (plus many more in this genre) are called *epic*. They tell an epic tale of epic men who accomplished epic tasks of epic proportions. Fictional characters find their way into my daily psyche by stepping into stories too big for them, and I begin to live my normal suburban American life with epic soundtracks in the background. Even as I type these words, Explosions in the Sky blares in my earbuds, and those around me have no idea of the epic adventure my heart finds itself in.

But why am I introducing Aidan to these stories? Is it merely for cultural education? Somewhat. However, far more than that, I want to introduce him to these stories' heroes: James J. Braddock, William Wallace, Jean Valjean, Maximus, Frodo and Sam, and more. I want him to begin crafting a schema in his head of what epic men are all about. And yes, as we watch the films, we discuss how these epic men fail as well.

I believe all men are called to be epic. I believe that, at the core of a man's life, he needs a purpose. He needs to know why he is here and what impact he is to make. He needs to know what he's fighting for and have a vision for how he wants the future to look. Far too many men find themselves approaching middle age, having done everything the world claimed would make them a "man," and yet they feel empty, purposeless, and hopeless. They've provided for their families, stayed loyal to their wives, and gone regularly to church. But the ache in their souls to *matter* has never been fulfilled. They have lived a tame tale, not an epic one. They have done all the right things but completely missed the point.

Brian is one such young man.[4] Fortunately, he is still in his early twenties, just about to complete a degree in biochemical engineering at the University of Michigan. All his life, academic success has come easy for him, and he has ridden on the wings of his intelligence rather than seek out purpose and direction. He spent the last semester Down Under as an international exchange student. His IQ landed him an opportunity to study under one of the world's most prominent scientists. When it comes to worldly success and upward mobility, Brian's already won the game. His heart, however, squandered the time overseas, surfing and chasing women because, as he told me, "at least those things had some semblance of conquest." For Brian, success has been his family's only request, and the story is just way too small to bring any excitement or challenge.

Recently, as we talked through his addictions to pornography, alcohol, and hooking up with girls, I asked him a simple question: "What is your life *about*?" He looked at me, dumbfounded, the only time he has been speechless in months. "I don't know," he responded. "I just don't know." Unless something changes now, Brian will go the way of far too many men, and live a self-focused life centered around comfort, pleasure, and pension. Yes, he is a Christian. Yes, he goes to church. Yes, he has a conscience. But no, he does not have a clue what the life of a true man is all about.

All of the great epic tales throughout history, both fiction and nonfiction, have primary characters who live for something greater than themselves. Their purpose far exceeds their own lives, and they take on a deeper meaning to their existence.

- For James J. Braddock in *Cinderella Man*, what began as a fight to provide milk for his family ended with his rallying the crowds toward hope in the midst of the Great Depression.
- For William Wallace in *Braveheart*, what began as vengeance of his wife's murder ended with a fight for national freedom from oppression.

4. Name and details changed.

- For Jean Valjean in *Les Misérables*, what began as a cover for an escaped convict became a way of life filled with integrity, goodness, generosity, and kindness.

- For Maximus in *Gladiator*, what began as a fight to survive became a calling to represent the true meaning of Rome in the face of violence and tyrannical leadership.

- For Frodo and Sam in *The Lord of the Rings*, what began as a road trip to the neighboring town transformed into a quest to save all of Middle Earth.

All men long for deep meaning in life, yet few find it amongst the common, comfortable worlds we construct. We must look beyond this world into the next to find our purpose. We must live in the tension of the kingdom both now and not yet.

Meta-Narrative

As fathers, we must instill in our sons a deep love and conviction of the meta-narrative of God's story. For boys to become true men, they must come to understand that life's purpose is ultimately designed to be intertwined with God's purposes and God's kingdom. There are a million possible flavors and applications of this, but at the core, a man's life is most deeply lived when it is lived on behalf of the King. This core aspect of manhood is kingdom focus.

My friend Greg is teaching his nine-year-old son, Jude, the Westminster Shorter Catechism in preparation for his eventual Man Year. At first I considered this a bit of overkill. Surely Jude was learning about God from their Jesus-focused home and church life. But then, one day as we all hiked through the backcountry, I heard Jude murmur under his breath, "What is the chief end of man? Man's chief end is to glorify God, and to enjoy him forever."[5] I stopped in my tracks. Here among the majestic Maroon Bells peaks of Colorado, this little nine-year-old stated one of the most profound truths in the universe. He knew that "I am on this earth to give honor to the King, forever."

This earth is not the point. This stuff is not the point. Nor is this role, this idea, this career, this house, this car, this grade, this retirement. None of

---

5. "Westminster Shorter Catechism," line 2.

this comes close to the point of life. No, our chief end is to glorify God and enjoy him. That's it. Honor the King, always, and we've achieved our highest calling. Live for him. Be about his business. Strive to enjoy him. Find every possible way to find life in him. That is the reason for our existence.

What does this mean for your son? It means applying the masculine strength imprinted in him by the Father toward the things on earth that God cares most deeply about. It means moving to protect the vulnerable, feed the hungry, father the fatherless. It means living out the truth of the good news in such a way as to represent the grace and goodness of Jesus. It means bringing the truth of Life to those who suffer under death. It means holding out hope for the kingdom "not yet" while doing everything possible to usher in the kingdom now.

Ultimately, it means arranging everything in a man's life to orbit around the story of the kingdom, both now on earth and the kingdom to come. It's a perspective many men believe they have when they check off "went to church" or "did devotions" on their to-do lists. But, in actuality, they completely miss the potential for a radical reorientation to make them truly *epic* men. As a result, many men settle for lesser stories, and then wonder why their hearts and lives are empty of meaning. Left to their own devices, men lose sight of the larger story, in which they are offered far greater roles than they could ever imagine for themselves.

C.S. Lewis puts it this way: "We are half-hearted creatures, fooling about with drink and sex and ambition when infinite joy is offered us, like an ignorant child who wants to go on making mud pies in a slum because he cannot imagine what is meant by the offer of a holiday at the sea. We are far too easily pleased."[6] We settle for smaller stories, believing that life is all about *us*.

What sort of story would there be if Braddock had settled for milk? What would have happened if Wallace had merely avenged the death of his bride, tit-for-tat? Where would Marius and Cosette be if Valjean had simply hidden amongst the crowds? What might have happened to the entire Roman empire if Maximus had not defied the emperor? What story would there be if Frodo and Sam had stopped at the edge of the Shire? And where would we be had Jesus not looked past the painful cross with a keen eye toward the coming redemption of his beloved sons and daughters?

When men live for a greater narrative far beyond themselves, things change radically. Empires shift. Tyrants fall. Innocents are rescued. Evil is

6. Lewis, *The Weight of Glory and Other Essays*. 1–2.

defied and brought down. Wrong is undone. Death no longer stings,[7] and, in fact, it starts working backwards.[8] When life becomes about more than ourselves, the pressure to perform is no longer on our shoulders. Instead, we experience relief.

The Relief of Not Being God

When we become focused on the minutia of our lives, the day-in-and-day-out monotony that dictates our existence, we fall asleep to the deeper realities of life. Our minds and hearts go numb, and we forget to hold onto the foundational truths of life as God intended. We become burdened with the weight of the world, as if we have to push through and play the hero. And, for the most part, we just don't know how.

Just the other week, the complexity of multiple ongoing projects, the difficulty of navigating business ventures and nonprofit funding issues, combined with the hit-my-head-against-the-wall parenting hamster wheel of purposeless repetition, and the unmet desire to find time for a date with my wife overwhelmed me to the point of tears. I crumbled in a literal mess on the living room floor. When my focus becomes merely putting one foot in front of the other, I forget myself and the greater narrative. I become so focused on the path, one foot in front of the other, that I lose sense of the horizon.

Richard Rohr states, "I do not have to figure it all out, straighten it all out, or even do it perfectly by myself. I do not have to be God. It is an enormous weight off your back. All you have to do is *participate!*"[9] I do not have to write the story. I do not have to push my way through. I do not have to always know what to do. I do not ultimately play God. Though my heart so easily slips into that role, the story belongs to God. I have the beautiful freedom and relief of mere participation.

When God is the storyteller, and the ultimate responsibility for this life, this planet, and this people fall squarely on his shoulders, I am freed up to play. I am granted the gifts of curiosity and wonder as I engage with the world, knowing that he has interlaced goodness and mercy in every corner of life's tapestry. Indeed, I have a significant part in the narrative, but

7. See 1 Corinthians 15:55.

8. See C.S. Lewis's *The Lion, The Witch and the Wardrobe*. Aslan (the Christ figure) comes back to life after laying down his life for Edmund. When this happens, he says, death starts working backwards.

9. Rohr, *Adam's Return*, 61, italics added.

it is only a *part*. God calls us all to "seek first His kingdom."[10] And he even throws in the rest for good measure.

What an overwhelming relief. "My life is not about me," Rohr continues. "It is about God. It is about a willing participation in a larger mystery."[11] This is the essence of maintaining a kingdom focus. The writer of the book of Hebrews describes it like this:

> Therefore, since we are surrounded by such a great cloud of witnesses, let us throw off everything that hinders and the sin that so easily entangles. And let us run with perseverance the race marked out for us, fixing our eyes on Jesus, the pioneer and perfecter of faith. For the joy set before him he endured the cross, scorning its shame, and sat down at the right hand of the throne of God. Consider him who endured such opposition from sinners, so that you will not grow weary and lose heart.[12]

Jesus is the "pioneer and perfecter of faith." He is the one *to* whom all creation belongs, and the one *for* whom all creation longs. What he has begun, he will bring to fullness of beauty and absolute completion.[13] Ultimately, the story belongs to him. What a relief!

In his Daily Prayer, John Eldredge wrote a fantastic line that catches me every time I pray through it. It says, "I worship you, bow to you, and give myself over to you in my heart's search for life. You alone are Life, and you have become my life. . . . I confess here and now that it is all about you, God, and not about me. You are the Hero of this story, and I belong to you."[14] I find myself and the purpose of my life when I zero in and focus on his kingdom.

The world offers our sons nothing but small stories. If we want a generation of men to show up and change the world, to bring life and healing and restoration, then we must intentionally connect them to the greater narrative of God's kingdom. If we lose on this front, we lose altogether.

Kingdom Focus: keeping a laser-like lock on the kingdom of God

---

10. Matthew 6:33, NIV.

11. Rohr, *Adam's Return*, 66.

12. Hebrews 12:1–3, NIV.

13. See Philippians 1:6.

14. Eldredge, "Daily Prayer," lines 8–11. Available for download at www.ransomedheart.com.

Living Lesser Stories

Why then do we so deeply struggle with life in the here and now? What so easily captures our hearts, drawing us away from the relief of participation and into the slavery and tyranny of the urgent?

The reality is that things need to get done. The electric bill needs to be paid, the tires need to be rotated, the e-mail needs to be sent, and the proposal needs to be submitted. I get it. I really do. It's my life too. We are humans, after all.

Yet when we allow these earthbound concerns to bind us to an earthbound story, we forfeit the most important portions of our souls. Our lives were never meant to be about paying bills, mowing the lawn, or even going to church. The greater narrative tells us that you and I were made for something far beyond this world. To live with a kingdom focus is one of the foundational aspects of true manhood. Despite the inundation of advertising designed to capture our hearts and bind us to a lesser story, we were not created for this fallen world.

The other night, our family gathered around the TV to watch *Sunday Night Football*. We rallied and cheered for our team, yelled at the screen when refs threw erroneous flags, and whooped and hollered when the ball crossed the goal line. But, as everyone knows, football comes with an overwhelming number of commercials. My middle daughter commented, "Why are there so many commercials, in the middle of already watching football, about *watching football*?" She was right. Sixty percent of the commercials were about enhancing the football-watching experience. Greater HD. More games. Better beer while watching football. Deeper coverage and analysis of the game. It went on and on and on to the point of nausea. While we wanted a simple evening of family entertainment, the advertising aimed to convince us that football is life. Bigger. Better. Stronger. Faster. The four horsemen of the marketing apocalypse, seeking to entangle all who need a story to live.

We cannot forget our true country and our deeper citizenship.[15] In the end, we were all meant to participate in an epic story. *The* story.

15. See Hebrews 11:13–16.

Knowing the Grand Narrative

But do we even know what that story is about? In order to know our place in the grand narrative, we must first become familiar with the story.

Many of us have participated in *The Lord of the Rings* marathons. Hour after hour, extended version after extended version, we have taken in and become fluent in the language, lore, and plot of Tolkein's classic masterpiece. Our culture has been so sufficiently inundated with the story that previously unknown words like *hobbit* and *orc* have become part of everyday vernacular.

Similarly, the biblical narrative must penetrate our minds and hearts so deeply that we view our daily commonplaces through the lens of God's story. The unfortunate use of flannel-boards and puppets in Sunday school, while useful and convenient in the telling of Bible stories, has emasculated and domesticated Scripture to such a degree that many have come to treat it as fairy tale and fiction. But if we read the narrative of God's history as it really happened with real people in real time, a whole new experience emerges.

Noah, for example, is not the kindly old zoologist who constructs a boat to sail the seven seas. He is the recipient of odd instructions from an odd God to do odd things. While he and his family are safe in the ark, they witness the largest and most devastating divine genocide ever known to humanity, all while scooping elephant poop and dealing with seasickness. Noah had to do hard things, have massive amounts of faith, and put up with a lot of confusion and complaining. He also had to watch thousands of people clamor and drown at the edge of the ark as the water submerged the earth and swallowed them whole. Hard, hard choices, yet Noah was a man clearly committed to the call of God.

Or consider the apostle Paul, a man who found his way to the top of his class in every way. "I was advancing in Judaism beyond many of my own age among my people and was extremely zealous for the traditions of my fathers," he says.[16] Paul gives an impressive résumé of spiritual and cultural achievements,[17] and yet concludes, "Am I now trying to win the approval of human beings, or of God? Or am I trying to please people? If I were still trying to please people, I would not be a servant of Christ."[18] Admittedly, Paul spent much of his life people-pleasing, living a lesser story

16. Galatians 1:14, NIV.

17. See Philippians 3:4–6.

18. Galatians 1:10, NIV.

for his own gain. But, somewhere along the way, the message of Christ so deeply captured his heart that he "considered everything a loss because of the surpassing worth of knowing Christ Jesus my Lord, for whose sake I have lost all things. I consider them garbage [literally, *crap*]."[19] His life became so profoundly God-focused that all the rewards of society were like a port-a-potty compared to the magnificence of living for the King.

For our sons to become men, we must open up the grand narrative to orient them to life as a man of God. This means teaching them about the gospel, the forgiveness of sins, and the redemption Jesus offers—but it is so much more than that. It means living life in light of the truth that God is who he says he is, and he is going to do what he has said he's going to do. Period.

Imagine if a trustworthy friend of yours worked in the upper echelons of Homeland Security. One afternoon he calls you out of the blue and says, "I can't tell you any details. I'm already risking everything to call you now. But, whatever you do, get your family and leave town now. Go somewhere, out to the wilderness or something. Just get out. Something is going to happen." What would you do? In all likelihood, you would live as if his words were true and hightail it out of there.

In the same way, living with kingdom focus compels us to live our daily lives not for the lesser stories we are so often tempted to serve, but for the greater and grander narrative told by the One who says, "I am the beginning and the end." If we live *as if it is true*, things change. We may even do something radical.

Donald Miller summarizes this well: "[God] said to me I was a tree in a story about a forest, and that it was arrogant of me to believe any differently. And he told me the story of the forest is better than the story of the tree."[20] When we live out the story of just our trees, we are only individual trees. We may be good trees, but in the end, we are merely lumber. But when we consider the bigger picture and remember the forest, the story gets much, much bigger and much, much better.

God's Global Story

I get very frustrated with ethnocentrism. Maybe it is because I've had the privilege of living and traveling overseas. Maybe it has to do with the

19. Philippians 3:8, NIV.

20. Miller, *A Million Miles and a Thousand Years*, 198.

number of years I lived in diverse cities and neighborhoods. Regardless of its origin, when I hear any of my children talking as if the United States sits at the center of the universe, my blood starts to boil and my face quickly turns sour.

In some ways, I can't blame them. We live in Fort Collins, Colorado, a city ranked in the top ten for almost everything: *Forbes* rated it among the best places for business and careers; Livability.com named our downtown the best in the country; Gallup-Healthways called it the healthiest mid-size city in the United States; and even *Yahoo! Travel* ranked it the best vacation city for beer lovers. No doubt, we live in a great small town. (Please don't move here. You can only visit.)

But the King's meta-narrative far exceeds our northern Colorado borders. As part of Aidan's Man Year experience, I wanted to blow his categories of where God is at work. My hope is that he sees the world as deeply broken yet deeply loved by the Creator. I want him to consider the expansiveness of God's love and the global kingdom of God's people. First-world problems fill our days when we live in the suburbs. For many, the greatest worry we have is if we remembered to charge our iPhone or thaw the chicken.

What is faith? Where we live, it's of little consequence. In the vast majority of the world, faith means getting the next meal, surviving the night, or hoping to learn to read.

What is poverty? Where we live, it means free or reduced lunch at school. In other places, it means rooting through garbage heaps in hopes of finding a scrap of food or a piece of cardboard for shelter.

What is fear? Where we live, it's wondering if we left the garage door open. For others, it means quietly worshipping Christ in a back-alley basement to avoid detection.

I decided to travel internationally with Aidan to expose him to a world without God, a world without money, a world serving other gods, and a world in desperate need of the kingdom. I wanted to awaken in him the potential of who he can be and how he can make a significant impact as he focuses his life on the kingdom of God. During this segment of Aidan's Man Year, we met persecuted missionaries, traveled through impoverished parts of international megacities, and engaged with gypsies and homeless children selling packets of tissue on the streets. In the end, my hope was to open his eyes to the suffering of the world and the purposes of God to bind up the brokenhearted and set the captives free.[21]

21. See Isaiah 61.

Not all fathers can plan an overseas trip. But eye-opening experiences abound just around the corner. Over this past year, on two separate occasions, our family hosted two "vulnerable" youth. A man in his early twenties and a thirteen-year-old girl lived in our home for extended periods of time. Both had their own stories of pain, confusion, rejection, loss, and hopelessness, and we sought to provide them some semblance of stability during a difficult transition in life. Aidan gave up his room for the homeless young man, and my eldest daughter sacrificed hers for the suicidal seventh-grader. We did not have to leave our home to expose our children to the pain of the world while offering the hope of renewal. In those months, they were able to see the kingdom come.

Needless to say, none of us will ever be the same.

Your Story

This is a hard quality to engage because it first requires you to take an inventory of your own life—as you are living it now—and determine the places where you have kingdom focus and where you have lost it. You must ask yourself, "For what story am I living?"

Be careful not to dismiss or judge yourself. We all get caught in the world's attempts to lure our hearts away from the true narrative. But consider this a tremendous opportunity for you to realign your heart to the One who gave you life and breath. You may ask your wife or friends for thoughts and feedback. You may also consult your calendar, checkbook, e-mail inbox, and entertainment schedule. These do not often lie about where our hearts find their treasure.

At the same time, take an inventory of your life as a boy. What messages were you taught about the meta-narrative? Anything at all? If you did receive some insight into God's bigger story, how was it communicated? Was it epic, or a domesticated flannel-board version of the gospel? How did you receive it? How did that shape your life, for either good or ill?

And finally, what is your hope for your son with regard to kingdom living? Are you willing to join him? What you do here may change his life and yours forever.

His Story

Of all the characteristics of manhood presented in the Man Maker Project, kingdom focus will likely be the hardest one for your son to identify in his own life. Yet there is an innate desire in his heart to live for the bigger picture. He *wants* to be epic. He knows that living for the small narratives will leave him unfulfilled in life, but he may not know how to move toward bigger stories. Your son's life is likely filled with messages that attempt to persuade and distract him—owning the newest smartphone, wearing the right ski jacket, playing the newest video game, or achieving in school. There is nothing inherently wrong with any of these things. But, as you know, they are a far cry from the epic tale that God designed him to live.

In many ways, the discussions and experiences he has now as part of this rites of passage process will constitute the stories of kingdom focus for him. This, I believe, is tremendous.

At the same time, some young men have already tuned into kingdom frequencies, and find themselves aware of issues more important than themselves. If this is the case for your son, lean into this area with him and ask him to teach you what he has discovered about the nature of his epic story.

Questions for Your Journey

1. How do you respond to the epic man movies? What happens in you?

2. In what ways have you been captured by lesser stories? Have you?

3. When you consider having a kingdom focus, what changes might be necessary in your own life?

4. What breaks your heart? What are you doing about it?

5. How well do you know the greater narrative? Is it an ancient myth or an ever-present daily reality?

6. In what ways do you want to bring the kingdom into your everyday?

CHAPTER 12

Protective Leadership
Sacrificial Strength and Hopeful Vision

Anyone who neglects to care for family members in need repudiates the faith. That's worse than refusing to believe in the first place.[1]

—1 TIMOTHY 5:8

The Lord is a Warrior. The Lord is His name.[2]

—EXODUS 15:3

It is in my nature to be kind, gentle and loving . . . But know this: When it comes to matters of protecting my friends, my family and my heart. Do not trifle with me. For I'm the most powerful and relentless creature you will ever know . . .[3]

—HARRIET MORGAN

MY WIFE AND I got lost almost right away in the ancient, winding streets of Venice. The narrow passageways meander left and right, up and over small bridges and underneath nondescript archways. From the moment we left the train station, I knew we would not find our way without some serious help.

1. The Message.
2. NIV.
3. "Harriet Morgan Quotes & Sayings," quote 1.

Two young newlyweds, we had embarked on a grand Italian adventure for our honeymoon. With a lust for life and travel, and with nothing to lose, we spent the first several days of our marriage wandering the streets of ancient Italian cities and exploring the richness of the Tuscan countryside. It was the perfect way to launch our lives together—a quintessential beginning to lives of adventure, challenge, and wonder. Now approaching our twentieth anniversary, we are saving up for a return trip.

While immeasurably romantic and overwhelmingly beautiful, Venice proved to be a navigational nightmare. For hours we wandered the streets and circumnavigated our hotel several times before finally catching a glimpse of the old wrought-iron sign at the end of a long channel. Just before dark, we made our way inside to safety.

In the Middle Ages in Venice, these labyrinthine passageways were dark and dangerous. Bustling with foot and water traffic during the day, these paths proved foreboding at dark, and any sensible person stayed inside after the sun gave in to night. In the event that a nighttime excursion became necessary, however, one would hire a *codega,* a man well-versed in the maze of Venetian passageways, to carry a lit lantern and guide the way. His role was to provide light, protection, and leadership, offering courage and confidence against the darkness and the thieves who sat waiting for easy prey. Travelers with a codega made it safely to their destination. Those without a codega were often found the next morning, floating facedown in the waterways.

In his divine design, God intended men to act as the codega, to stand in the gap between the innocent and the darkness, between the hunter and the hunted, and between the precious and the thief. Acting as the shielding bulwark against evil, men are called to provide protective leadership to the world.

Power Versus Strength

As boys become men, their bodies grow in muscle mass and definition. Their coordination, physical acuity, and stamina increase, and what was once an awkward and gangly teenager quickly becomes a force to reckon with.

Every morning, before departing the house, I pull my boy close to my chest and give him a powerful hug. I want him to know that I am not afraid of showing him man-to-man affection. Every morning, he returns the hug.

It is a truly tender moment for both of us. And, as is the case for many fathers and sons, a bit of wrestling shows as much or more affection as a tender embrace. The other day, just after the father-son hug ritual, I reached out and attempted to capture Aidan in a quickly executed half nelson—a move that has regularly worked to my advantage. To my surprise, however, I was the one who ended up nearly pinned to the floor, licking my shoes. Sometime since the previous day, my son's physical prowess had achieved a new level of strength.

His shoulders are broadening. His feet now fit my shoes, and his eyes nearly meet mine. Tufts of hair sprout from his armpits, and his voice is now mistaken for mine instead of his mother's. My boy has transformed into a man right before my eyes.

This is all by design—beautiful design. Just as my daughter's body will transform with suppleness and tenderness as she gracefully moves toward womanhood, my son's body lengthens and hardens as he prepares for manhood. There is something deeply spiritual about puberty. In many ways, anatomy reflects spirituality. As he grows, his strength increases. It is vital, however, for him to know the difference between masculine strength and masculine power. It is this difference that changes the course of things, both for him and for the world around him.

In 1887, historian Lord Acton made an authoritative observation about powerful men across time. In a letter to Bishop Mandell Creighton, he wrote, "Power tends to corrupt, and absolute power corrupts absolutely. Great men are almost always bad men, even [i.e. especially] when they exercise influence and not authority."[4] Throughout history, men with unbridled power have left a swath of destruction in their wake. Hitler. Stalin. Bin Laden. Al-Gadaffi. Shwe. Kim Jong-Il. Mugabe. Ho Chi Minh. Hussein. Nero. Pharoah Khufu. King Ahab. The list is almost endless and spans all of human history.

Masculine power leads men down a path of destruction. It is a fearful force that decimates, seeking to overpower others and gain control in order to consume and reduce. In many ways, ungodly and unchecked masculine power is at the core of most of the world's pain.

There is a vast difference between *masculine power* and *masculine strength*. Whereas power seeks to overwhelm and overcome, the calling of masculine strength is to guard and protect. Both require force, but the force of power is selfish and mercenary. Strength, on the other hand, always acts

4. Letter to Archbishop Mandell Creighton, paragraph 7, lines 3–4.

on behalf of another. Strength is unselfish and generous. It stays, stands firm, endures difficulty, and holds ground.

As we seek to shape the minds and hearts of our sons, it is vital to teach them to direct their innate forcefulness toward the defense of the defenseless, to create a force field around those in their domain, and to offer their strength toward restoration rather than destruction.

I will never forget John's face as we talked about the vast difference between manliness and machismo.[5] Over the course of the past year, John and I have delved into his story as he longs for healing in his masculine friendships. As a boy, he suffered from a verbally and physically abusive father. His dad would yell, throw tools, call him names, and treat him worse than the family pet. Violence and power were used as a weapon to annihilate John, to cut him down and forcefully put him in his place.

Over time, John found safety and retreat in the home of another family in the neighborhood. They welcomed John in and treated him with dignity. At their house, he was safe. Or so he thought. He unknowingly found himself caught in a web of emotional bondage, as this neighborly father figure began to experiment sexually with John, mixing the supposed kindness of their home with the loss of innocence and genital shame. In John's boyhood mind, masculinity and manhood became synonymous with the violent machismo of his father and the seductive forcefulness of his abuser. Masculinity became equal to power—a power that always sought to destroy or consume.

As we talked about the true nature of manliness, and the difference between masculine power and masculine strength, John sat with mouth agape. A masculinity that swelled in strength rather than in violence or abuse seemed unfathomable. "I only know about power," he said. "When someone crosses me, I only know how to react with anger. When someone does something irritating, my only response is to yell. Are you saying that there's another way that won't make me weak?"

"Yes," I responded. "You don't have to be violent or powerful to be a man."

"What's left, then?"

"Strength. You don't have to be an aggressor, and you don't have to run away. Strength is the force to *stay*."

---

5. Name and details changed to protect his identity.

Strength to Stay

In the conclusion of his letter to the Ephesians, Paul provides us with a few final words of instruction and admonition. He employs military language and lists what he calls "the full armor of God." He says, "Finally, be strong in the Lord and in His mighty power,"[6] and proceeds to describe various attributes of heavenly protective covering. Proceeding from head to toe, he describes spiritual armor: the helmet of salvation, the breastplate of righteousness, the belt of truth, the shoes of peace, the shield of faith, and the sword of the Spirit. He describes the enemy as the rulers, the authorities, the powers of this dark world, and the spiritual forces of evil, and calls believing men to military action. As he does so, he peppers his language with a conspicuously repeated word: *stand*. Four times in four verses, Paul calls the defenders of the gospel to stand. In the heat of battle, he says, put on the armor of God and stay put. Don't move. Stay. Though the battle will intensify, and though all the powers of hell will be turned fully against you—stay.

Fascinating. To be a godly warrior, Paul says, is to stand your ground in godly strength. Aren't men supposed to be aggressive and violent? But, then again, the gospel is often paradoxical.

What would the world look like if men employed their forcefulness in the direction of *staying*? To solidly plant their feet and hold? What if men stood firm and provided impenetrable protection against evil?

What is the difference between a powerful man and a strong man? Consider the common idiom "He's like a bull in a china shop." A powerful man decimates and destroys, even unknowingly, because his masculine force is unleashed without regard to the fragility of his surroundings. A powerful man bulldozes and steamrolls, and leaves a swath of destruction in his wake. Though he may gain much in life, the cost to himself and others is devastating.

A strong man, however, holds. He stands. He stays. He provides shelter, protection, and fortitude. He builds rather than destroys. He creates rather than decimates. He plants rather than uproots. A strong man turns and faces evil and says, "Here is where I stand. Come no further. You shall not pass!"[7]

When a powerful man enters the room, fear and agitation increase.

When a strong man enters the room, there is a collective sigh of relief.

---

6. Ephesians 6:10.

7. Yes, another reference to Gandalf from *The Lord of the Rings*.

Consider the strong man described in Isaiah 61, the passage Jesus read aloud at the inauguration of his ministry of restoration and redemption:[8]

> The Spirit of the Sovereign Lord is on me,
>
> because the Lord has anointed me
>
> to *proclaim* good news to the poor.
>
> He has sent me to *bind up* the brokenhearted,
>
> to *proclaim* freedom for the captives
>
> and release from darkness for the prisoners,
>
> to *proclaim* the year of the Lord's favor
>
> and the day of vengeance of our God,
>
> to *comfort* all who mourn,
>
> and *provide* for those who grieve in Zion—
>
> to *bestow* on them a crown of beauty
>
> instead of ashes,
>
> the oil of joy
>
> instead of mourning,
>
> and a garment of praise
>
> instead of a spirit of despair.
>
> They will be called oaks of righteousness,
>
> a planting of the Lord
>
> for the display of his splendor.
>
> They will *rebuild* the ancient ruins
>
> and *restore* the places long devastated;
>
> they will *renew* the ruined cities
>
> that have been devastated for generations.[9]

The actions of the strong man are to proclaim, bind up, comfort, provide, bestow, rebuild, restore, and renew. These can only be accomplished by a man who *stays*. He is called an "oak of righteousness, a planting of the Lord."[10] His strength is as firm, permanent, planted, and solid as an ancient oak tree.

---

8. Jesus reads Isaiah in Luke 4.

9. Isaiah 61:1–4, NIV, italics added.

10. Isaiah 61:3, NIV.

How does a man root himself in masculine strength rather than masculine power? How does he become an oak tree rather than a bulldozing mercenary? Hearken back to Paul's words in Ephesians 6:1. Just prior to defining the armor of God and making the call to stand firm, Paul slips in an interesting phrase that is often overlooked: "Be strong in the Lord and in His mighty power."[11] Here in one simple sentence, we have both words: *strength* and *power*. Paul commands us to be strong, and then includes two subsequent phrases to qualify our strength: in the Lord and in his mighty power. The location of our strength, the ground in which we root ourselves and plant our feet, the nourishment for the force and strength of our masculinity comes from somewhere else. It does not come from us. We are commanded to be strong in the Lord and in the mighty power that belongs to him. It's his. Not mine. Not yours. His.

We get this so mixed up.

As men, our strength comes from him who *is* strength, and from him whose power is both immeasurable and immensely kind. There is no corruption in the Lord's power, only goodness, mercy, kindness, love, grace, tenderness, protection, and glory aimed at the restoration and redemption of those he loves. This is key. Don't miss this. Godly strength is *always* combined with tenderness and kindness. Theologian Douglas Wilson puts it this way: "Masculine toughness has to lay underneath masculine tenderness. It is a velvet-covered brick."[12] If men are to truly mirror the King to this earth, we must root ourselves in the balance of strength and tenderness. Fallen strength is violence. Fallen tenderness is weakness. True, oak-like men withstand the fiercest of storms and also provide shade for Sunday afternoon picnics.

On Behalf Of

The nightly news rarely highlights good news. The sensationalism of primetime television draws our attention through tragedy and violence, and, like peeping toms, we willingly participate in the voyeurism that has come to be our "news."

The other night, however, a news story nearly knocked me off my couch. An organization of rough and gruff bikers called Bikers Against

11. Ephesians 6:1.
12. Parnell, "Leading the Home: Quotes from Doug Wilson," quote 7.

Child Abuse (BACA) encircled a young girl and her two brothers.[13] Victims of emotional and physical abuse, these youngsters lived in fear of a father who operated from a place of power rather than strength. Then BACA came to their aid. Riding loud Harley Davidsons and donning black leather, BACA's members pursue the mission of protecting innocent children from stupid men. Their motto: no child deserves to live in fear. This is strength manifested on behalf of the weak.

BACA joined these three children in the courtroom at their father's child-abuse trial. This is the girl's account of the protective presence of these gruff heroes:

> Actually, I had one trial that I had to go to and sit. And when [my father] went up to the stand, I had so many mixed emotions of fear and hatred toward the guy. And then BACA was just sitting right next to me and just kinda patting my leg. As soon as I looked over at them and they looked at me, I realized he is never going to be able to hurt me and my brothers again."[14]

Strength is always employed *on behalf of another*. BACA deploys its riders to come to the protective aid of the vulnerable. To protect others is one of the highest callings on a man's life. Strength is designed by God to be wielded on behalf of another. True men create a protective force field around those they love, and it extends to any who need to be defended. Protection involves not only employing physical strength, but it includes all areas of life—the emotional, mental, financial, and spiritual. For a man to protect others is for that man to live more fully into his God-given strength.

First to Die, Last to Leave

When I work with couples in marriage counseling, I start with a warning. I directly address the man, saying, "I want you to know that about 80 percent of my focus will be on you. That's not to say that you are 80 percent of the problem. Rather, it's to say that if there is any hope for movement out of the difficulties your marriage faces, it's going to have to come from you." More often than not, wives have unnecessarily borne the burden of the relationship, which their husbands abdicated years ago. Most calls for marriage counseling come from over-functioning and overwhelmed wives who have

13. Learn more at bacaworld.org.
14. Murray, "Gruff Heroes Come to Aid of Child Abuse Victims."

come to the end of their rope with their uninvolved husbands. How's that for a start to counseling?

At first, my approach catches guys off guard. They squirm and question, and some even get upset. But the more I look them squarely in the eyes and call them to show up, I can see a visible change in their demeanor and stature. Their chests begin to swell, and fire starts to burn in their eyes. Many of them shift their body posture toward their wives rather than remain in their previously defensive positions. When they realize that our work together is not going to be a power struggle, that I am committed to calling forth their strength rather than wrestling their egos, they lay down their weapons and plant their feet. It is remarkable to see. When they know I am not going to emasculate or demean them, they join me in believing that, if anyone in the room has the strength to plot a new course and actually change things, it's *them*. Inevitably, they rise to the occasion.

There is something in the heart of a man that longs to rise to protective leadership. Though this desire may be long forgotten and dormant, it's there, and it needs to be dug up and resuscitated. He wants it. She wants it. But neither realizes this because they have both lost touch with the true meaning of leadership.

One of the most misused and misunderstood passages of Scripture in regard to the marriage relationship is Ephesians 5. In many circles, these verses are used to inappropriately place women in a subservient role to men, to give husbands carte blanche authority over the wife, or to devalue women to a place of submission rather than elevate her to her God-given place of quintessential beauty and royalty. While this is not a discourse on marriage,[15] I want to point out some very important aspects of Paul's arguments with regard to leadership. Just as far too many men confuse power and strength, they also often cross wires with regard to leadership and authority.

Paul starts this portion of his letter to the Ephesians with this sentence: "Follow God's example, therefore, as dearly loved children and walk in the way of love, just as Christ loved us and gave himself up for us as a fragrant offering and sacrifice to God."[16] Paul then spends the next several sentences identifying the kinds of partners that will lead to death and destruction,

---

15. That might be a segue way to another book.
16. Ephesians 5:1, NIV.

such as sexual immorality, greed, and drunkenness. In verse 7, he states clearly, "Do not be partners with them."[17]

Far too often we jump to the verses about wives and husbands, and lose sight of where Paul begins. His first admonition for godly relationships is to "walk in the way of love" and mimic Christ in his self-sacrificing offering to God. The foundation of human-to-human relationships, therefore, is love and sacrifice. Too many Christians focus on who's in charge rather than on who "gives himself up as a fragrant offering."

Mirroring the "just as Christ loved and gave himself up" language of verse 1, Paul repeats himself as he directly addresses husbands. "Husbands, love your wives, just as Christ loved the church and gave himself up for her . . ."[18] According to the apostle Paul, the calling on husbands to lead their wives is in the way of death. How did Christ love the church? By dying first. By sacrificing first. By giving himself up. By stepping in the way of death and taking the blow so that she could be saved.

Masculine leadership, therefore, is about dying first. It believes so strongly in the hope of life, resurrection, and redemption that it takes the deathblow so others may live. Far too many men strive for authority and headship, fully missing God's calling to lead through sacrifice. Christ loved the church by dying. *That* is masculine leadership.

We know this and we don't know this. Imagine a burglar invading your home at night. Who grabs the baseball bat and confronts him? When the Titanic sinks, who gets on the lifeboats last? When the tire blows out on a dark and rainy night, who gets out to fix the flat?[19] On one level, our natural manly inclination is to step up to protect and lead. But on another and likely more important level, far too many men flounder in sacrificing first when it comes to relationship, spirituality, or emotions. Men know to show up with a bat, but we fail to show up with our hearts.

Leadership, therefore, has little to do with authority and far more to do with a willingness to step in, take the risk and bear the brunt of decisions, and die to self on behalf of others. The opposite of leadership is

17. Ephesians 5:7, NIV.

18. Ephesians 5:25, NIV.

19. Please hear me correctly. In no way am I insinuating that *only* men can or should do these things. In fact, I have many female friends who are far more handy and brave than their husbands. My point is merely that if there is a place where self-sacrifice needs to be made, it is *his* place to make it first. He may suck at changing tires or chasing burglars, but if he is to love his wife as Christ loved the church, he is to be the one to sacrifice first.

not followership. The opposite of leadership is passivity. While our society views leaders as those at the helm, giving orders and directions to others, true spiritual leadership involves much more sacrifice and servitude than our world would like to admit. A man who leads is a man who willingly puts himself in front, not out of pride or power, but out of a desire to absorb the brunt of whatever is to come.

As a result, any time I get a call from a man for marriage counseling, I wholeheartedly commend him, praising his movement forward and giving him as many kudos as I possibly can without being weird. When I call men to take 80 percent of the burden for the redemption of their marriage, I see men rise up and become more manly, and I see women relax with relief that they no longer have to be the one to continually die first.

Raising Strong Men

Aidan has a unique relationship with one of his younger sisters. Though they have their normal sibling conflicts, she looks up to him with great admiration. And he likes it. He pretends he doesn't, but deep down, I know he wears her esteem like a badge.

The other day, she told us she had been bullied by a boy on the bus. While we could not decipher whether the boy meant to verbally harm her or to awkwardly manage his middle-school-boy crush on her, both Aidan and I knew something had to be done. He and I talked about what to do in private, and then, with a gleam in his eye, he looked at me and said, "Dad, I got this one."

As fathers, our goal is to raise boys who will step into the realm of protection with kindness and strength. Aidan did not go beat the boy up, nor did he confront him without provocation. He did, however, sit with his sister on the bus as a physical reminder that someone larger, stronger, and braver stood between his sister and harm. Aidan's strength and tenderness, his velvet-covered-brick, showed up. In the end, he said nothing to the boy—his protective presence alone made his point. The boy never spoke to her again.

But what about the boy who is scrawny, bullied, shy, or withdrawn? What about the boy who doesn't develop the stereotypical musculature or commanding presence? Some boys are naturally more reserved, quiet, or inhibited. Can we still raise them to be protective leaders?

As Paul reminds us, we are to be strong in the Lord first and foremost. As a father training his son in the craft of manhood, I believe that *all* boys, regardless of muscle mass or personality type, must be raised to find their footing and rooting in the power and presence of God. Many of the heroes of faith were stutterers, hiders, and small-statured men.[20] Even the prophet Samuel focused on physicality while searching for King Saul's replacement. He considered Eliab, David's older brother, a likely candidate for king because of his stature and physique. God admonishes Samuel, "Do not consider his appearance or his height, for I have rejected him. The Lord does not look at the things people look at. People look at the outward appearance, but the Lord looks at the heart."[21] Regardless of how they bring themselves to the world, boys who learn that their strength comes from a spiritual place deep within will stand as solid oaks of the kingdom

Being a protective leader may mean sitting with his sister on the bus. It may mean writing a thoughtful discourse on the tragedies of homelessness. He may produce art that inspires action or create iPhone apps that screen unnecessary phone calls. The protective leader might rally votes for the humane society or join the military to fight for the freedom of our country. Regardless of the outward action, the core of protective leadership rests in the boy's heart. As Douglas Wilson states, "Masculinity is the glad assumption of sacrificial responsibility."[22] In raising our sons, we must inspire them to take on the mantle of responsibility for the world around them. In so doing, they ally with God in the protection, stewardship, and sacrificial leadership of the future.

Protection:
creating a barrier between threat and innocence

Leadership:
the call to take the first sacrificial step toward a better future

Protective Leadership:
wisely, boldly, and sacrificially creating direction and safety for others

---

20. Consider Moses with his speech impediment, Gideon with his winepress hiding place, and Nicodemus and his tree-climbing antics. God's "man" has far more to do with God's presence in his life than with the man's own natural ability or strength.

21. 1 Samuel 16:7, NIV.

22. Parnell, "Leading the Home: Quotes from Doug Wilson," quote 6.

Your Story

One of the challenges in addressing this topic with your son is that *he* has been the benefactor of your protection—or not. It has been your role to protect and lead him. In a real and raw way, you can engage him in an honest conversation about how you have embodied this aspect of manhood *with him.*

In fact, embracing and leading your son through this rites of passage process is a protective leadership issue. You are protecting him from the emptiness most boys experience as they transition from boyhood to manhood. You are protecting him from false notions of manhood and creating for him the mental file folders necessary to live well as a man. Your leadership in this area not only affects him, but all whom he will lead and love in the future.

In addition, it is important for you to share your struggles in the areas of power versus strength. Tell him stories of how you failed or succeeded in these areas. You may also ask your wife to share her experience of your protective leadership, or lack thereof. Share with him your experience of your own father, uncles, and coaches. How did they protect you? How did you see them "die first"? How did they miss the mark?

Throughout this process, remember that you are also becoming. Learn with your son and confess those areas where you need to embrace protective leadership, especially the sacrificial aspect, even more than you already do.

Who knows? You might find yourself in marriage counseling.

His Story

Most boys have stories of protection. Boyhood games often involve imaginary battles with makeshift swords or bows and arrows. Rock outcroppings or city sidewalks become "realms" in need of conquering, and playgrounds transform into castles to defend or spaceships designed as warships. In the heart of most every boy lives a little warrior.

Now is the time to ask him to tell you his stories of conquest and share with you the times and places he has won bright battles or defended his tree house. But, more than that, invite him to share stories of bullies at school or on the football field. If he has siblings, ask him how he has or has not protected them, and how he may do that in the future. In all likelihood, he has experienced times of vulnerability, where he has not been protected, or where a man's power (maybe yours?) has harmed him in some way. These stories are vital and need to be shared. Be aware that he may be ashamed to share his perceived weakness in the face of power or harm, or that he may not want to share how he cowered away from sacrificing himself on behalf of another. Gently encourage him to learn from the past and lay the course for a better future.

Questions for Your Journey

1. In what ways do you struggle with the differences between power and strength?

2. How has masculine power been used against you, wounding you in the process?

3. Consider the strength Christ displayed as he stayed on the cross. Though he had the ability to end it all, he stayed and died on our behalf. How are you challenged by his example?

4. In what new ways is God calling you to protectively lead your family?

5. For what do you need to humbly ask forgiveness with regard to your lack of protection or lack of leadership?

6. What do you think would happen in our society and in our churches if we raised a generation of strong men?

CHAPTER 13

Purity
Wholly Holy

How can a young person live a clean life?
By carefully reading the map of your Word.
I'm single minded in pursuit of you;
don't let me miss the road signs you've posted.[1]

—PSALM 119:9–10

Finally, brothers and sisters, whatever is true, whatever is noble, whatever is
right, whatever is pure, whatever is lovely, whatever is admirable—if anything
is excellent or praiseworthy—think about such things.[2]

—PHILIPPIANS 4:8

It is the image of God reflected in you that so enrages hell;
it is this at which the demons hurl their mightiest weapons.[3]

—WILLIAM GURNALL

BEFORE ME SAT A crowd of a hundred young men, all preparing to give
leadership to one-year international missions teams around the world.
These recent college graduates aimed their not-so-excited eyes in my direc-

1. The Message.
2. NIV.
3. As quoted in Eldredge, *Wild at Heart*, 155.

tion as the emcee introduced me as the speaker for the compulsory "men's time" of their missionary training regimen. In Christian circles, *men's time* immediately connotes some form of "the sex talk" that always includes the word *don't*. Don't. Don't. Don't. Don't lust. Don't look at porn. Don't be inappropriate. Don't. And that is what these young men expected me to say.

But it's not what they got.

Sending young men into co-ed international situations with little accountability and high accessibility to the temptations of the flesh is a ludicrous idea from the start. Despite devout intentions and personal purity commitments, *any* young man will face an overwhelming battle to keep himself pure, no matter where he lives. But relocating these Christian missionaries into some of the world's darkest megacities to bring hope and light stands as one of the most ridiculous notions I have ever considered. Yet this is how God is advancing the kingdom around the world in our generation—through young people.

My task that evening was to address these hormonal twenty-somethings with "the talk" in hopes that it might dissuade them from serious indiscretions during their time abroad—an impossible undertaking from the start. But, being the brazen disruptor that I am, I began with this sentence: "God has given every one of you in this room a powerful tool to worship him and reach the world for Christ. It's your penis. And you know what, guys? *I encourage you to use it.*"

Immediately, the chatter in the room ceased, a hundred sets of unblinking eyes locked with mine, and the blood drained from the emcee's face as he instantly regretted inviting me to speak. What had I just said? This was supposed to be the men's talk, and that is *not* how men's talks go.

I believe that Christian men today suffer from an epidemic of *don'ts*, especially when it comes to the issue of purity. We are constantly told what we should not do, how to limit our desire and avert our eyes. Recent books portray a man's engagement with purity as a battle,[4] and have popularized the passage from Job 31:1: "I have made a covenant with my eyes not to look lustfully at a young woman."[5] While these truths have their benefits for mankind, they also dangerously dichotomize and demonize desire as

---

4. In particular, the *Every Man's Battle* series. While these books have some excellent content, I find them somewhat anemic when it comes to helping men *embrace* their bodies rather then subject them to unnecessary disdain.

5. NIV.

bad, evil, and to be routed out rather than a God-given aspect of manhood[6] to be celebrated as part of his unique image in men. It is my desire to turn twenty-first-century Christian men's notion of purity away from the *don'ts* and more toward the *do*. I find it far more effective to call men toward godly action than to harp on their failures.[7]

Purity itself has been reduced to being synonymous with sexuality. For a man to be pure, he must pursue wholeness and holiness in all aspects of life, not just in his sexuality. Purity in the sexual realm is an outward expression of a man's internal heart-level purity. Just as a body's high fever indicates a deeper infection, wayward sexuality is an external symptom of internal impurity. To tell a man "don't" with regard to his sexuality merely skims the surface of the deeper calling of God to pursue wholehearted purity. Treating the symptom does not treat the disease. We must elevate purity to its rightful place of *whole-life holiness*.

As I crafted Aidan's passage into manhood, I knew that I needed to address issues of purity. No rites of passage process is complete without honest and direct conversation about the power of the penis. Every young man needs fatherly guidance in how to appropriately engage sexuality and pursue holiness with regard to his body. But sexual purity is a subset of a greater category, one that is built on the shoulders of the other biblical aspects of manhood. A man of courage, a man of integrity, a man of excellent action, a man of kingdom focus, and a man of protective leadership *yields* a man of purity. In this way, purity is grown and nurtured along the way rather than mandated or regulated. Therefore, I decided to address issues of purity in Aidan's final segment of his Man Year, knowing that most of the groundwork would already be laid by the previous months of conversations. While there had to be a direct conversation about sexuality, it would rest on the foundation of the larger context of all that came before.

6. Naturally, this also includes womanhood and the beautiful sexuality of the feminine. However, my focus here is on men.

7. At the same time, I do not shy away from clear correction when it is needed. Some men need to be hit upside the head and called to the carpet for their stupidity. But I have found that most Christian men are intimately aware of their failures. They need to be reminded of who they can be and called into *that*.

Image Reflector

"I encourage you to use it." After I made this statement to the crowd of would-be missionary men, the room was pregnant with both curiosity and disdain. Men are rarely encouraged to use their penises for the glory of God. If you ever need to capture the interest of a young male crowd, say the word *penis*, and you will have their undivided attention.

But I believe our masculine anatomy is a metaphor for the image of God in men. Consider Genesis 1:27: "So God created mankind in his own image, in the image of God he created them; male and female he created them." The author of the Genesis account poetically and clearly unites humanity's image-bearing with our maleness and femaleness. He finds it so important and compelling that he restates it again a few chapters later in Genesis 5:1.[8] As the pinnacle of creation, God creates humanity and clearly states that they bear his image him as male and female.[9]

The ancient Hebrew word here for "male" is *zakar,* which holds an interesting pairing of meanings. First, *zakar* means "pointed" or "sharp," and in both modern-day Hebrew and Arabic it still refers to men and the male organ. Secondly, and possibly more interestingly, *zakar* also means "to mark so as to be recognized, and to properly remember or stand as a memorial."[10] Inherent in the maleness of mankind is the memory and marking of God. Here is a sentence you may never read elsewhere: penises are reminders of the mark of God on men.[11]

When you consider the phrase "stand as a memorial" you can't but think about the correlation between erecting an altar or memorial and the penile erection. Consider the spiritual correlations to this physical response. Men are called to stand up, to be strong yet gentle, to reach out and bring life, to sow seeds of hope and life, to extend that which is vulnerable, and to harden that which is soft. In his infinite wisdom, God provides every

---

8. Genesis 5:1–2 states, "This is the written account of Adam's family line. When God created mankind, he made them in the *likeness of God.* He created them *male and female* and blessed them" (NIV, italics added).

9. While an equal discussion of *female* is more than a worthy task, it falls outside the parameters of this book.

10. *Strong's Concordance and Lexicon of Hebrew and Greek,* #2142.

11. I know this sort of direct discussion about penises may be difficult for some readers. Some of you may completely disagree. I welcome your thoughts and push-back, as well as your wholehearted "Yeah!" Please contact me.

man with daily reminders, a physical memorial, of God's presence and purpose for men.

During this evening conversation with these soon-to-be missionary men, one young man dared to ask me, "So what do we do then when we wake up with an erection?" My response: "Remember him whom it memorializes."

Is it any wonder, then, that God chose circumcision as the "mark" of his people? What sets the Hebrew men apart from all others is surgery in the most tender of spots. It is a calling to remember both the God and community to which the man belongs. Every time he uses his penis, whether to pee or engage sexually, or merely to adjust for comfort, he is called to remember. God knew where to put his mark and keep a man's attention.

Ancient pagan worship always included an element of perverse sexuality. Artemis had a hundred breasts. Priapus's phallus was larger than his arm. Ancient rituals of temple prostitution purified the land. Asherah poles that worshipped the fertility goddess desecrated the holy places of the Hebrews, making God rather upset.[12]

It comes down to this: penises are spiritual.

Now, I am not a theologian, nor am I a Hebrew scholar. But the correlation between male sexuality and the worship of God is too uncanny to overlook. It is in this context and with these much larger definitions that the issue of purity, especially sexual purity, finds even greater significance. My sexuality and my purity is not my own. Neither is yours nor your son's. It is connected to something far greater.

It's Bigger Than That

A few weeks ago, our family left the natural beauty of Colorado to explore the great American histories lining the East Coast. For a ten-day spring break trip, our overzealous family of five ventured from New York to Philadelphia, through Annapolis and on to Washington, D.C., and then down through Richmond and into Jamestown and Williamsburg. We wanted to learn and experience the origins of our country, and to be witness to the greater narrative that defines the United States of America. After the trip, we came home, exhausted and with blisters on our feet, but with a quiver full of tales.

12. Do a quick Bible search for *Asherah poles*, and you will find that God is not too keen.

The day we left Colorado and headed east, we were American citizens—at least on paper. As a result of our encounter with the greater narrative of battles, liberties, sacrifices, declarations, revolts, and solidarities, we returned to Colorado as American *citizens*. The experience of our heritage elevated for us what being American truly means. And while that definition has morphed through the years of our country's existence (especially on the international scene), the exploration of our origins gave us a deeper sense of who we are because of who *they* were. The sacrifice and courage of our predecessors reminds us of who we can be today.

In the same way, when we elevate our citizenship as male image-bearers of God and remember the larger narrative of how and why he created us male, we can't but participate in his greater calling toward holiness. Purity means far more than sexual chastity. It points us directly to our citizenship and participation in bearing the image of God. As a result, rather than squelch a man's desires with an unending list of *don'ts*, I believe we should remind him that his purity is directly tied to how he reflects God to the world.

So, yes, I encourage young men to use their penises in their pursuit of God. If we can encourage young men to be purposeful in engaging with their penises (and by this I don't just mean their male anatomies but include their masculine hearts as well), and choose to use them for goodness, holiness, and worship, then we connect them to the greater narrative. Godly purity is less about what we avoid and more about what we pursue. It is bigger and more important than we ever imagined.

In discussions with my son about purity, I have extended the concept far beyond sexual purity to include mental, emotional, behavioral, and spiritual purity. In every aspect of life, I want him to pursue a purity that is God-inclined and God-infused. Instead of *don't*, I have attempted to help him decipher that which is true, noble, right, pure, and admirable amongst all that is not. We analyze movies, video games, friends' texts, and Instagram postings through the lens of purity. We evaluate his motivations to determine whether or not they are pure. For example, why does he want to play football, star in the school play, be a part of student council, or go to camp? Are the intentions behind these activities, which in and of themselves are neither moral or immoral, God-inclined and God-infused? Are my son's intentions, therefore, pure? If they are, then he should apply the best of his strength, courage, intention, energy, and devotion to them.

Pure men exert their God-ward masculinity because they are characters in a much larger narrative.

When it comes to sexuality, the conversation is no different. As you apply your penis to these activities, do you represent the King? Are the places, spaces, relationships, and representations you engage sexually also where God longs to be memorialized? Does your understanding of your citizenship and participation in the kingdom increase through the use of your body there? Again, here's what I said to those missionary men: "God has given every one of you in this room a powerful tool to worship him and reach the world for Christ. It's your penis. And you know what, guys? *I encourage you to use it.*"

I would rather have my son use his penis on purpose than by mistake. In my conversations with Aidan about sex, I often refer to a fantastic analogy I heard before: The burning desire for sex is like a fire. When it is properly built and tended in a fireplace, it offers warmth, comfort, romance, ambience, good smells, and good feelings. But take that same fire and place it in the matchstick dryness of the Colorado forest, and it quickly becomes an out-of-control blaze that consumes, destroys, and burns. Fire in its appropriate place is meant to be used, stoked, and fed. In the same way, man's burning drive for sex and intimacy is meant to be used in those places where God designed.

The Attack

Masculine purity sits in the crosshairs of the enemy. As William Gurnall states, "It is the image of God reflected in you that so enrages hell; it is this at which the demons hurl their mightiest weapons."[13] If the enemy had one sure-fire way to obliterate the masculine image of God on earth and eradicate the positive impact of men, it is through a direct attack on their purity. There is no greater way to reduce a man to nothing but an impotent bystander than to attack the very nature of how he images God—through his maleness.

Where God designed potency, strength, and a divine memorial, the enemy aims impotence, self-serving addiction, and the pursuit of hedonistic pleasure.

Where God created love and the desire to provide and protect, the enemy tempts toward lust and the inclination to steal, kill, and destroy.

13. As quoted in Eldredge, *Wild at Heart*, 155.

Where God established marital harmony and worshipful vulnerability, the enemy designs discord and fear.

We must be both honest and hopeful as we teach our sons about their rightful place as God's male image-bearers. Purity is about much more than sex. It's identity and purpose. More than the *don't*s, we must teach them about the high calling of the *dos*.

Psalm 119:9–11 states, "How can a young person stay on the path of purity? By living according to your word. I seek you with all my heart. Do not let me stray from your commands. I have hidden your word in my heart that I might not sin against you."[14] The pursuit of purity is far more an *action* than a *reaction*. According to the psalmist, the pure person lives, seeks, and hides in his heart the word and identity of God. He needs to know who he is in order to live well in the world. The psalmist's answer to purity does not include the word *don't*. Instead, the path of purity is one of intention and action.

Consider also Philippians 4:8–9: "Finally, brothers and sisters, whatever is true, whatever is noble, whatever is right, whatever is pure, whatever is lovely, whatever is admirable—if anything is excellent or praiseworthy— think about such things. Whatever you have learned or received or heard from me, or seen in me—put into practice. And the peace of God will be with you."[15] The apostle Paul is not shy in sharing his thoughts and concerns with the sexually wayward. He very clearly directs us to flee immorality (1 Corinthians 6:9–10 and 6:18; 1 Thessalonians 4:3–5; Ephesians 5:5; Colossians 3:5, to name but a few). At the same time, he encourages us to remember the truth and pursue that which is holy. He has been a model of purity for his disciples, and encourages them to live into purity from the start. It's about what we pursue more than what we avoid.

Attitudes that Elevate or Destroy

From the start. Here's where it gets even more tricky.

After King David's epic fall into adultery with Bathsheba, the prophet Nathan confronts David on his sin and calls him to repent.[16] David recognizes the depth of his impurity and comes to God with sincere agony and contrition. And while he asks forgiveness for his sin in Psalm 51, he

14. NIV.

15. NIV, italics added.

16. See 2 Samuel 11–12.

never once mentions his fallen sexuality. He talks of his waywardness and transgression, and cries out for cleansing, but does not once refer to adultery or murder (of Bathsheba's husband, Uriah). Instead, the core of his prayer is "Create in me a pure heart, O God, and renew a steadfast spirit within me."[17]

David recognized that the hole in his purity was a matter of *heart* and *spirit*. More than the sexual sin, David's cry to God involved renewing in him a heart that was pure and a spirit that was steadfast. For David to commit adultery with Bathsheba, he first had to have a low view of women—co-image bearers of the King—that un-dignified and dehumanized them, and saw them as objects for his own pleasure. Prior to Bathsheba, David had seven wives and a multitude of concubines. Over time, his attitude toward women became unclean, and his actions followed. It was not a big step for David to sleep with Bathsheba when she represented nothing more than an object of his sexual pleasure. In his repentance, he cries out, asking God to restore his heart-level purity and spiritual steadfastness.

A man's sexual sinfulness begins with his attitudes. If a man has a high view of women and views them as dignified co-image-bearers of God, then he is far less likely to objectify them and take them for his pleasure. But if a man has somehow come to believe that women are less-than or merely a means to his pleasurable ends, then he will be far more likely to abuse them.

These objectifying attitudes are rife within our current masculine culture. As boys, we are told, "Don't throw like a girl" or "You're crying like a sissy." Girls and femininity are used to degrade and reduce boys to nothing more than objects. In the heart of a boy, these attitudes grow into an unthoughtfulness or unconcern for how he treats women. From this unconcern, it is a small step toward pornography, in which he uses women for his personal masturbatory pleasure. From there, a small step toward sexual actions, and, from there, a small step toward supporting prostitution or even sex trafficking. In *End: Engaging Men to End Sex Trafficking*, I recently wrote, "Sex trafficking exists to satiate the demand that pornography creates."[18] Like David, the man who engages in these actions is doing more than giving in to a momentary lustful indulgence. His heart is wayward and his spirit disloyal.

Therefore, as fathers intending to raise boys with a commitment to godly purity, we must address the area of sexual *actions* and train our boys toward a heart-level commitment to internal *attitudes*. Women do not exist

17. Psalm 51:10, NIV.

18. Bruno and Bruno, *End: Engaging Men to End Sex Trafficking*, 28.

for the pleasure of men. They equally reflect the glorious image of God on earth, and deserve the ultimate elevation of beauty and dignity. We must stand against a culture that seeks to dehumanize and un-dignify women, and lead our boys into a purity that stems from, as David prayed, a "pure heart" and "steadfast spirit."

Furthermore, while purity often involves other people (particularly a man's involvement with a woman), it is far more connected to his relationship to God and his own soul. In Psalm 51:3, David states, "Against you, you only, have I sinned and done what is evil in your sight." David's sinful action of adultery is primarily an affront to the integrity of God. And while there are earthly victims (Bathsheba and her husband) and earthly consequences of his actions (the death of their child), David is aware that his most dire sin is his insult to the image of God in him *and* her. Additionally, Paul encourages the hypersexual Corinthians to "flee from sexual immorality. All other sins a person commits are outside the body, but whoever sins sexually, sins against their own body."[19] There is a deep connection between our sex and our souls, between our masculinity and the image we bear. Sexual sin is directly related to the image of God.

For fathers to speak into this difficult and often awkward topic of purity, we must remind our sons of the image of God in them and call them to live according to this truth. This is a tall, tall order. But if we are to change the course of manhood for our sons, we must take the high road.

Purity: a heart-level commitment to masculine holiness

Your Story

Oh boy. Of all the sections in this book, this is the one that will likely be most read or most skipped. In your intentional pursuit of your son's development as a man, I am asking you to consider your own story of purity—and impurity.

Enter shame, stage left.

The very nature of purity and integrity requires the teacher to live according to the high calling he proclaims. A father pontificating about purity but living his own life without it will nullify his every word and harden the heart of his son. In order to adequately usher your son into godly manhood, he must know that you too are in pursuit of the heart of God. And while you

19. 1 Corinthians 6:18, NIV.

may be tempted to paint a picture of your perfection, it is far better to allow him to see behind the curtain of your shame and failings, especially in the area of purity. For if he knows your stumbles and your continued pursuit, he will have hope that he too can walk the difficult journey of purity.

Your son needs to know. He needs to know that you are tempted, when you are tempted, and how you are tempted. He needs to hear about your misdeeds and failings as a teenager, and how you gave in to the lusts of the flesh. He needs to see your face as you talk about your indiscretions, and hear about the momentary pleasure that opened the doorway to decades of pain. He wants to understand how to navigate the daily assault on *his* masculinity as he joins you in understanding *yours*. One author states, "What was silent in the father speaks in the son, and often I found in the son the unveiled secret of the father."[20] He longs to know how to struggle and succeed and struggle again. And he needs to know how deeply pervasive the assault on purity is for grown men—from sex to taxes, from white lies to spiritual pursuit, from internal motivations to how you make tithing decisions, from masturbation to music choices.

At the end of the day, if he does not see you honestly wrestle for your own purity, then he will not wrestle for his. This may require you to do some intensely personal work with a trained therapist or a trusted friend. You may need to honestly review your life and join David in praying for a clean heart and steadfast spirit. Far too many fathers hide behind good intentions and empty statements. Recent news articles quote a Canadian study, published in the *Archives of Sexual Behahiour*,[21] indicating that Bible-belt states have overwhelmingly higher pornography usage statistics than other American states. Just being a "Christian" does not exempt you from facing the reality that you too need a Savior.

His Story

The sad reality for young men today is that their purity has already been compromised. The challenge to "live in the world but not of it" means that, no matter how strenuously we strive to stay pure, we are inevitably marred by the fallenness of the world, the assault of the enemy, or the internal sabotage of the flesh. Regardless of how sheltered your son may have been up to

20. Believe it or not, this quote is attributed to Friedrich Nietzsche at Thinkexist.com.

21. MacInnis and Hodson, "Do American States with More Religious or Conservative Populations Search More for Sexual Content on Google?"

this point, he *already* has stories he needs to tell. His masculine purity has already been drawn into question, and he lives with both fear and shame for what he has done, what he has seen, or what has been done to him. Fathers must boldly draw their sons out of the shadows toward the One who forgives our sin and removes our shame.

Very gently, with an invitation of strength mixed with kindness, invite your son to tell you his stories of struggle. Ask him when he has experienced shame. Invite him to talk openly with you about those moments where he has succumbed to temptation. Be curious about his heart, mind, spirit, and body.

Many fathers ask me when to have "the talk." I believe there is no single talk but a lifetime of talks. From the moment your son begins to notice his anatomy, he needs his father to teach him about it—what it means, what it does, and how to use it. I encourage dads to use real language with regard to anatomy, and to help boys know the beautiful differences between males and females. By the time he hits puberty, he should know most everything there is to know. Fathers should be ahead of the curve of playground sex education, health class, locker-room banter, or television shows. For fathers who have engaged in these conversations before, inviting your son to talk about purity will not pose a significant hurdle. For fathers who need to start at square one, I encourage you to do so. For this, I highly recommend Stan and Brenda Jones's four-part series called *God's Design for Sex.*

At this stage in the game, fearful fathers will leave their sons to wander through the world of purity alone, loading on a pile of *don'ts* and hoping their insistence is enough. I believe boys needs dads *all along the way* to help them navigate the choppy waters of purity. And though our Western culture no longer utilizes circumcision as a communal reminder of solidarity with one another and the King, we can create for our boys a community of masculinity that speaks wholly and holy about a purity connected to a much, much greater narrative than "just don't."

Questions for Your Journey

1. How do you react to the notion that men should use their bodies rather than focus on all the *don'ts*?

2. What do you think about God's choice to mark his people with the sign of circumcision?

3. In what ways have you considered penises spiritual?

4. In your opinion, why has purity been a primary focal point of attack by the enemy?

5. In what ways do you need to reconsider the purity in every category of your life (including but not limited to sexuality)?

6. What work do you need to do in this area of your own life?

7. How will you go about doing that before you address these issues with your son?

PART IV

Man Maker Project

Creating a Rite of Passage Journey for Your Son

CHAPTER 14

Preparing a Man Year

Plotting a Course

If you don't care where you are going, any road will take you there.[1]
BRIAN MOLITOR

IN A CULTURE WHERE prescribed male rites of passage do not exist, where we do not have a template or a system in place, modern-day fathers must establish their own. I have spoken with many fathers who desire to do something for their sons but have no idea where to start. The task feels monumental, and many quit before they begin. It is for this reason that I have attempted to create a structure and process for fathers to adopt and adapt to their specific family and their specific sons. There is no one right way to do this, but my hope is that, while reading the previous chapters, you have thought, wrestled, prayed, and processed. The time has now come for you to take action.

More Than a One-Time Event

Ancient passage rituals involved a series of events over the course of an extended amount of time. There was a beginning and an end, but these rites often extended over the course of several weeks, sometimes months. Today, if our hope is to both affirm the manhood in our sons and teach them what that means, we need more than a single event or ceremony. We need a plan. True rites of passage are more than a moment. John Eldredge says, "We need more than a moment, an event. We need a process, a journey, an epic

1. Molitor, *Boy's Passage, Man's Journey*, 135.

story of many experiences woven together . . . . We need initiation. And we need a Guide."[2] These experiences build on one another and progress toward a well-planned culmination. God designed the experience of living as a man to be epic. So should the process of becoming one.

Therefore, I believe the rites of passage process should act as a springboard into the greater narrative of the boy's life. It should create a greater community of men with whom he builds long-standing relationships. It should offer him a biblical background of manhood, taught by a variety of men other than the father, but initiated and managed by the father. It should be filled with experiences—*wild* experiences—that break him free from the confines of his boyhood and open his eyes to the world of possibility, dreams, and a future. He needs to be pushed, pulled, prodded, and tested over the course of time, and given the opportunity to reflect and talk about his experience with others.

To accomplish all this for my son, I needed time. A lot of time. As I wrestled through all I wanted to achieve as part of Aidan's rite of passage, I decided I would take the time I needed rather than rush through. Given the six aspects of manhood I desired to instill in him, I determined I needed a full year. As a result, I created what I called his Man Year, a yearlong process that would culminate in a well-thought-out ceremony.

I also realized this Man Year would be merely the *first stage* of his growth into manhood. Every man faces new challenges with each life stage; the Man Year is simply for the first. I plan also to mark three other significant moments in his life with similar, though not as elaborate, intention. When he graduates from high school and heads off to college, I want to ritualize his step toward independence. As he graduates from college, he will need an affirmation of his responsible place in society. And when he marries, I want to mark his entrance into covenant relationship. At each of these stages, and at every moment in between, he will need his father. And while his level of independence and individuation will increase over time, the strength of the father remains a bulwark for children as long as they live. Thus, this is just the beginning.

The Man Year needs to look different for each father and each son. You are both unique individuals with unique stories in unique places. To simply copy and paste what I have done may actually be a disservice. Take the time to prayerfully create a rites of passage process that uniquely honors *your* son. One mother I know has three sons. The oldest is outdoorsy, the middle

2. Eldredge, *Fathered by God*, 8.

one is an energetic extrovert, and the youngest is reserved and nerdy. Each of these boys will need different rites. It is up to the father to know his son and design a passage process that will meet the child's heart.

In the previous chapters, I have laid a foundation of four atmospheric conditions necessary for a rites of passage process and six aspects of manhood. I believe they are ubiquitous across all shapes and types of men. Some current men's literature, for example, idealizes men who hunt, ride motorbikes, fly-fish, or scale mountains. While some men identify with the courage required to do these things, other men need courage to step on stage and sing opera or apply for a PhD program. The foundation in both scenarios is courage. The application is vastly different.

You may find *Man Maker Project 101: A Father's Field Guide for Initiating His Son* helpful in this process.[3] It is my hope here to give you the scaffolding on which to build your unique process for your unique son. The possibilities are endless, but the most important ingredient of all is the father's intentionality to make it happen.

He can't do it alone. He needs you.

Timing and Time: When to Begin

At the age of thirteen, boys enter the awkward time when they rapidly become men. Physically they grow taller and develop larger muscles, and they are mature enough to handle greater responsibility. I chose my son's thirteenth birthday as the day that would stand as a marker for him between boyhood and manhood. From that point, I simply worked backwards, beginning his Man Year on the day of his twelfth birthday and planning for the final ceremony around his thirteenth.

For me, stepping into the world of teenagers means something. With today's daily advancements in technology and media, teenagers are exposed to controversial issues and the underbelly of humanity at increasingly young ages. I wanted to preempt many of these influences in my son's life by giving him a godly lens through which to view the world, himself, and his life and role as a man. I decided that, at the age of twelve, he was

3. *Man Maker Project 101: A Father's Field Guide for Initiating His Son* is available as a free downloadable PDF resource. This workbook will walk you through a step-by-step process to help you create a unique rites of passage process for your son. Get it now at www.restorationproject.net.

old enough to handle the experience and still young enough to learn and appreciate it.

Some men have told me, "I've missed it. My son is already in his twenties. What do I do now?" To this I say, "It's never too late." The hunger for initiation and the father's blessing lasts a lifetime. One man has a married son in his thirties. As this older father took the challenge to actively initiate and bless his adult son, their entire relationship changed. What had been fragile and hostile soon softened into affection and connection. Even the son's relationship with his mother changed. Another man in his late twenties *asked* his father to lead him in an initiation process. Naturally, the rites of passage process looked vastly different for these families, but it's never too late, and something is always better than nothing.

I designed Aidan's Man Year as a full year because I was committed to the idea that much more is "caught than taught." This allowed for high times and low times, times of activity and conversation, and time for things to sink in. During the year, we had specific moments where we would address certain issues. At other times, issues arose organically, allowing us to take real-time experiences and filter them through what he was learning. Time, therefore, became our friend. In a hurry-up-and-get-'er-done world, we took our time.

Qualities of Manhood: Where to Lead Him

In Part III, I walk through the six foundational categories of godly masculinity I feel are crucial to a boy's passage to manhood. While these are the ones I chose for my son, the list of possible characteristics is truly long: honor, respect, stewardship, generosity, hospitality, loyalty, brotherhood, perseverance, humility, servanthood, and kindness, to name but a few. I believe what is important to the father should be passed to the son, while taking into account the son's demeanor, personality, and struggles. Consider the various aspects of godly manhood and determine for yourself which qualities you would like to focus on during the year. Then, spend some time researching and reading about them, and come up with a game plan for how you will go about teaching them.

I found that I had to narrow my list to six. At one point, I had twelve and endeavored to focus on one a month. My friend Greg gently stepped in and corrected my overachiever goal. Thanks to him, I limited it to six.

Be careful that you don't fall into the same trap. Too much and it may be overwhelming for you; too little and your son is left hungry for more.

I decided on the six characteristics of manhood detailed in Part III—*courage, integrity, excellent action, kingdom focus, protective leadership,* and *purity*—after talking with other dads; voraciously reading about rites of passage across time; asking moms to share their thoughts, needs, and concerns with regard to their boys; and speaking with young men about the modern-day challenges they face. It is around these six categories that I have developed the Man Maker Project materials and resources.

Our sons learn about math and reading from school, but there is no school that intentionally teaches our children about courage, integrity, and other godly characteristics of manhood. While they may see these characteristics in your life, they may not know what it is they see. Even in Sunday school, they most likely learn the stories of biblical characters without deep attention to the internal qualities of the heart. They learn about Noah and the "arky-arky," but do they grasp the significance of his courage and kingdom focus? The reality is that we must actively teach our sons. During these months, you are giving your son language and categories for the qualities of a man's life that go beyond the surface into the deeper levels of true heart.

Ultimately, he will not learn everything there is to know about being a man through this one-year project. The goal is to help him create schema through which he can interpret and experience the world. These mental file folders may not be full or complete by the end of his Man Year, but at least the folders will exist and he can pull them out, refer to them, and fill them as he grows.

The Company of Men: Father-Directed, Not Father Alone

No man is an island. The ancient literature about rites of passage insists that a boy's initiation include a larger community of men. While the father acts as the key driver to the process, he needs a group of other trusted men to join him in the journey. As young men grow into adulthood, they need a diverse group of older men to whom they can relate and whom they consider friends. The father alone cannot provide everything the son needs. Young men need models, mentors, and older friends with whom they have deeper relationships. There will be times in your son's life that he needs to talk with someone other than you. By involving a company of men in his rites of passage, you are offering him the freedom to seek wisdom, guidance, and help from men you trust. You may not be part of those future conversations, but you can know that these men will honor you and your son.

A wise father chooses well. Key characteristics of these men should include: a strong commitment to God; the potential for lifelong connection to the boy; being worthy of emulation; a good reputation with other men *and* with women; humility and a willingness to learn as much as they are willing to teach; and an existing love and commitment to your son and his future as a man. Ideally, these men will also have done some prayerful reflection on their own lives and stories, and are able to speak from a place of being internally settled. They don't need to be perfect men, but they should be men who are actively seeking God and the restoration he brings.

It is also important to think about family legacy. I believe it is vital for boys to know their family narrative and to build relationships with the men who have come before them. Our boys were born on a moving train, and it is crucial that they know the stock they came from. Even if you desire to break free from dangerous family histories and significantly alter the direction of your family tree, your son needs to know his past. The Scriptures are full of long lists of lineage, encouraging each new generation to remember their forefathers.

It was important for me to involve Aidan's two grandfathers. While neither of them are intimately involved in his daily life or cornerstone elders in their church, I wanted to take advantage of this rites of passage process to invite them to the table to participate. They may not have had a tremendous *manhood* influence on Aidan, but he had the unique opportunity to spend one-on-one time with his grandfathers. This, in itself, was a win in my book.

For the Man Maker Project, you will need to *choose five men*. As a team of six (you + five), you can divide and conquer the six topics and other experiences you have designed for your son. Likely, one of the more difficult tasks in developing a Man Year for your son will be asking other men to participate. You are asking them to give of their time, money, and focus—three resources that are in short supply for most men. I recommend asking each of your selected men personally to join your team on behalf of your son. Take them out for coffee or a beer and lay out your plan for your son and your desire for them to participate. Tell them *why* you want them and paint a picture of the grand scheme.

The six men I asked to be part of Aidan's Man Year live all around the country. They are his two uncles, his two grandfathers, and my best friend.

Asking all of them face-to-face was a geographic impossibility. In order to cast a vision for my plans and invite them to participate, I wrote a letter and sent it via e-mail. Then, within a few days, I spoke with each one on the phone to answer any questions and formally ask him to join in. Here is a snippet from that letter:

> Dear Chris, Brian, Dennis, Dad, and Greg,
>
> This year, Aidan will be entering his twelfth year. It is so hard to believe that the little bugger has grown up so quickly . . . but he has. Every day I see more of a young man in him—his boy-like features are fading, and signs of teenager-hood are emerging left and right. Though he hasn't yet hit full-on puberty, he's getting taller and broader, his voice is deepening, and he's gaining independence (sometimes too much). This fall, he'll be in seventh grade.
>
> I'm writing the five of you (his uncles, grandfathers, and friend) to ask you to be part of his transition into manhood. I think it is vital for every boy to have a collection of men intentionally usher him into the man-circle. As I have thought and prayed about how to best do this for him, I wanted to invite you to play a crucial part. I trust each of you implicitly, and I believe you have Aidan's best interests in mind. I think you have an important role in his life, and I want to foster that for him as much as possible.
>
> Aidan looks up to each of you—all in different ways and for different reasons—but each one of you is extremely important to him. And each one of you has something crucial to offer him as he becomes a man.

Ideally, your men will live in proximity to you and be able to gather for conversations, plans, prayer, and camaraderie. But if your situation is like mine, with men living far away, make sure to communicate regularly, provide them with a copy of the Man Maker material, and do the best you can to establish a sense of togetherness. Distance also creates an additional barrier for your son to spend one-on-one time with them. I bit the bullet and worked a weekend job to afford extra plane tickets for Aidan to visit his mentors. In the end, putting him on a plane alone only added to the epic adventure.

However you choose to do it, you need other good men.

Developing a Plan

As the pieces start to fall into place, you can now plot out a specific course for your son's Man Year. The essential elements are:

- *Timing and Time:* When will you begin this process for your son, and when will it end? How long will the entire process take? Pick specific dates. They may coincide with certain other events, such as birthdays, holidays, or the school year. As I've said, I suggest during the year between his twelfth and thirteenth birthdays. I also suggest taking an entire year.

- *Qualities of Manhood:* Decide on the specific qualities of manhood on which you will focus during his initiation. I have provided you with the six I chose, which I found to be a manageable number.

- *The Company of Men:* Whom will you ask to participate? When and how will you ask them? I suggest asking them at least 3–6 months *prior* to your start date to give all of you enough time to prepare and plan together.

Once you have determined your course of action for each of these elements, it's time to start planning the specifics. For Aidan's Man Year, I broke his year into two-month segments, assigning a different manhood topic and a different mentor to each. As I did so, I prayerfully thought through the lives and stories of the men, and attempted to pair each with the topic I thought he could most easily and adequately address. For some, this meant that they actively modeled the characteristic. For others, it meant that they had struggled with it in the past. Remember, the key for a boy's passage is not the guidance of perfect men, but that of men who are willing to talk about their successes and failures, normalizing the ups and downs, joys and pains of manhood.

During his assigned two-month window, I asked each mentor to spend 2–3 days of intentional one-on-one time with Aidan. For this time, I asked the mentors to create the appropriate conditions needed for a boy's passage to manhood, as discussed in Part II. These conditions are: *intentionality, removal from the feminine, risk and danger,* and *blessing.* I helped brainstorm ideas that would be meaningful to Aidan and easily accessible to the mentor.

During their time together, each mentor was invited to address the character quality assigned to him and find ways to *experience* it with Aidan in practical ways. How this looked turned out to be quite simple. Some took him camping. Others took him golfing. He went sailing with one and on an overseas missions trip with me. The point of this time together is less about teaching the manhood quality and much more about helping the boy create *mental file folders* for the qualities. It is impossible for a twelve-year-old to fully grasp the full meaning of integrity or kingdom focus, for example, especially in just two months . But it is vital for him to develop a schema for what these qualities are, so that he can return to them and begin coloring in the details as life gives him the opportunity to do so.

I firmly believe that boys are designed by God to learn in a variety of ways, and as fathers it is important to know our sons' preferred learning modalities. Some boys are readers. Others balk at the idea of a book. Some boys can watch a YouTube video on knot tying and instantly become proficient. Other boys will struggle with this. It is important to know your son and help the other men engage with him accordingly. However, there is something extremely powerful for anyone who is able to "taste and see" through the lens of experience. The more you can create experiences for your son to come face-to-face with the concepts, the more he will learn and remember. You can tell your son about jail as you teach him about integrity, but the sights, smells, and memories of actually visiting a jail will forever be emblazoned in his mind. It is the classic difference between telling versus doing. By all means, *do*.

Throughout the year, I never left the driver seat. Remember, it is the father's intentionality, supported and subsidized by the greater company of men, that creates the passage process. Though Aidan spent 2–3 days with each mentor, I also watched movies with him, asked questions, and had late-into-the-night discussions regarding each topic. I told him stories and asked him for his. The burden of the passage year remained on my shoulders, while the other men supported the process by taking him for a few days for more focused time away. I provided them with the information for their respective character qualities (see Chapter 15 for resources to give your men), and then entrusted Aidan into their hands for a few intensive days.

You might find it helpful to create a chart such as this:[4]

4. Charts like this are available in a free PDF download called *Man Maker Project 101: An Intentional Father's Guide to Initiating His Son* from www.restorationproject.net.

Months	Manhood Quality	Mentor	Intensive Time with Mentor
	Man Year Begins on Twelfth birthday —Opening Conversation with Aidan		
June–July	Courage	Greg	3-day High-country Back-packing Trip
August–September	Integrity	Grandfather B.	Fishing and Camping Trip
October–November	Excellent Action	Chris P.	Sailing, Flying and Military Intensity
December–January	Kingdom Focus	Chris B.	Missions Trip to Turkey
February–March	Protective Leadership	Grandfather P.	Golfing Trip
April–May	Purity	Brian	Weekend Retreat
	Man Year Ending Ceremony on Thirteenth Birthday		

Man Year Journal: Preparing for the Test

I knew the year I had planned for Aidan would be epic, and I wanted him to have a place to record his thoughts, experiences, and stories. He's not much of a writer, but I know that he often finds inspiration in brief quotes or impactful stories. I also informed him that he would be tested at the end of his yearlong experience, and that he should be prepared to remember what he had learned. This motivated him to take notes and strive to remember the definitions offered, the topics covered, and the stories shared.

As a receptacle for these reflections, I created a simple Man Year Journal for him. I bought a nice, small, leather-bound journal from the bookstore, and then created six sections with paper clips and dividers. Whenever Aidan spent time with a mentor, I made sure his journal accompanied him. Together we wrote down ideas, quotes, stories, and conversations from his experiences with me and the other men. At times I asked him to do additional research on a topic and record his thoughts.

As a symbol of the beginning of the process, I gave him the journal during our first conversation about his Man Year. During our walk in the Black Hills, I explained the value of a man in the eyes of God, and the challenge young men have in becoming true, godly men. I shared about the group of men I had asked to be part of his year, and then told him about the times he would spend with each. I then handed him the journal and said, "So it begins."

On the first pages of the journal, I wrote the following:

Dear Aidan,

You are about to enter into a new season of your life. As you turn twelve, you are leaving behind boyhood and entering into manhood. This is far more than going through puberty. It is far more than getting taller or heading into a new grade in the fall. It is the call of God on every boy's life to become a man—not just physically, but spiritually, emotionally, relationally, and morally. It means leaving behind boyhood things and fully embracing who you are as a man.

Being a man in our world today is confusing. What does that even mean? As you know from our conversations in the past, it is my desire as your father to usher you into manhood in such a way that you *know* you are a man—where there is no doubt in your mind or in the minds of those around you. You have what it takes to be a true man. Now is the time to become him.

This is not an easy transition. In fact, it is extremely difficult. But you are not alone. Throughout your twelfth year (from your twelfth birthday to your thirteenth birthday), I have designed a year of experience and adventure. I have gathered together significant men in your life to come alongside you in this transition, to help teach and mentor you into manhood. These men are: both your grandfathers (Pop and Grandpa), both your uncles (Chris and Brian), Greg, and myself. Together, the six of us will be your guides. Each one of us has a different perspective, different experiences, and different stories we want to share with you. Each one of us loves you and wants to see you succeed.

I have set out six different "man" topics for you to learn and experience this year. Each of us will take one of these topics and teach you what we know about it. You will have specific movies to watch, things to read, places to go, and adventures to take. I'm sending you to spend time with each of these guides. You will be traveling to each one to spend a few days together—just you and him. That means that I'm sending you to Virginia, Florida, California, and on two trips in Colorado. I'm also planning a trip with just you and me.

Our goal is to prepare you for your thirteenth birthday—the day you transition into manhood. There are other important markers in your future as well—when you turn eighteen and leave home for college, when you graduate from college and set out on your own, and when you get married and take responsibility for a bride. But we'll get to those later . . .

This journal is meant to be your field manual for your "Man Year." I want you to keep track of your experiences. Write down important things these men teach you. Keep record of what they say and the stories they tell. Write your questions, doubts, and wonderings. By the end of this year, my hope is that this journal will be full of great wisdom for you to look back on for years to come. Oh, and you will be tested on what you learn before we officially welcome you into manhood. Be ready.

Aidan, your name means "little fire." My hope for you this year is that your fire will become a blaze, and that you will embrace all that God has for you as a true man of the King. Your time has come.

Love,

Dad

Your Story

There are few things more thrilling and terrifying for a father than to begin the process of inviting his son into manhood. I have already mentioned my own fear and trepidation. Truthfully, this is a lot of work, and it takes tremendous dedication to see it through. At this juncture, I wish to remind you of *why*. Why is this important? What does your son stand to gain from this amount of planning, resourcing, and creating?

Consider your own story of masculine initiation. For most grown men today, their story involves little intention, an absence of emotional engagement, and a lingering and haunting question as to just what manhood truly means. Yet we have little idea of how much we have missed.

I spoke once with a man who claimed, "My parents were perfect. They loved us well, gave us everything we needed, and provided a great foundation for faith and life." Then, just a few moments later, he said under his breath, "My mother was condescending and my father was complacent." Naturally, I paused him and drew attention to his blatant contradictions. With a slip of the tongue, he had broken through the façade of his boyhood and begun to face the realities of the emptiness he truly experienced in his "good and perfect" home. He had never been initiated. He never received the intentional pursuit of his father and spent the majority of his life pursuing degree after degree, culminating in a PhD, with the hope of achieving purpose and affirmation. He lived his life in a relational void, longing for marriage but not finding a woman until well into his fifties. This man had to create a manhood construct on his own.

That is what this is all about. You have the divine assignment to set the course for your future family tree. Regardless of what you have inherited, the legacy you leave is up to you. Look deeply into the heart of your son and know that he is asking you the core question: *Am I a man?* But more than that, look into the future to *his* sons and *his* grandsons. Your actions this year will have a lasting effect that far outlives your time on earth. Answer his question now, and change the future forever. It's really that big.

Questions for Your Journey

1. When you consider embarking on this initiation journey with your son, what are your hesitations and fears?

2. What are your dreams and hopes for your son after this process?

3. In what ways do shame or inadequacy creep up in your mind and heart?

4. How does it feel to you to ask other men to be part of this year?

5. What unique circumstances do you need to consider for your son's Man Year (i.e. you live in an urban setting, your son has a physical

limitation, your financial resources are stretched, etc.)? How might you go about managing this?

6. What does your son's mother think about this whole proposal?

CHAPTER 15

Man Maker Playbook

Step-by-Step Guides to Conversations with Your Son

The superior man is he who develops, in harmonious proportions, his moral, intellectual, and physical nature. This should be the end at which men of all classes should aim, and it is this only which constitutes real greatness.[1]

—DOUGLASS JERROLD

IN THE FOLLOWING PAGES, you will find a step-by-step conversation guide for each of the six godly characteristics of manhood discussed in this book. While not exhaustive, I have attempted to offer conversational starting points for the various phases of this journey.

As a father, you need to take the lead in each of these areas. At the same time, choose other men to intentionally pursue your son's heart with regard to one or more of these characteristics. I encourage you to ask each man to read this book. You might even consider leading your group of chosen mentors through a series of intentional discussions about each section, answering the questions at the end the chapters, to build cohesion and purpose. I also recommend asking each man to commit to regularly praying for you and your son through the entire process. This will be where theory meets practice.

Each of the following sections is divided into the following categories:

- *Biblical Examples*: This highlights biblical characters who either succeed or fail in the specific manhood quality. References and a brief summary are provided. More than Sunday-school-felt-board conversations, fathers must mine the Scriptures for beautiful and tragic

1. As quoted in Edwards, *A Dictionary of Thoughts*, 325.

stories to orient our lives and navigate our world. Be sure not to domesticate the Bible. It's tragic and often rated R, and your son needs to experience the rawness of God's Word. Discuss these characters with your son on hikes, in a canoe, late at night, at the dinner table, or whenever God provides you the opportunity.

- *Movies*: Film is a powerful tool for this generation. As modern-day poetry and storytelling, movies can offer us language and shared experience with our sons. Using these stories, characters, and situations as a tool in teaching and discussion can help solidify concepts and open up new topics. I've included a few suggested films to watch together and discuss with your son. Please note that these movie suggestions have a variety of ratings, and not all content may be suitable for all audiences.[2] As a result, you may need to address difficult issues as they come up. I believe it is better at this age (12+) to expose young men to questionable content (within reason) and intentionally discuss it between father and son rather than avoid these topics. The reality is that he *will* be exposed. Better for him to engage with his father than to reach conclusions on his own.

- *Topics, Questions, and Conversations*: Here I provide some sample conversation starters. We all know the agony of asking our sons questions, only to be met with blank stares and one-word answers. These open-ended questions are designed to elicit more than a single sentence. Realistically, this is going to be hard. While I've done my best to throw you the ball, it's up to you to catch it and run.

- *Experience and Gift*: This offers ideas for creating meaningful experiences for your son. Naturally, one experience may cover multiple character qualities, but I encourage you to walk through each one deliberately to solidify your son's mental file folders for each. In this one year he will not learn the totality of what each means. (Do any of us know?) But an intentional experience will sear his heart and provide him with a mile-marker in his journey that he can refer to for decades to come. In addition, a small but meaningful gift for each section of his year will offer him a physical memento of his experience. I've provided a few ideas here. By no means is this exhaustive. Be creative and

2. I leave it up to the father to determine what is appropriate for his son to watch. I do not condone much of what comes out of Hollywood, and by providing this list I am not giving any sort of "thumbs up" to these films other than for the purpose of providing a platform for discussion between father and son.

particular, knowing who you are, who your son is, and what would be meaningful for the two of you.

Each of the following sections should be read and utilized in concert with its corresponding chapter in the book. As you talk with your fellow mentors, discuss how you would like them to engage your son around these movies, Scriptures, and questions.

Courage

Definition: *having the guts to do hard things despite your fears*

Biblical Examples of Courage

Joshua (Key passage: Joshua 1–6)

We have a tremendous example of courage in the Old Testament book of
Joshua. After the death of Moses, Joshua faces the great challenge of leading
the wandering Israelites into the Promised Land. His lifelong mentor has
passed away, and the overwhelming tasks of leadership and battle fall to
him. In the first sixteen verses of the book of Joshua, how does God speak
to this man? Five times God tells him to have *heart*.

> Be courageous.
>
> Be courageous.
>
> Be courageous.
>
> Be courageous.
>
> Be courageous.

"Joshua," God says, "the task before you is great. But, as you take on
this mantle of leadership and step into the role as commander-in-chief of
the Israelite army, have courage. Why? Because, my friend, *I am with you.*
You got this."

Take time to read Joshua 1–6 and meditate on the reality of his fears
and the deeper reality of God's promises and presence with him. Without
this courageous man, the Israelites would still be wandering in the desert.

Courage

Jesus (Key passage: Luke 22:39—24:53)

Throughout his life, Jesus showed incredible courage. Of any man to walk the earth, he is our greatest example of what it means to live with heart. There is no more powerful example of courage and trust than when he faced a painful death on the cross. Moments before his betrayal and arrest, he prays in the Garden of Gethsemane—broken, alone, and anxious to the point of sweating blood. Yet his inner courage overcomes his fear. He rises from prayer, returns to the crowd, and allows himself to be arrested. He could have fled. He could have worked powerfully to avoid a death reserved for criminals. Instead he faced his destiny with courage.

The strength of Jesus' courage comes from his connection to the Father. His trust in the goodness of God runs so deep that he is willing to put aside his fears and believe that God's will is right and good and necessary. "Not my will, but Yours be done," he says.[1]

Movies of Courage

There is no end to the fantastically instructive, personal conversations that can result from mutually engaging in good stories. Below are just a few ideas. Watch the films together, and then ask your son this open-ended question: "Where did you see courage in this movie?"

- *We Bought a Zoo* – Talk about the "20 seconds of courage" that a person needs to face the difficult things in life.

- *Kingdom of Heaven* – Focus on the "oath" the main character must take, and how he later uses that oath to give *heart* to the people.

- *The Lord of the Rings: The Fellowship of the Ring* – Reflect on the courage Frodo must have to begin his journey, and then again when he offers to take the ring.

- *Courageous* – Note the courage each man needs to live boldly in his world, especially on behalf of his family.

- Classics like *Braveheart* and *Gladiator* – Discuss the courage these men have to stand for what is right, even though the decision leads to their deaths.

1. Luke 22:42, NIV.

Discussion Topics and Questions

The following questions are merely suggested conversation-starters about courage. Successfully initiating boys into manhood requires leading conversations with a point.

- What are the differences between bravery, courage, and recklessness?
- When in the next year do you think you will need courage?
- What is the difference between courage and bravado?
- Where is the line between courage and self-centeredness?
- Is it okay for a man to be afraid? What do courageous men do with fear?
- What is the connection between having courage and being strong?
- In what situations do men require courage? (i.e. work, relationships, faith, etc.)
- Where do men get courage when they don't feel like they have enough?

An Experience and a Gift

Crafting an experience for your son that engages the characteristic of courage may seem daunting. It can actually be quite easy. Whether you choose something simple or complex, your son must face a situation where his heart is challenged, where fear emerges, and where he can act courageously *with a man watching*. He needs to come to the end of himself and overcome both the obstacle and his fears, and experience the delight of being seen and celebrated. Keep in mind the necessary atmospheric conditions that create an initiatory scene: *intention of the father, removal from the feminine, risk and danger,* and *blessing.*

Some men might choose a physical challenge for their sons, like rock climbing, waterskiing or scuba diving. Others might decide to create a social challenge, like engaging people from a different culture or socioeconomic background. Or the experience might involve trying out for the middle school musical or riding along in a police car. Regardless of the actual experience, the boy must be challenged to face his fear, and overcome.

To mark and celebrate the experience, consider giving a gift that symbolizes courage and will remind him of his accomplishment. For example, if rock climbing, give him a carabineer engraved with the date and his name; if scuba diving, give him a shell; if riding along in a police car, a badge or a gun. Any object can be a memento if you ascribe meaning to it.

I asked my friend Greg to take Aidan on a high-country journey. Having grown up in predominantly urban and suburban areas, my son hadn't experienced a multi-day backpacking trip. He had hiked and camped, but he had not backpacked. As an entrance into the multiple Man Maker experiences I had in store for him, I wanted him to experience both the terror and the delight of sustained exposure to the elements.

Greg carefully planned a three-day, 26-mile backcountry packing trip for just the two of them. Prior to their departure, the three of us talked about the itinerary, the trail, and the experience. But, far more, we discussed the courage it would require: the courage to go on a several-day journey with another man, *alone;* the courage to be "off the grid" for several days; the courage to be exposed to the elements, rain or shine, with no possibility of escape; the courage to face the seemingly unending trail; and mostly the courage to experience the pounding quiet of his own thoughts without the distractions most teenagers use to anesthetize their fears. It would be an epic adventure that marked his departure from boyhood toward manhood—a literal journey I would send my boy on, with the hope that he would return a few clicks closer to being a man.

Greg gave Aidan a one-man hammock-tent for their journey. It served as shelter during their trip and a reminder of my son's courage to string himself up like a living bear-bag and sleep between the trees *alone.*

Integrity

Definition: *honoring yourself and others by being wholly* you, *even when it hurts*

Biblical Examples of Integrity

Samuel (Key passage: 1 Samuel 12:1–4)

People want to know their leader can be trusted. As with any leader, Samuel has the power and authority over the Israelite nation to take things for himself. He can require whatever he likes of the people, using his position as God's prophet and last of the judges for his own selfish gain. Yet, at the end of his life, in his farewell speech, he asks the people to show him where he has been dishonest or taken anything that does not belong to him. They respond with "You have done nothing wrong." What an incredible measure of a man's integrity.

Pharisees (Key Passage: Matthew 23)

A stunning example of hypocrisy, dishonesty, and *dis*integration are the Pharisees. In his most flaming sermon, Jesus condemns the Pharisees for their lies and two-faced approach to God. He says to the crowds, "But do not do what [the Pharisees] do, for they do not practice what they preach. They tie up heavy, cumbersome loads and put them on other people's shoulders, but they themselves are not willing to lift a finger to move them."[1] Jesus goes on to boldly speak seven "woes" against them.

Read through this chapter of Matthew together, and discuss how and why the Pharisees' lack of integrity so enrages Jesus.

---

1. Matthew 23:3–4, NIV.

Joseph, father of Jesus (Key passage: Matthew 1:18–25)

Joseph was like any other guy. A common carpenter from a little town called Nazareth, he looked forward to his wedding day with great anticipation. He followed the Jewish traditions carefully, honoring his family by holding to the customary courting and betrothal process with a young woman named Mary. He was an upstanding man, full of integrity. Then his wife-to-be announces that she is pregnant and makes the wild claim that the child is from God. Joseph faces a choice: listen to Mary (and later the angel) or end the betrothal, leaving her in shame and protecting himself from public ridicule. Even before the divinity of the Christ Child was made clear to him, Joseph was "faithful to the law, and yet did not want to expose [Mary] to public disgrace, [so] he had in mind to divorce her quietly."[2] After the angel confirmed Mary's story, he, as a man of integrity, chooses to honor himself, his wife, and his God, despite the ridicule that will certainly ensue. What hurts his reputation in the short-term eventually enters him into the eternal archives of great and honorable men.

Movies of Integrity

- *Les Misérables* – Protagonist Jean Valjean provides a tremendous example of integrity. He also lives his life hiding from the law, providing discussion opportunities about integrity from both angles. (There are several versions of this film, including the cinematic version of the musical. I personally prefer the dramatic version starring Liam Neeson.)

- *Cinderella Man* – After learning that his son has stolen from the grocer, the father steps in, makes him return the stolen goods, and promises to provide.

- *Courageous* – A character faces a difficult choice: lie and keep his job, or tell the truth, which would honor God, his wife, and himself but force him to pay the price.

- *What About Bob?* – Although venerated by society, the psychiatrist consistently shows his lack of integrity, while Bob, who is continually ridiculed and brushed aside, shows his integrity.

2. Matthew 1:19, NIV.

- *The Mission* – Despite external pressures, the missionaries stand up for what is right, sacrificing their own lives in the process.

Discussion Topics and Questions

Talking with your son about integrity can be exciting and difficult. He may feel that you are attempting to corner him or catch him in a lie. Be careful to approach these topics with openness and honesty yourself.

- What would happen in our world if men did not uphold truth and what is right?
- What have been some situations where you have had to make a hard choice?
- What should a man do when telling a little lie might actually make a situation better?
- How do we know what is right?
- What happens if we don't agree with the law? Do we uphold it or stand for what we believe?
- What happens to a man's life and heart if he makes a habit of breaking integrity?
- How does society deal with dishonesty? What have you heard about the term "little white lie"?
- Why is integrity such a big deal?

An Experience and a Gift

As you create an experience to codify the characteristic of integrity for your son, you will not have to go far to find the effects of lies and dishonesty. Throughout your son's Man Year, I challenge you to repeatedly expose him to the reality of the world's pervasive deception. Having the background and experience of courage under his belt, he is now equipped to examine the difficulty of living in this world as a man of integrity.

What sort of experience can you create for your son that will punctuate a man's call to live with integrity? You may remember that my father worked as an attorney for his entire adult life. As part of this process, he took Aidan to visit the courtroom, where he could observe the proceedings and process of law. He was able to hear the testimonies from the witness stand, watch the prosecution and defense make their cases, and see the judge wrestle with weighing the evidence in order to find the truth. Is there a similar experience you can craft for your son to absorb the value of integrity and honesty in his own life?

My dad and Aidan also went camping and fishing, sitting together at the lake's edge. Their time together held few words, I'm sure. But, in the end, my dad gave Aidan a compass, a gift of deep symbolism as he navigates the choppy waters of life. The meaning you attribute to the gift will, ideally, forever remind him that the heart of a true man always holds tightly to integrity, even when it hurts. Let truth and integrity be your true north.

Excellent Action

Definition: *making an extraordinary impact*

Biblical Examples of Excellent Action

Adam (Key passage: Genesis 3:1–24)

Naturally, the first man Adam is *not* a winning example of excellent action. Quite the opposite. He is the prime illustration of the devastation that results when a man is passive. In Genesis 3:6, we see that Eve is tempted by the serpent, eats the fruit, and then hands it to Adam *who was with her the whole time*. Adam stood by, and humanity fell.

What might have been the fate of humankind if Adam had appropriately stepped up to the plate and *acted excellently*? As sons of Adam, all men struggle with a level of passivity that perpetuates the first man's inaction. Theologians call the "fall" of all people the "sin of Adam" rather than the "sin of Adam and Eve" for this very reason. He caved. And we still suffer the consequences.

Daniel (Key passage: Daniel 1)

The young man Daniel is captured by the Babylonians and carried away for training in the king's service. Resolving not to defile himself with the food and culture of his captors, Daniel refuses to partake in the richer foods and trusts the Lord's provision . In time, he and three other Israelites ascend to higher roles of honor when the king "talked with them, and he found none equal [to them]."[1] Daniel is a tremendous model of excellent action for young men today who may be tempted to sacrifice their values in exchange for comfortable living.

Read the whole narrative of Daniel's captivity and his commitment to excellent action throughout his life.

1. Daniel 1:19, NIV.

Paul the Apostle

The pursuit of excellent action is all over the Scriptures, with Paul as a primary spokesperson. Take some time to look these up, memorize them, and then discuss these passages with your son. Here are a few great references:

- Ecclesiastes 9:10
- Philippians 1:9–10
- Colossians 3:23–24
- 1 Corinthians 10:31
- 2 Corinthians 8:7
- 1 Thessalonians 4:1

Movies of Excellent Action

- *The Incredibles* – Throughout the movie, the superhero characters struggle between wanting to blend into normal society and embracing their gifts and being extraordinary. In the end, they decide to act, saving the world in the process.

- *Captain America: The First Avenger* – Captain America must make a choice to remain on the sidelines or do what he can to rescue prisoners of war. From this turning point onward, he lives into excellent action and refuses to allow others to suffer on their own.

- *The Karate Kid* – Mr. Miyagi challenges his protégé to pursue excellence, even when he doesn't understand the training he's receiving. In the end, excellence wins the fight.

- *Braveheart* – William Wallace chooses to step in and lead his fellow countrymen in a battle against injustice. It leads to his death, but his movement toward action changes the course of history.

Discussion Topics and Questions

Fortunately, men who take action are venerated by our society. Movies are made about history-changing individuals, and many superheroes have recently found their way to the silver screen. The challenge for fathers is to help bridge the gap for our sons between the screen and the couch.

- Why would God want men to pursue excellence?
- How does God show his love for the extraordinary?
- What historical figures can you think of that settled for the status quo?
- How are men tempted to get by with being "good enough" versus pursuing excellence?
- What are some possible consequences of being passive in life?
- What common temptations do men have to *not* be excellent or active?
- What kind of commitment does it take for a man to strive toward excellent action?

An Experience and a Gift

Entropy works against us. The gradual decline into chaos and disorder fights excellent action every step of the way. Even as I labor to complete each section of this book, I fight my own temptation to allow "good enough" to pass. Finding an experience that concretizes the necessity for excellent action in a man's life can be difficult. It's just so much work.

I wanted Aidan to experience the rigor of military life. As a result, I sent him to spend the weekend with his uncle Chris at the Naval Post-Graduate School in California. I asked Chris to show him the rules for properly wearing his uniform, what "be on time" means for his military classes, and how to bounce a quarter on the bed—twice.

During their time together, Chris challenged Aidan to push his limits. They ran up a mountain, scurried along cliffs and caves, sailed the ocean, and flew a Cessna over Monterey Bay. They slept little and ate a lot. Aidan returned home exhausted yet full of tales.

There are many tremendous models of excellent action. Consider your own world and the places where excellence and action collide. You could show him how you conduct business or demonstrate the difference between a fine craftsman and a factory assembly line. He may need to see the disparity between a thriving, successful, clean restaurant and a struggling, dirty one. You might present him with a variety of sample résumés and discuss how you decipher excellent action. Take him to your city's version of Broadway and discuss what it takes for an entertainer to land the part. Opportunities for him to immediately embody this characteristic of manhood exist everywhere, from his own schoolwork to his hygiene, from his pursuit of sports to his music practice. Together with your son, discover what it means to step in, reject passivity, and "excel still more."[2]

2. 1 Thessalonians 4:10, NIV.

Kingdom Focus

Definition: *keeping a laser-like lock on the kingdom of God*

Biblical Examples of Kingdom Focus

Abram (Key passages: Genesis 12:1–9 and Hebrews 11:8–19)

Shortly after the Tower of Babel, Abram receives instructions from the Lord to set out and move his entire clan to an unknown place. In this era, such a trek meant danger and battle, and involved a significant amount of risk. The writer of Hebrews further illuminates Abram's journey of faith, indicating that "he was looking forward to the city with foundations, whose architect and builder is God."[1]

While Abram failed on many occasions throughout his life, he represents a man who kept his eyes fixed on the kingdom of God.

Paul (Key passage: Philippians 3:7–14, 20–21)

Other than Christ himself, there is no better example of living with a kingdom focus than the apostle Paul. Enduring hardship after hardship, Paul continually reminds us in his letters to hold firm to the faith. In Philippians 3, we find a tremendous summary of this exhortation, and Paul's ultimate focus on the coming kingdom.

An extremist, Paul indicates the absolute high value he places on living for the King through his words. He is willing to trade everything in life, and even face death, for the "surpassing value of knowing Christ Jesus my Lord, for whose sake I have lost all things. I consider them garbage, that I may gain Christ."[2]

These are fantastic words to commit to memory, and to challenge both yourself and your son to live accordingly.

1. Hebrews 11:10, NIV.
2. Philippians 3:8, NIV.

Moses (Key passage: Exodus 1–15; Hebrews 11:23–29)

We all know the story of Moses, rescued by Pharaoh's daughter from a floating basket in the Nile. Adopted into Egypt's most powerful family, Moses soon discovers the horrific plight of his true brothers and sisters at the hand of his adoptive father. He flees to the desert, spending forty years in exile amongst the bushes and the sheep. There, God calls him to free the Hebrew people from slavery.

Though Moses struggles with his calling, the writer of the book of Hebrews venerates him as a kingdom-focused man. Hebrews 11:27 says that Moses "endured, as seeing Him who is unseen."[3] Moses' eyes remained fixed on the prize of Christ, and he changed the fate of Israel forever.

Movies of Kingdom Focus

In Chapter 11, I mentioned several movies with characters who lived in light of a greater narrative. Feel free to use those films, as well as the following:

- *The Mission* – Eighteenth-century Spanish Jesuits try to protect a remote South American native tribe in danger of falling under the rule of pro-slavery Portugal. Their focus remains on the bigger story rather than worldly gain.

- *Avatar* – A paraplegic Marine dispatched on a unique mission to the moon Pandora becomes torn between following his military orders and protecting the world he feels is his home. He decides to live for something more than just himself.

- *Oblivion* – A veteran assigned to extract earth's remaining resources begins to question what he knows about his mission and himself. He comes to realize that the story he's been living is a lie, and he must choose to live on behalf of a greater narrative.

- *The Matrix* – Computer-hacker Neo discovers the life he's known is not at all the reality of his situation. He struggles to believe but eventually steps into the battle for the salvation of all humanity.

---

3. Hebrews 11:27, NIV.

Discussion Topics and Questions

The difficulty with discussing this section is to avoid being "preachy." The goal is more to inspire than instruct. Conversations and questions should be aimed at opening up your son's eyes to the larger story. A framing question may be "What is really going on here?"

- What do you think God wants us to live for?
- What's the ultimate purpose of our lives?
- Does God want us to pay our bills and mow our lawns? Of course. But how can we do those small things in light of the bigger picture?
- Does God care about other places in the world? How do you know?
- What part do you want to play in making the world a better place?
- What kinds of temptations are there for you as a young man—things that vie for your attention and ask you to make them the point of your life?
- What happens when we live in light of God's story instead of our own?
- How can you tell if you are caught in something too small?
- At the end of your life, what do you want people to say about who you were and how you lived?
- How does that change how you act today?

An Experience and a Gift

Having lived and worked overseas as part of a missionary family, Aidan had already experienced much of his life outside of the United States. However, due to the clandestine nature of our work in the Middle East, my wife and I rarely shared the true nature of our lives and work. To him, I had a job in an office, we volunteered in our small church, and we just happened to live internationally.

When Aidan turned thirteen, I chose to take him with me on an overseas trip back to the land of his youth and expose him to the real story of why we sacrificed so much to live abroad. I took him back to our old neighborhood and the park where he played as a toddler, but I also took him to mosques, hidden churches, and crowded streets. As we stood among the crowds, I asked him to count out fifteen thousand people. Naturally, he balked at my request, and I responded, "That's how many people you'd have to meet here before you met even *one* Christian. To put it in perspective, that means there would only be ten believers in our entire town in Colorado." Naturally, his mouth stood agape, and he felt the weight of the church's struggle in this part of the world.

Part of the reason I returned was to speak and counsel ministers in the region. We joined a conference of missionaries, and Aidan experienced firsthand the stories of exhaustion and frustration alongside the tales of hope and miracles. He met one of my good friends, who told him about the fistfight from which he narrowly escaped after he shared the gospel on a university campus. Aidan saw the poverty and smelled the refuse in the streets.

While not all fathers can take their sons to an international missions location as part of this element of the Man Year, I highly encourage all dads to find places and ways to expose their sons to "the least of these." When a young man experiences the squalor and struggles of life, things change. Take him downtown. Introduce him to the man who pastors the church in the roughest of neighborhoods, and ask him to share why he ministers there. Bring vulnerable teens into your home and work together as a family to create an environment that will change the course of their futures. Find ways to help your son live into the bigger story, and call out the small stories our world offers.

In addition, consider a gift that will forever remind him of living in light of the bigger narrative. As part of our Middle Eastern adventure, I bought Aidan a Turkish water pipe and taught him how to use it. Not all fathers will agree with my decision, but I wanted to provide him with an appropriate man-like experience from this part of the world, while still reminding him that God's purposes are beyond our comprehension.

I also took him to a Turkish bath—an experience he will *never* forget.

Protective Leadership

Definition: *wisely, boldly, and sacrificially creating direction and safety for others*

Biblical Examples of Protective Leadership

Noah (Key passage: Genesis 6)

In the time of Noah, the world had become more wicked than God could stand. Yet one man remained faithful. God gives Noah the responsibility of building a massive vessel to deliver his family from the coming disaster. Noah believes God's word, builds the boat, and leads his family to life. He withstands immense ridicule and condemnation, yet stays true to his faith. He steps in and protects his family, leading them through disaster to the other side. Without Noah, none of us would be alive.

Jethro (Key passage: Exodus 18)

Though Jethro, Moses' father-in-law, may be an obscure character in the Scriptures, he plays a vital role in the salvation and governance of the people of God. After the exodus from Egypt, Moses is overwhelmed by the burden of responsibility. Jethro gently steps in and guides Moses—top dog and miracle worker of God—to consider a new approach to leadership. Jethro's wisdom and willingness to speak protective truth to Moses saves Israel from poor governance.

Movies of Protective Leadership

As I stated previously, we get protective leadership and we don't get it. There are many movies that represent the protective-leadership nature of men. These movies are often celebrated and held up as quintessential "man movies."

- *Captain Phillips* – The captain of a modern-day cargo ship captured by pirates off the Somali coast, Captain Phillips protects his crew at the cost of his own safety.

- *Saving Private Ryan* – A band of men save a young private's life at the risk of their own.

- *The Pursuit of Happyness* – A father makes incredible sacrifices to provide for his son.

- *The Lion King* – Simba learns that he must step in to protect the kingdom from encroaching evil and lead his subjects to regained life and freedom.

Discussion Topics and Questions

Boys respond well to this topic. They know the place in their own lives and hearts that longs to be the warrior. The key is to help them know that sacrificial leadership is God's calling to men, and is not to be confused with senseless violence.

- What is the difference between power and strength?
- In what ways do you already desire to protect others?
- What happens when a man turns away and chooses not to protect?
- If you see someone being threatened in some way, what do you do?
- How do men hurt other people?
- What is the difference between a strong tree and a powerful bull?
- How are men (especially husbands and fathers) called to "die first"?
- What are some common temptations for men to *not* protect or lead?
- What happens in a community or country where men seek power over strength?
- In what ways can you be a protective leader starting today?

An Experience and a Gift

Recently, a situation arose with a family close to us. The husband and wife are headed toward divorce. While I don't know all the reasons, Aidan and

I were witness to the destructive effects of the man's poor decisions. Overnight, his wife and daughter were forced to flee because he "escalated," and the situation went from tense to terrible in a matter of minutes. After verifying that the family was safe from the harmful effects of his violence, I said to Aidan, "Don't grow up to be a jerk. This is where a man uses his power to harm rather than his strength to protect."

Real life offers a wealth of opportunities for us to show our boys the difference between protective leadership and violence. You will not have to search very far to find experiences that punctuate the importance of this aspect of biblical manhood. These experiences speak loudly.

At the same time, physical representations abound. Give him a gift that can be used either for good or for harm. Find a metaphor that is meaningful to you, and talk through your gift with him. You might consider everything from a knife or gun to kung fu lessons. Your son needs to know that his masculinity has a deep effect, and it is up to him to determine how he will use it.

Purity

Definition: *a heart-level commitment to masculine holiness*

Biblical Examples of Purity

David (Key passages: 2 Samuel 11–12; Psalm 51)

The Scriptures are full of men who did not succeed in the area of purity. I have already referred to King David and his sinful choices with Bathsheba. I believe it is important for us all to take heed of those biblical references in which men have fallen. We should discover how and why they fell, and watch either God's restoration in their lives or the destruction that follows. David is a fantastic example of both.

King David falls prey to the lusts of life. His impure choices lead to severe consequences, including the death of a trusted soldier, the abuse of a woman, and the death of a baby. The prophet Nathan confronts David, re-awakening him to the calling of God for pure-heartedness. David repents, yet the ramifications of his sin continue.

Joseph (Key passage: Genesis 39)

Joseph is a man who believes in purity to such an extent that he suffers false accusation as a result. The wife of Potiphar, his master, attempts to seduce Joseph, and still "he refused to go to bed with her or even be with her."[1] He stands as a great example of believing in the larger narrative of the purity of God, and is eventually elevated to high position because of his commitment to staying pure.

---

1. Genesis 39:10, NIV.

Amnon (Key passage: 2 Samuel 13)

I find it immensely interesting that *just* after the account of David's sexual impropriety in 2 Samuel 12, the author of 2 Samuel relates the story of the fall of Amnon, David's son. This is a clear indication that what remains untransformed and unredeemed in the father is transmitted to the son. In this passage, Amnon becomes smitten with his half-sister (also a result of David's sexual exploits). He is so overwhelmed with lust that he lures and rapes his sister, and is then engulfed in rage against her. This is a classic example of sinful masculine attitudes toward women—they are to be consumed and discarded.

Movies of Purity

This is a tough one, especially for this age. Movies about purity are few and far between. If there are movies, they usually have to do with the *lack* of purity.

- *Legends of the Fall* – This is the tale of three brothers and their insatiable love for one woman. These brothers struggle with the elements of purity, and find themselves in a battle for love. (This movie is rated R).

- *Shall We Dance?* – A middle-aged man discovers life once again as he pursues dancing. While initially lured in by the beauty of a woman, he rediscovers what his heart truly longs for—his wife.

Discussion Topics and Questions

It is important for fathers to boldly yet carefully discuss issues of purity with their sons. I highly recommend that the "sex talk" happen long before these conversations occur. However, if they have not yet happened, take the time to directly address sex.

- How do you see or hear your friends talking about sex? How do your teachers at school handle the topic?

- It's completely normal for you to be interested and curious about sex and girls. In what ways do you see men treating women? How might God want us to treat them?

- Did you know that God created a direct connection between your brain, your heart (spirit), and your penis? What do you think that connection is?

- What do you typically see in movies with regard to men and their desires, especially sexual desires?

- What are some ways you can pursue purity in your mind, heart, and body?

- Who are some men you know whom you would consider "pure"?

- Is it wrong to have desire?

- What do you think is the reward for living a pure life?

- Where do you imagine being the most challenged in the area of purity?

An Experience and a Gift

As with all segments of the Man Maker Project, it is important to concretize the conversation with a specific experience and a notable gift. Of course, in the area of purity, this can be incredibly tricky. How do you expose your son to the importance of purity without also exposing him to the world of impurity? In some ways, you can't.

Remember that purity stands on the shoulders of the other five aspects of biblical manhood. It involves purity of heart, soul, mind, and body, and requires courage, integrity, excellence, kingdom-mindedness, and protection on all fronts. Perhaps one of the greatest challenges of purity is its pervasiveness in and amongst all other conversations. I suggest a culmination experience for purity that summarizes all the other characteristics, rather than a one-off, purity-only encounter.

Here's what I mean: During Aidan's Man Year, we watched several movies together, some with questionable themes or scenes. While we never ventured into the realms of R-rated films, we certainly came close. Rather than close his eyes or excessively fast-forward, we spoke about what we were seeing or being led to believe. We talked about how the men we saw engaged their world with either purity or impurity, and discussed the ramifications of their decisions on the stories of everyone involved.

In the midst of other Man Year conversations, I attempted to connect our thinking to issues of purity. For example, during our overseas trip together, we encountered a number of international newspapers with less-than-modest photographs on the front page. We walked past bars, nightclubs, and even brothels as we returned to the safety of our hotel. In the all-male Turkish bath, we encountered men who spoke about women disparagingly and how Aidan was developing into a real stud. Rather than avoid or minimize these situations, we addressed them head-on, talking about the choices we could make as men of the world versus men of the King.

Additionally, ask the other men in your group to address these issues as they come up. For example, during Aidan's backcountry camping trip with Greg, their campsite sat on the edge of a high mountain lake. As they sat together on the shore to take in the wonder of the majestic vista, another group of campers—two men and one woman—began to strip for a quick skinny dip. Naturally, Aidan's eyes were drawn to watch, and Greg kindly asked about this interest. They turned their seats to avoid a straight line-of-sight and talked about the beauty of the female form.

As you consider crafting an experience for your son with regard to purity, simply look around to find examples of impurity. You won't have to look far. Keep in mind that, while fathers need to have conversations about sexual purity with their sons, we must frame them in the larger category of heart-level purity: wholly holy. In everything we do and think we are to be without stain or blemish. Where can you take your son that will expose him to the dirtiness of impurity without infecting him with slime? I am convinced that these conversations must occur over time and with a variety of men and experiences.

Marking masculine purity with a gift reminds him of the extreme value of wholeness. This requires creativity on your part and will likely emerge out of organic conversations over the course of the year. Find a symbol that stands for purity, and give it to him as an emblem to symbolize his commitment to remain pure. For many years, fathers in Christian circles gave their children "purity rings." While a good idea, many well-meaning parents focused solely on sexual purity, leaving behind the greater focus on whole-life purity. Your son needs to know purity involves all areas of the heart.

Again, any object can take on meaning. For example, give your son an inkwell and discuss how one drop of ink in a gallon of water makes the whole jug impure. Or give him a television remote, and discuss how purity involves not just what we choose *not* to watch, but what we choose *to* watch. The brave father might find a small statue of Artemis and discuss with his son how the temptation to worship the idol of pleasure also means turning away from worshipping the true God.

CHAPTER 16

Finishing the Man Year

Culmination and Calling into Manhood

The blessing casts a vision and serves as a rough blueprint, a life map that a person can step into with confidence and hope.[1]

—JOHN SOWERS

W ʜᴇɴ ᴅɪᴅ ʏᴏᴜ "ʙᴇᴄᴏᴍᴇ a man"? Rarely in our experience do we have a specific moment when we know we made the transition from boyhood to manhood. And yet, most of life is split into a *before* and an *after*. Before you were married, and after the wedding. Before the birth of your child, and after you had children. Before you got a job, and after your first day at the office. Before baptism, and after a public proclamation of your faith. Before cancer, after chemo. Before the move to Colorado, and after the departure from Washington. Before 9/11, and after the world changed. Before the coming of Christ, after the revelation of the Messiah's greatest offer of love. We mark our experience as humans in time, and while our memory is stored only somewhat linearly, we remember many scenes of our narrative as *before* and *after*.

The purpose of a ceremony, therefore, is to mark. The passage to manhood is a transition over time, just as earning a college degree or falling in love occurs over the course of many months and a good degree of struggle. Yet every *before* and every *after* requires a hinge point, a step, a ceremony. Acting as priest for his family, the father has the responsibility and privilege of creating rituals and rhythms that mark the beginning and

---

1. Sowers, *Fatherless Generation*, 119.

end of significant stories in the lives of his family members.[2] In the initiation rites of boys, this requires a clear beginning of the passage process, and a declarative end that will, once and for all, answer the boy's heart-level question: *Am I a man?* From that moment onward, he will always know, "Yes, I am. My father declared it."

In order to ceremonially finish the Man Year and create a clear delineation between the before and after, two final elements are required: the *manhood test* and the *passage ceremony*.

Manhood Test

A father who invests his time, energy, and resources into creating a rites of passage process for his son wants him to take it seriously. Few things are more disappointing for a father than moving toward his son with such intentionality, only to be blown off or dismissed. In our society of entitlement, Xbox, and iTunes, teenagers are unfortunately apt to diminish important processes simply by their lack of attention. To combat this, I encouraged Aidan to reflect on his experiences throughout his Man Year, writing down thoughts, questions, stories, and definitions. From the beginning, I told him that he would be tested, and that he must face the challenge of manhood in order for him to be invited into the company of men. Then and only then would he receive the rights and privileges of a true man. My hope was to create in him a sense of anticipation and healthy fear, two essential ingredients to call out the best in any man. All ancient rites of passage include such an examination. I intended to build into this experience a process that would force Aidan to face himself and the aspects of manhood I presented to him, and to do so in front of other men. I knew he would need to prove himself, and I intended to create the space for this to happen rather than leave it to chance.

The elements of this test need to engage young men physically, mentally, emotionally, and spiritually. In order to mark his whole being, a young man needs to be tried on all levels. Physically, he needs to show that he no longer resides in a soft boy body but has inhabited the hardened body of a man. He needs to prove he can overcome a physical challenge, separating

---

2. Much more can be said about the role of priest. Jesus models for us what theologians call the *triplex munex Christi*, or "the offices of Christ." These are commonly known as Prophet, Priest, and King. I more fully explore how these roles apply to manhood in Restoration Project men's retreat called *Second Adam: The Adventure of Manhood.*

himself from boyhood and moving into the world of muscles and endurance. Mentally, he needs to show his acumen and ability to think well on his feet. He needs to have the mental wherewithal to remember information and employ it appropriately. Emotionally, he must have the ability to experience empathy and compassion, while maintaining a masculine strength that others can rely on. He needs to make difficult decisions in the furnace of real-time experience. And, spiritually, a young man must show that his purposes, perspectives, values, and faith are placed wholly in the Lord. He must have a deep sense of his capacity for depravity and his redemption as a son of the King.

Designing such a test is no small task. Some fathers may prefer to have a "council of men" who pose a variety of questions to the boy.[3] Other fathers may choose to whisk the boy away alone for a private conversation to fully examine the boy. As I began to conceive of Aidan's manhood test, I decided to employ a variety of elements, including a physical experience in the mountains and a case-study-based examination of real-to-life possibilities that would cover each of the six characteristics of manhood. I also decided to do all this with a company of men. I offer my example as merely a template for fathers to imagine and create their own version of the manhood test. Regardless of the specifics, a boy must have an experience that *proves* he is a man, and other men must *tell him he is a man.* In this manhood test, the boy needs all four of the atmospheric conditions to be met in order for his heart to grow: *intention of the father, removal from the feminine, risk and danger,* and *blessing.*

On the weekend of Aidan's thirteenth birthday, after he completed all six segments of his Man Year, I surprised him by picking him up from school and taking him for a one-on-one overnight camping trip in the mountains. He knew his manhood test was imminent but had no idea what it would look like or require. I imagine he pictured something similar to a math test. What I had planned for him couldn't have been more different.

We pitched our tent and climbed around the Alluvial Fan in Rocky Mountain National Park. We exhausted ourselves on that mountain and fully enjoyed stretching the limits of our endurance. Throughout our time together on the trail, I asked him to reflect on his year, tell me more stories of his times with his mentors, and ask me any final questions he might have about manhood. Knowing the test would be the next day, he asked me

---

3. This may look scarily close to a dissertation defense!

(without my prompting) to clarify and remind him of certain definitions and answer questions with regard to specific stories his mentors shared.

During that overnight, I mostly sat in my chair and asked him to take the lead in many of the camping responsibilities. Make the fire. Cook dinner. Fetch water. Bear-proof the food. In so doing, I wanted him to engage practically in the world of manhood, even if it just meant cutting some summer sausage and stoking the dying embers of our campfire. We had significant time playing in the river and hitting pinecones like baseballs out over the ravine. Yet when it came to taking care of things, I chose to hang back and allow him the space to step in. He rose to the occasion.

The next morning, I instructed him to break camp. Together we packed the car and set off for an unknown destination. His anticipation rose, and he continued to guess how and where the test would take place. Just as a man does not know what lies around every corner, I wanted to increase his sense of curiosity, anxiety, and preparedness. About mid-morning, I pulled into the parking lot at the trailhead of a route I had carefully selected weeks before. I got out and loaded a backpack with water, snacks, a two-way radio, and a map. My heart raced.

Prior to this weekend, I had scoped out an intersection of several trails that would lead him on a 4.5-mile hike through the high country, around several lakes, and with a one-thousand-foot elevation gain. I knew it would be a challenge for Aidan, one he could manage if he truly applied himself. I also created a series of ancient-looking scrolls. At the trailhead, I pulled out the first scroll, opened it with him, and read it aloud:

> After a year of manhood journeys, your Man Year is coming to an end. You have known that you will be tested with regard to all you have experienced and learned. You have had mentors along the way.
>
> Today is your day of testing. And, today, you must face it alone. No one will be coming with you this time. It's just you, the mountain, and the test.
>
> Your task is to get yourself from where I drop you off to Dream Lake. There is a map on the back. Along the way, you will encounter specific challenges. You will know them when you see them. Only after you adequately pass the challenge will you be allowed to continue on the journey.
>
> Aidan, through this process, may you know the goodness, harshness, seriousness, and playfulness of God.
>
> See you on the other side,
>
> Dad

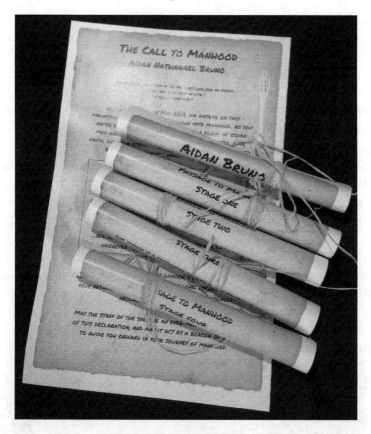

I told him, "You are about to prove that you are ready to become a man. You've known this day would come. Here it is." Then, I pointed at the map and said, "We are here. Your task is to get yourself over to here, where the X is at Dream Lake. All I can say is, may God be with you." At that point, I got back in the car and drove away. In the rearview mirror, I could see him look at me and then at the trail. He turned and started his ascent.

Unbeknownst to Aidan, I had arranged for three other men to be stationed along the trail. They awaited him on the mountain, each with a case-study scroll I had previously given them. I instructed them to intersect Aidan during his journey and sit with him in the woods while they discussed the contents of the scroll. On each, I had written a scenario, along with a few questions designed to test Aidan's ability to respond appropriately *as a man*. In the end, I did not care if he remembered the definitions of each of the manhood categories I offered him. What I wanted him to prove was that he knew, understood, and could put into practice these aspects of godly masculinity when life threw him a curveball. Scenarios offer the opportunity to respond as a unique individual, yet still indicate the state of the man's heart.

In addition to the case studies in the scrolls, I also wanted Aidan to experience the *weight* of being a man. While I know that he will not truly know the weighty responsibility of manhood until it is fully upon him, I wanted to symbolically show him that each of the six godly characteristics requires a man to bear a heavy burden. To represent this weight, I created six bricks, each with the name of a manhood quality. As Aidan encountered each mentor in the forest, had the case-study conversations and "passed," the mentor gave him the corresponding brick to carry with him the rest of the journey. At the beginning, adding only one brick to his pack made little difference. But with each subsequent manhood quality, the burden on his back increased, creating a physical reminder of the heavy spiritual concepts. By the end, he was dragging under the weight—exactly as I wanted. The definition of a *pilgrimage* is "a physical journey with a spiritual destination." This journey up the mountain was certainly physical, but the spiritual implications and reminders were designed to concretize Aidan's thinking and create a clear *before* and *after*.

Following are the five scenarios Aidan faced during his over-the-mountain journey. After engaging the situation adequately, he received his brick and was sent on his way.

Scenario #1: Case Study on Courage and Integrity

You are eighteen years old, hanging out with your friends one Saturday evening. One of them recently bought a car, and the five of you decide to take it for a spin to check it out. They all hop in, and the driver cracks a joke, saying, "Everybody buckle up. I'm not sure I can see straight after those beers I snuck from my dad. Let's see what happens!" He then guns the engine and the car lurches down the road. Everyone is laughing and having a good time.

It doesn't take long for him to get pulled over by the cops due to his reckless driving. When the officer comes to the window, he asks, "Have you been drinking?" Your friend answers, "No, of course not. I'm only eighteen." Everyone else in the car snickers.

What do you do?

Questions for conversation:

- What is your definition of courage?
- What courage is required of a man in situations like this?
- What is your definition of integrity? In what ways is integrity required here? What values do you need to uphold in this situation? What are the risks?
- What biblical role models do you have to guide you in courage and integrity? Tell me their stories.
- What other role models (from books, film, stories) do you have?

Scenario #2: Case Study on Excellent Action

It's finally the summer vacation after your sophomore year in high school. You are sixteen years old, and you have just landed your first job. After the first week or so of training, you've gotten a handle on things and find that you are pretty good at the work. Even your boss says so.

One evening, your boss gets a phone call from his wife. There is an emergency at home, and he turns to you and says, "I need to go. Can you close down the shop this evening?"

"Sure," you respond.

After he leaves, you are alone with one other coworker to close the shop. The other guy says, "Well, that's awesome. I'm getting out of here early!" And he takes off, leaving you alone. The shop is pretty clean already, and it looks decent enough to leave it till morning.

What do you do?

Questions for conversation:

- What is your definition of excellent action?
- How does your manly commitment to excellence affect your choice?
- Who are some biblical role models of excellent action?
- What about other role models (from movies, books, etc.)?

Scenario #3: Case Study on Kingdom Focus

One person is a missionary serving in the remote jungles of Bolivia. He has been there for over ten years, has learned the language, planted a church, and serves as the only medical doctor in a twenty-five-mile radius. Yet he's sarcastic, cynical, tired, and resentful of everyone who comes to him with any kind of need. But he's a "missionary" serving God.

Another person lives in Chicago and works as a lawyer for one of the most prestigious law firms in the Midwest. Because of his job, he doesn't have much time to attend church, serve in the community, or share about Christ with other people. He loves God deeply, prays regularly for the world, gives money away like crazy, and teaches Sunday school when he is in town. But he's *not* a missionary serving God.

Which man would you rather be?

Questions for conversation:

- Which man is most pleasing to God?
- Why did you answer that way?
- What is the definition of kingdom focus?
- How does having a kingdom focus affect how you make decisions in your life?
- Who are some biblical role models of kingdom focus?
- What about other role models (from movies, books, etc.)?

Scenario #4: Case Study on Protective Leadership

You are traveling in a remote part of China with your wife and two elementary-aged children. This has been the trip of a lifetime, and all of you have fully enjoyed the scenery, history, food, and exotic locations.

Suddenly, a large truck rams into your taxi, sending it careening off the road. It hits an embankment and comes to an abrupt stop. The taxi driver is dead on impact, and the rest of you are alive but badly hurt. Your wife is alive but unconscious. For whatever reason, all you have are a few scrapes and bruises.

You manage to get everyone out of the car. Two ambulances come, and you quickly learn that they will be taking your family members to two different hospitals because of the nature of their injuries—your wife to one and your kids to another. No one in your family speaks a word of Chinese. They begin closing ambulance doors and starting the engines.

What do you do? Where do you go?

Questions for conversation:

- What is your definition of protective leadership?
- How do you make a decision in this moment based on what you've learned?
- Who needs your protection most in this situation?
- What biblical models of protective leadership do you have ?
- Other models?

197

Scenario #5: Case Study on Purity

The first year of college is always a lot of fun. For the first time, you are on your own and able to make your own decisions about where you go, when, and with whom. In all likelihood, you will make a whole new bunch of friends and also meet some very interesting and attractive girls.

You and your roommate are invited to a party at a friend's house. At first, it's just the guys hanging out, throwing the football, and playing video games. There is no drinking going on, and it seems like it's going to be a great evening. Sometime around 10 p.m., however, one of the guys you don't know calls everyone in and says that he's rented a video to watch. Excitedly, he puts the DVD in and says, "You guys are gonna *love* this."

On the large TV screen, images of naked women start to dance around. The guy says, "And it gets better!" Soon, these women are engaged in all sorts of sexual experiences with a variety of men in subtle but tantalizing scenarios. Your roommate turns to you at one point and says, "Awesome, huh?" You yourself start to feel aroused.

What do you do?

Questions for conversation:

- What is your definition of purity?
- What is wrong with these types of videos?
- What happens to a man's life and heart when he allows these types of scenes into his mind?
- What are some of the first clues that this may have been the direction of the evening?
- How do you handle your own arousal response to the movie?

Final Blessing Ceremony

I waited for Aidan at the end of the journey, wondering how he was doing and how his experience shaped up. While I had set up and facilitated the entire process, in the end, I had little control over what would actually transpire. I had to rely on the providence and love of God to truly usher Aidan into manhood. At the end of the trail, I anticipated what I would say when I saw him trudging up the mountain. By this time, he carried six heavy bricks, had encountered several men along the trail and had difficult conversations, and hiked about five miles at close to 10,000-feet elevation.

Nothing can compare to the overwhelming feeling of excitement, relief, and pride a father has when he sees his son emerge from the dense forest of testing. As I sat on a boulder next to the trail, I smiled so broadly it hurt. I leapt down and embraced Aidan heartily. He had made it. He had passed the test. He was ready to be deemed a true man. With exhaustion in his eyes, he looked at me and said, "I will never forget."

The final blessing ceremony embodies the fullness of God's design for a father to formally, ritually, and verbally bless his son, once and for all answering his heart's deepest question: *Am I a man?* The blessing ceremony brings finality to his question and opens up new categories of possibility in the life of the boy. A blessing involves meaningful touch and "continues with a spoken message of high value, a message that pictures a special future for the individual being blessed, and one that is based on an active commitment to see the blessing come to pass."[4]

As fathers, we have the ability to honor, shape, and create a future for our sons through our words. And though we long to hear the blessing of our own fathers over our lives, far too few fathers initiate meaningful blessing over their sons. We have lost the art of blessing. It is here that the powerful masculine substance is passed from an older man to the younger, and something deep within him shifts and awakens. These moments, these words from father to son, are the pinnacle of the rites of passage experience. When a man reaches out and touches the boy with strong and gentle hands and speaks words of life and hope into the very core of his being, his heart leaps and he breaks free from the cocoon of childhood—in a mysterious transformation—into man. Fathers who overcome whatever awkwardness they feel and step into the powerful place of blessing their sons change the course of history. Our words are life, and we must aim them well.

I designed an official ceremony for Aidan, as I wanted to live into the realities taught by the ancient rites of passage. Boys need a marker in time to which they can always refer. When did he become a man? It was *that* day, at *that* time, in *that* place, with *those men* present, and spoken by *his father* in clear and undeniable terms.

The men who tested him gathered at a favorite spot on the edge of Dream Lake in Rocky Mountain National Park. We ventured out on a rock

4. Smalley and Trent, *The Blessing*, 30.

outcropping, surrounded by the majesty of the rugged peaks, massive boulder fields, and fierce skies of the Colorado high country. The scene was perfect. God joined us in his splendor.

Prior to this, I had gathered thoughts and reflections about my son from a variety of other people. These included his mother, his Man Year mentors who could not be present, his grandmothers, a few of his teachers, his principal, and more. I began the ceremony by reading these words to him. I encouraged him to simply listen to the words of encouragement and blessing offered by these important people. I then asked the men present to speak directly to him any words they had prepared, thoughts they had about the masculine journey, or important warnings they might offer to him with regard to his future.

What is most important during this time is that the company of men together witness your son's ceremonial transition into manhood, and together hold that memory for the rest of his life. At any moment in the future, then, they are able to remind him that *he is a man* whenever he needs encouragement, help, correction, or hope. To step into manhood alone is terrifying, but to have other older and trusted men for backup is invaluable.

While nothing overly eloquent needs to be spoken, the boy must hear the sincerity of the father's heart. There is a combination of gravity and levity, seriousness and playfulness, that welcomes him and blesses him. The reality is that we have no idea what will transpire in his life. All we can offer are our few words of faith, hope, and love as we release him from boyhood and hand him over to God's greater narrative as a man. I believe that, as men do this with boys, they step out of their father's story and into their own. It is at this point that the boy moves from struggling with masculinity and begins the process of maturity. Without this step, he will forever wrestle with manhood and never truly step into the life of a mature man.

Marking significant moments with a gift seals the moment in memory. Much like a wedding ring, these items stand as a lifelong reminder of monumental moments. Aidan already had a collection of gifts from his Man Year mentors. I wanted to give him a capstone gift.

In my own life, with all the various messages of what true manhood may be in the church and in the world at large, I have personally chosen to aim for the *sage*.[5] More than the typical images of warrior or king, I believe

5. Restoration Project has a men's weekend experience (and soon-to-be book) called "Epic Man." It focuses on the six biblical stages of a man's life based on six Hebrew words for *man* in the Scriptures. The last of these, and the biblical pinnacle of manhood, is *zaken*, or *sage*. It literally means "gray beard." Sages are the pylons of society, upholding

that the wise, old sage represents the pinnacle of manhood. As an icon of this aim, I have a picture of Gandalf from *The Lord of the Rings* on my computer desktop as a constant reminder of my aimed-for destiny. Throughout Aidan's Man Year, I shared with him the importance of the sage, watched all the movies, and discussed Gandalf's ability to offer wisdom, engage in battle, and consult with kings and moths and hobbits alike. He is powerful yet humble, wise yet playful, mysterious yet simple, and has no concern for his own reputation but instead always seeks the good of others. *That* is the man I strive to be, and it is an image of manhood I endeavor to impart.

As a result, I wanted to give him a final gift that represented the fullness of manhood in the sage. I knew I wanted to give him a gift that would symbolize Gandalf, and was thrilled to find a replica of his staff. As a pinnacle of his Man Year collection, I knew it would be a treasured item for the rest of his life.

After the other men finished their words of encouragement and blessing, I called him to come stand before me on that mountaintop at Dream Lake. I offered him the staff and reminded him of the weightiness of manhood. As Aidan reached for the staff, his weary back straightened and his eyes lit up with amazement and delight. He knew what it meant as his fingers wrapped around the shank.

Finally, I had one more scroll to offer him. It was the "blessing scroll," on which I wrote the following words:

The Call to Manhood - Aidan Nathanael Bruno

"Be watchful, stand firm in the faith, act like men, be strong. Let all you do be done in love."[6]

1 Corinthians 16:3–4

On this 25th day of May 2013, we gather on this mountain to call you from boyhood into manhood. As you enter your thirteenth year, we, along with a cloud of other men and women, bear witness to your character, your faith, and your strength. Aidan, you have what it takes to be the godly man you were created to be.

---

truth, order, commerce, grace, family, and faith. In our modern world, "gray beards" retire and go south. I believe we lose the most powerful and important men to the golf course. In my own life, I have set my sights on being the sage. I've even grown a beard (which happens to be gray already) to live into this desire.

6. NASB.

PART IV—Man Maker Project

You are hereby called to:

- Act courageously in the face of fear (Courage)
- Live with integrity and walk in truth always (Integrity)
- Strive for excellence and pursue action over passivity (Excellent action)
- Focus your life, heart, and actions on God's kingdom (Kingdom focus)
- Protect the innocent and lead boldly (Protective leadership)
- Keep yourself pure in mind, body, and soul (Purity)

. . . all in order to bring godly strength and tenderness wherever you go and to whatever you do.

As of this moment, you are no longer a boy. Though the road toward fullness as a man lay long before you, I, your father, Christopher Frank Bruno, unequivocally declare you a *true man*.

May the staff of the sage be an ever-present reminder of this declaration, and may it act as a beacon of hope to guide you onward in your journey of manhood.

I laid my hand on his head, and the other men gathered around as we prayed together. Of course, as I read the final scroll and prayed a blessing over my son, I was undone in almost every way. My hopes and dreams for him filled my heart. My soul filled with amazement and gratitude at all the potential embodied in the young man who stood before me. My own story of loss, masculine struggle, and hope came crashing over me and nearly knocked me off my feet. There on that rock outcropping, my past, present, and future, as well as the past, present and future of my son, collided in that God-infused moment of blessing. I could barely stand. It was indeed holy ground.

I can honestly say that I have been in few places more sacred than that. Each of us in our own way delivered this young man into the hands of the Father. I firmly believe that Jesus himself joined us there on that majestic mountaintop. He was smiling, laughing, crying, and extremely pleased.

My boy had become a man.

And I, his father, became a man again.

After spending a good while basking together in the glory of the moment, in the stories from the year and that day's trail, and in our own stories of manhood, we turned our eyes downhill and descended.

Our goal: massive amounts of barbeque ribs to feed our man-sized appetites—Aidan's request.

His Man Year was complete, yet his journey into manhood had just begun. But it *had* begun.

CHAPTER 17

Returning the New Man

Reincorporating Him Back into Society

*Reincorporation. In this phase, the initiate, having passed the tests neces-
sary and proving himself worthy, is reintroduced into his community, which
recognizes and honors his new status within the group.*[1]

—BRETT AND KATE MCKAY

ON THE FIRST FRIDAY night of every month, our little city hosts "The
Gallery Walk" in the Old Town. Art galleries feature a host of local artists
of every genre of visual art, from photography to oil painting, from sculp-
ture to glass blowing, and from watercolor to metal work. Musicians line
the streets and the festivities of the cool summer evening create a magical
atmosphere that make one feel light, loving, and creative.

As a family, we try to have a family night at least once a week. Recently,
we joined the artsy-fartsy crowd and hit the galleries. I was struck by how
our world bursts with amazingly creative men and women. Some I appreciate as I stand in front of their pieces for several minutes, taking in the
splendor of the art. Others leave me asking, "Is *that* art?"

That night, however, nothing struck me more than watching Aidan
and his mother as they meandered through the galleries, playfully crossed
streets, and laughed during a cheese-tasting adventure at our local cheese
monger's store. Now tall enough to put his arm around his mother's shoulders, Aidan walked side-by-side with her in intimate conversation. They
touched in ways that were tender, kind, fun loving, and sweet. They simply
delighted in one another. The mother-child bond still exists between them,

1. McKay and McKay, "Coming of Age."

204

but what I witnessed was a lighthearted yet engaging relationship that has grown in safety and affection over the past several months. It is a beautiful thing to watch.

In the ancient rites of passage literature, we see a clear calling on the elders of society to train their boys in the ways of men, and to temporarily remove them from the public sphere in order to initiate them into manhood. This is a protective measure for the culture as a whole, as wayward manhood poses a large threat to the safety and security of the people. On the drastic end, just recently an angry man with an eye toward vengeance and delusion opened fire in the Navy Yards in Washington, D.C., killing thirteen. More common, however, are unfinished men like Scott, a typical man with whom I speak weekly, who is struggling to overcome his propensity to demean and verbally attack his wife;[2] or Curt, a typical man wrestling with his soul-link to sexual addiction.[3] Rites of passage are society's method of harnessing the masculine strength and channeling it in the right direction.

But, after the passage process has occurred, boys who have become men need to be *returned*. After the declarations of their manhood have been spoken and they have proven themselves to be men, they need the opportunity to fully live into their new identities. They do not re-enter society in the same way. Not only is there a shift in their own soul, but there must also be a shift in how society, and especially their *mothers*, interacts with and views them. In 1 Corinthians 13:11, Paul states, "When I was a child, I talked like a child, I thought like a child, I reasoned like a child. When I became a man, I put the ways of childhood behind me."[4] For many boys, these "ways of childhood" involve mother much more than father. For them to step into newness as a man, they must redefine their relationship with their mothers. This is a vital transition from mother's duty to mother's delight.

From Duty to Delight

For the first years of a boy's life, his mother typically oversees his this-is-how-to-live-in-the-world instruction. She teaches him to say *please* and *thank you*, to brush his teeth, to pick up his dirty socks, to bathe on a regular basis, to feed the dog, and to use a fork. She attends his parent-teacher conferences and oversees his homework. Mom monitors his screen-time,

2. Not his real name.
3. Not his real name either.
4. NIV.

his language usage, and his bedtime. It is her role and mother-duty to nurture him toward adulthood.

On a semi-regular basis during Aidan's early years, my wife would sit me down on the living room couch after the kids were in bed and share her thoughts, concerns, and fears about Aidan's behavior, and her forecasts of his future. "If this [insert attitude, offense or oversight here] continues like this, he'll be in deep trouble when he is a teenager, let alone when he's a grown man. We've got to work on this now, or we are sunk." Her concerns and prophecies were 100 percent true, and shaped much of our intentional parenting with him as a boy. Out of a deep love for her son, his mother wanted to influence his future by small (and some not-so-small) course corrections in his youth.

Throughout the teenage years, and even after the completion of the first stage of the initiation process, he will continue to need correction and instruction in the ways of life.[5] As a small example, Aidan seems to have an inability to turn off lights and pick up his socks from around the house. His mom and I are determined to train this out of him. More significantly, he still needs to develop increasing levels of self-control, thoughtfulness, discipline, and kindness toward his sisters. He needs to learn how to budget, how to take care of his property, and how to manage his time. Rites of passage do not complete his life training once and for all.

But, for the young man, parenting takes on a whole new meaning. Rather than viewing him as a child who needs to be corrected or instructed, we can now expect him to co-participate in his own growth. Whereas before he stood as a blank slate onto which we wrote our instructions or guidelines, now he is a coauthor in his own destiny and future. His mental functioning, his emotional maturity, and his spiritual integrity are such that he now responds more to a vision and a discussion about his life than simple commands and behavior modifications. While he may need a parent to bring his attention to his waywardness, he now has internal categories of behavior and attitude to which he refers.

---

5. Keep in mind that the Man Year is the first of several steps toward true manhood for a boy. This first step is designed to create mental file folders of manhood for him and call him to something bigger than the self-centered comfort our Western world aims to offer men. The next stages include a *transition to independence* when he goes to college; a *transition to society* when he graduates college and starts his first career-focused job; and a *transition to intimacy* when he marries. We can't expect thirteen-year-old boys to be full-fledged men after they experience such a rite of passage. But we do expect them to know what manhood means and to be on their way.

As a result, mothering takes on a different connotation at this life stage. Many mothers continue to relate to their teenage sons, and even their grown sons, in the same way they always have. Smothering mothers attempt to keep their boys close, small, and dependent. Teenage men need to learn from their mothers a new set of skills, including how to treat a woman, listen to her heart, and honor her feminine beauty and dignity. They need to learn how to date, how to be a gentleman, and what it means to protect the heart of a woman. Yet the greatest gift a mother can give her teenage son is her *delight*.

Boys naturally long for the delight of a woman. It is part of the internal workings of man's heart. As he steps into adolescence and young adulthood, he will naturally become far more drawn to the female form and desire female attention. He will need both mother and father to guide and teach him to navigate the world of relationships, but the experience of receiving delight from his mother will mean far more than teaching and instruction.

Does she notice him? Does she *like* being with him? Does she joke with him, touch him, play with him? Does he catch her looking at him with eyes of affection? Does she chase him with water balloons or sit down at the piano and play "Heart and Soul" with him? Does he know that he is worthy of a woman's full delight?

This is a man's *second question*. Whereas the father-directed rites of passage process is designed to answer his heart's most core question (*Am I a man?*), the delight of the mother in the young man is designed to respond to *Am I worthy of a woman's attention?* The father answers the first. The mother answers the second.

Too many men are left with unanswered questions. Steve is one such man.[6] In Steve's home of all boys, the masculine atmosphere dominated the scene as father and sons developed good and deep relationships. To this day, Steve talks with his father almost daily and has significant friendships with each of his four brothers. In his manhood, Steve is settled. Yet he recently told me, "I want to have relationships with women, but I just don't know how. I'm not even sure women like me. I know what to do with guys, but I don't know what it's like to be in relationship with a woman. I mean, I've had girlfriends, and I was even engaged. But I freak out when a woman gets close. What do I do?" Steve was asking the second question. While his father adequately ushered him into manhood, Steve needed his mother to *delight* in him, not mother him. More than training a man to treat a woman well,

6. Name and details changed to protect his identity.

the delighting mother gives him the experience of receiving wholesome, heart-level affection that frees him to be the man he is without fear.

The delighting mother is the first woman in the young man's life to call manhood out from him. She joins the father in recognizing the strength and tenderness in her son, begins to treat him with honor and respect, and expects him to rise to the manhood occasion with courage, integrity, protection, and more. Once the father tempers the steel of the boy's heart through the initiation process, his mother is the first one to venture out on the bridge to test its merit. Her approach to him is altogether different.

There is something deep within a young man's heart that swells with wholesome pride when he makes that shift from boy to man in the eyes of his mom. She confirms what dad has declared: "Yes, you are indeed a man. And I like you. I don't have to mother you any longer. Now we can really enjoy life."

While much of my work with men centers around their father relationships, a good majority of the heart-labor also involves their mothers. When fathers have been inadequate husbands, far too often mothers turn to their sons to meet their emotional needs. Boys become triangulated in an emotionally incestuous relationship with mom that confuses and obscures their masculine development. Over the years, as fathers have become more and more absent and the fatherless epidemic has skyrocketed, this mother-son dynamic has come center stage.

In one recent month, two emotionally incestuous mother-son situations found their way into my office. The first involved a young, newly married pastor from Kentucky, who struggled with intimacy in his marriage because of his deep heart-ties to his mom. The other involved an older man from Wyoming, who raged at everything that breathes because of the suffocating emotional vacuum of his mother's presence. Both men never experienced the father's intentional removing of them from the feminine space, nor did they ever receive the gift of returning to their mothers in an experience of delight versus demand.

Mothers are vital to a man's life. After he becomes a man, her relationship with him must change in order to make space for him to develop other female attachments. Smothering mothers are the bane of the daughter-in-law's existence. Yet it is the mother who opens the door, through *delight*, for the son to develop good relationships with other women. It is a move from motherly duty to motherly delight.

Delivering the Man Back to the World

The rites of passage process is designed to remove the boy from the world and usher him into the world of men. The point, however, is not to help the boy self-actualize or "find himself." It is not to induct him into the exclusive man-club or elevate him to a place of dominance. The ultimate purpose of this initiation is to deliver him back to society as a proven man who will lead, protect, love, provide, and restore the world. The rite of passage is an induction into masculine humility and servant-leadership. The boy is taken away, but the man is returned, and is now expected to take on the mantle of manhood in alliance with God on behalf of the greater kingdom. A true rites of passage process returns the boy back to society as a man who mimics Christ and "lays down his life" for another.[7]

The young man receives more respect and greater responsibility. He is held to a higher standard, and is invited to contribute in ways that are meaningful and important. He is expected to participate in decision-making conversations and is invited to offer thoughts and opinions even if they far exceed his awareness or abilities.

In the end, modern-day rites of passage are designed to create the physical, mental, spiritual, emotional, and relational space for boys to answer the apostle Paul's call on men in 1 Corinthians 16:13–14: "Be on the alert, stand firm in the faith, act like men, be strong. Let all that you do be done in love."[8]

What would the world look like if men truly lived into this calling, where strength and love combine?

Fathers, we have the opportunity to change the face of society for generations to come. We can choose to devote ourselves to our political leanings, our economic nest eggs, or even our faith communities. But nothing, absolutely nothing, is more vital to and effective in altering the future direction of our world than our fatherly investment in our children.

Be a world changer. Father well.

---

7. John 10:11, NIV.
8. NASB.

Epilogue

ONE OF THE GREATEST benefits of this rites of passage process for my son has been my *own* growth and development as a man and father. The men with whom I have had the privilege of collaborating, the conversations that have ensued, and the relationships that have been forged gift me with a richness I did not have before I began. I have found that as I bring up the topics of manhood and masculine initiation, people's eyes open and their hearts swell.

The other day, I had a conversation with a female counselor who also happens to be a mother. She asked about this material, and, as I gave a two-sentence summary of the topic and purpose, she immediately began to tell me about her hopes for and disappointments in her three sons. She indicated that she has a "good" husband, but that he has been struggling to know what do to and how to navigate these realms as a father.

"I want that," she said. "No, I need that."

I believe that my son has grown and developed significantly through the Man Maker Project. I see daily evidence of it in his life. His mother uses this language. His sisters seek his protection. His relationships with the other Man Year men have taken on their own life apart from me. He texts them, works for them, and has been invited to be part of *their* sons' initiation process. Aidan has successfully entered manhood. For this I am grateful.

But, the fact is, so have I. I have benefited. I have been stretched. I have stepped further into my manhood. I have been regularly challenged in my own understandings of myself. From the beginning, I knew that I would be fathered as I fathered my son. I knew, and yet I didn't expect. Those places that have remained unfinished, wounded, or empty in my soul have begun to heal, and I have a new outlook on my own future and family. I view men completely differently, and I certainly view my friends in a new light.

Fathering my son fathers me. Fathering each other fathers us all.

Epilogue

I choose to be among those fathers who turn their hearts toward their children, and it is my great desire to challenge a generation of fathers to join me.

Now I turn hopefully and humbly toward my daughters. For they too need a father. And that father is *me*.

Bibliography

Arnold, Patrick. *Wildmen, Warriors, and Kings: Masculine Spirituality and the Bible*. New York: Crossroad, 1991.

Bikers Against Child Abuse International. http://bacaworld.org.

Bittman, Mark. "How to Eat Now: The Truth about Home Cooking." *Time* magazine (October 20, 2014) 48-54.

Bly, Robert. *Iron John: A Book About Men*. Jackson, Tennessee: Da Cappo, 2004.

Bruno, Beth, and Chris Bruno. *End: Engaging Men to End Sex Trafficking*. Fort Collins, CO: Restoration Project, 2014.

Bruno, Chris. "Unintentional Abuse: Rites of Non-Passage." Unpublished manuscript, The Seattle School of Theology and Psychology, 2009.

Cathy, S. Truett. *It's Better to Build Boys Than Mend Men*. Decatur, Georgia: Looking Glass, 2004.

Chadwick, Clifton. "Seven Minutes a Day: The Modern-Day Excuse for a Parent." *The National* (November 14, 2011). http://www.thenational.ae/thenationalconversation/comment/seven-minutes-a-day-the-modern-day-excuse-for-a-parent.

Crabb, Larry, et al. *Silence of Adam: Becoming Men of Courage in a World of Chaos*. Grand Rapids, MI: Zondervan, 1998.

Dalbey, Gordon. *Healing the Masculine Soul: God's Restoration of Men to Real Manhood*. Nashville: W Publishing Group, 2003.

Dalberg, John Emerich Edward. "Letter to Archbishop Mandell Creighton." http://history.hanover.edu/courses/excerpts/165acton.html.

Dobson, James. *Bringing Up Boys: Practical Advice and Encouragement for Those Shaping the Next Generation of Men*. Wheaton, IL: Tyndale, 2001.

Edwards, Tryon, ed. *A Dictionary of Thoughts*. F.B. Dickerson Company, 1908.

Eldredge, John. "Daily Prayer." http://ransomedheart.com/prayer/daily-prayer.

————. *Fathered By God: Learning What Your Dad Could Never Teach You*. Nashville: Thomas Nelson, 2009.

————. *Wild at Heart: Discovering the Secret of a Man's Soul*. Nashville: Thomas Nelson, 2001.

Farrar, Steve. *King Me: What Every Son Wants and Needs from His Father*. Chicago: Moody, 2005.

"Friedrich Nietzsche Quotes." http://thinkexist.com/quotation/what_was_silent_in_the_father_speaks_in_the_son/336802.html.

Graham, Stedman. *Diversity: Leaders Not Labels: A New Plan for the 21st Century*. New York: Free, 2006.

"Harriet Morgan Quotes and Sayings." http://www.searchquotes.com/quotes/author/Harriet_Morgan/.

Bibliography

Hicks, Robert. *The Masculine Journey: Understanding the Six Stages of Manhood*. Colorado Springs: Navpress, 1993.

Hughes, R. Kent. *Disciplines of a Godly Man*. Wheaton, IL: Crossway, 2001.

Jones, Stan, and Brenna Jones. *God's Design for Sex*. 4 vols. Colorado Springs: Navpress, 2007.

Kasulke, Calvin. "Everything You Always Wanted to Know About Transgender People but Were Afraid to Ask." http://www.buzzfeed.com/sbkasulke/everything-you-always-wanted-to-know-about-transgender-peopl.

Kiley, Dan. *The Peter Pan Syndrome: Men Who Have Never Grown Up*. New York: Dodd Mead, 1983.

Krienert, Jessie. "Masculinity and Crime: A Quantitative Exploration of Messerschmidt's Hypothesis." *Electronic Journal of Sociology* 2 (July 2003). http://www.sociology.org/content/vol7.2/01_krienert.html.

Lee, John. "Part I: Passivity and the Male Psyche." http://www.talkingaboutmenshealth.com/passivity-and-the-male-psyche/.

Lee, Patrick, and Annie Lucas Wolinski. "Male Teachers of Young Children: A Preliminary Empirical Study." *Young Children's Journal* 28 (August 1973) 342-53.

Levinson, Daniel. *The Seasons of a Man's Life*. New York: Ballantine, 1978.

Lewis, C.S. *The Lion, the Witch and the Wardrobe*. The Chronicles of Narnia. New York: Harper Collins, 1950.

———. *Mere Christianity*. New York: Harper Collins, 1952.

———. *The Screwtape Letters*. New York: Collier, 1961.

———. *The Weight of Glory*. San Francisco: Harper San Francisco, 1949.

Lewis, Robert. *Raising a Modern-Day Knight: A Father's Role in Guiding His Son to Authentic Manhood*. Wheaton, IL: Tyndale, 1997.

MacInnis, Cara C., and Gordon Hodson. "Do American States with More Religious or Conservative Populations Search More for Sexual Content on Google?" *Archives of Sexual Behavior* (October 3, 2014). http://link.springer.com/article/10.1007%2Fs10508-014-0361-8#page-1.

McGee, Robert S. *Father Hunger*. Ann Arbor, MI: Servant, 1993.

McKay, Brett, and Kate McKay. "Coming of Age: The Importance of Male Rites of Passage." http://www.artofmanliness.com/2008/11/09/coming-of-age-the-importance-of-male-rites-of-passage/.

Meade, Michael. *Men and the Water of Life: Initiation and the Tempering of Men*. San Francisco: Harper San Francisco, 1993.

Michaelson, Peter. "How Inner Passivity Robs Men of Power." http://www.whywesuffer.com/how-inner-passivity-robs-men-of-power/.

Miller, Donald. *Father Fiction: Chapters for a Fatherless Generation*. New York: Howard, 2010.

———. *A Million Miles in a Thousand Years: How I Learned to Live a Better Story*. Nashville: Thomas Nelson, 2009.

Milliken, Caleb. "Rites of Passage for Michael Milliken." https://www.indiegogo.com/projects/rites-of-passage-for-michael-milliken.

Molitor, Brian. *Boy's Passage, Man's Journey*. Lynnwood, WA: Emerald, 2004.

Moody, W.R., ed. *Record of Christian Work*. Vol. XXXVI. East Northfield, MA: Record of Christian Work, 1914.

Moore, Robert, and Douglas Gillette. *King, Warrior, Magician, Lover: Rediscovering the Archetypes of the Mature Masculine*. New York: Harper Collins, 1990.

Bibliography

Morley, Patrick. *Seven Seasons of the Man in the Mirror: Guidance for Each Major Phase of Your Life*. Grand Rapids, MI: Zondervan, 1997.

Murray, Erin. "Gruff Heroes Come to Aid of Child Abuse Victims." http://www.wowt.com/news/headlines/Gruff-Heroes-Come-to-Aid-of-Child-Abuse-Victims-225903221.html?ref=221.

National Fatherhood Initiative. "Statistics on the Father Absence Crisis in America." http://www.fatherhood.org/media/consequences-of-father-absence-statistics.

Parnell, Jonathan, ed. "Leading the Home: Quotes from Doug Wilson." http://www.desiringgod.org/blog/posts/leading-the-home-quotes-from-doug-wilson.

Pittman, Frank. *Man Enough: Fathers, Sons and the Search for Masculinity*. New York: Berkley, 1993.

Raphael, Ray. *The Men from the Boys: Rites of Passage in Male America*. Lincoln, NE: University of Nebraska Press, 1988.

Rohr, Richard. *Adam's Return: The Five Promises of Male Initiation*. Chestnut Ridge, NY: Crossroad, 2004.

Sawyer, Scott. *Earthly Fathers: A Memoir*. Grand Rapids, MI: Zondervan, 2001.

Sowers, John. *Fatherless Generation: Redeeming the Story*. Grand Rapids, MI: Zondervan, 2010.

"St. Thomas Aquinas Quotes." http://www.art-quotes.com/auth_search.php?authid=2541.

Trent, John, and Gary Smalley. *The Blessing: Giving the Gift of Unconditional Love and Acceptance*. Nashville: Thomas Nelson, 2004.

Tufferson, Terry. "GoPro: Man Fights Off Great White Shark In Sydney Harbour." https://www.youtube.com/watch?v=-m3N_BnVdOI.

Weber, Stu. *Tender Warrior: God's Intention for a Man*. Sisters, OR: Multnomah, 1993.

"Westminster Shorter Catechism." http://www.reformed.org/documents/wsc/index.html?_top=http://www.reformed.org/documents/WSC.html.

About the Author

ONE OF THE FEW actual natives of Colorado, Chris Bruno lives along the Northern Front Range of the Rocky Mountains with his wife, Beth, and their three awe-inspiring children, Aidan, Ella, and Sophie. Together they spent the good part of a decade serving in missions in the Near East. Their international wanderlust and love for the exotic permeates their home and dinnertime conversations. All five are go-getters, and can often be found traveling, tackling a mountain, battling on behalf of the vulnerable, or snuggling on the couch.

Chris received a bachelor of science in communication and a master of arts in speech from Northwestern University in Evanston, Illinois, and a master of arts in counseling psychology from The Seattle School of Theology and Psychology. He is a licensed professional counselor, and the founder and director of Restoration Counseling Center of Northern Colorado. In 2010, he founded Restoration Project, a ministry dedicated to calling men to heal their wounds, know their God, and restore their world.

Chris and Beth coauthored *END: Engaging Men to End Sex Trafficking*, a power-packed manual that equips men to combat human trafficking in their own backyard. Chris also wrote *Brotherhood Project: A Journey Toward Brotherhood*, a ten-week men's experiment in developing masculine relationships. He blogs at restorationproject.net and restorationcounselingnoco.com. Chris travels all over the world, speaking at retreats, conferences, and workshops—always dedicated to calling men to *show up* and restore the world.

Additional Resources

For more information about the Man Maker Project, including additional fathering resources, online conversations, father-coaching opportunities, podcasts, videos, supplemental father-son conversations, and prayers, visit:

www.restorationproject.net/man-maker

Don't miss out on Restoration Project's new father-son offering called Restoration Expeditions. Utilizing the Man Maker Project material, these guided and facilitated backcountry trips engage fathers and sons in unforgettable experiences in the wilderness, on the trail and off the grid. For more information, visit:

www.restorationproject.net/expedition

Restoration Project exists to call men to heal their wounds, know their God, and restore their world. We create experiential spaces for men to dive deeper into the places of the heart, align themselves with God's great narrative, and bring restoration to the world. We challenge men to *show up.*